MOBSTERS, MOGULS, MOVIE STARS AND MORE

Roger Rossi

La Maison Publishing, Inc.
Vero Beach, Florida
The Hibiscus City
www.lamaisonpublishing.com

Acknowledgements and thanks . . . .

La Maison publisher Inc., Janet Sierzant for her ongoing editing and advice.

To my best friend and wife Sal, for all her help, love and patience.

Initial Editing; Albert Colletti and Marcia Yudkin

To all of those I wrote about, thank you for enriching my life through our shared experiences.

DEDICATED TO . . .

My wife, best friend, and soul mate Sal.
She's been there and stood by me through it all.

FOREWORD

I am a full-time professional musician. Playing the piano is all I've ever done. I am neither famous, nor great. If you were to take a consensus of opinions, by all the people in all of the audiences for whom I've played, I am sure some thought me great, while others rated me closer to lousy. But the majority would probably rate my playing ability as *a slightly-better-than-average* professional. That is where I rate myself. I would also suggest that my vocal talent does not even rank that high.

That is precisely why I undertook this mini-autobiography. You see, if I were great or famous, or still better, both, then you and I could understand why I have had such unique experiences and encounters with such great and famous people. My possessing simply average skills, and being totally unknown to most people, makes that interplay with so many celebrities border on the astonishing.

Recalling my many wonderful memories after sixty years of making a living tickling the ivories—I do go back before plastic keys—I am amazed at how many famous and notorious people I've encountered. Many of these experiences occurred under bizarre and embarrassing circumstances.

How many slightly better than average pianists can lay claim to actually witnessing, right under their noses, the great crooner Perry Como accidentally drenched by a tray of spilled cocktails? And all this while the star applauded that pianist's performance? It happened to me, my vocalist wife Sal, and our band. How many unknown musicians can say that Robin Leach of *Lifestyles of the Rich and Famous* has been a guest at their house? How many people can say they knocked one of the world's premier concert violinists, Itzhak Perlman, right on his rear, and then added insult to injury by the apology! How many unknown piano players are past presidents of the local Rotary Club, having been awarded the *Paul Harris Fellowship;* was the resident pianist at a Roman Catholic Church for 15 years; and pianist-organist at a Lutheran Church for (to date) 3 years and counting. And yet, on the other side of life's coin, have had a close friendship with a notorious member of the Carlo Gambino crime family who was a catalyst to the downfall of the Godfather, Paul *"Big Paulie"* Castellano?

These stories, and more, are in this book. Some are short, others more elaborate. There are stories involving sport stars, recording, television and movie celebrities, royalty, and underworld crime figures. Occasionally I tell of friends who, while not famous, have their own unique and interesting stories.

However, please realize, I was born in 1940, and most of my encounters occurred between 1957 and the late 1990's when I was 17 to 60 years old, so I never met today's stars like Lady Gaga, Floyd Mayweather Jr, Tiger Woods, Brad Pitt, or Jay Leno because they were not yet born, or stars. Instead, my stories focus on past encounters that were comparable, if not bigger, like Liberace, Joe Louis, Jack Nicklaus, Shelley Winters, Princess Diana, Tony Bennett, and Rodney Dangerfield.

My book is for everyone. In some areas, I've added areas, that dwell on "Records and Accomplishments" that for some will be enjoyed with enthusiasm, but for others can easily be ignored by simply bypassing their "facts." Older readers will automatically relate to my book's content. For younger readers, I suggest you buy this book for an older loved one's birthday, or facsimile, but first, carefully read it yourself before gift-wrapping it for your older loved one. You and they will enjoy gleaning information about America's great stars of the past, including: Julius La Rosa, Tennessee Ernie Ford, The Shangri-Las, Vic Damone, Ray Bolger, Evel Knievel, Rick Mears, Johnny Mathis, John Kennedy Jr, Gabe Kaplan, Jimmy Hoffa, Rocky Graziano, Mel Tillis, George Raft, Errol Garner, Woody Herman, Whitey Ford, The Ink Spots, Donald Trump and more, much more.

All of these stories are true, and exactly the way I viewed them; mostly from the piano bench.

ROGER ROSSI
Palm City, Florida

Contents

PART ONE: The Personalities

Rodney Dangerfield
Lindsay Nelson
The Flame
Tip O'Neill
Ray Bolger
Shelley Winters
Cornel Wilde
Gabe Kaplan
Princess Diana & Prince Charles
Robin Leach
Jerry Lewis
Alexander Haig
John Kennedy, Jr.
John Patrick
Donald Trump

Rodney Dangerfield

Two very famous people came from my hometown, Babylon, New York. One was the Fox News Correspondent Geraldo Rivera, the other Jacob Cohen, who later changed his name to Rodney Dangerfield.

I never met Geraldo, who, like me, also graduated from West Babylon School. He was in my brother, Paul's class. I did meet Dangerfield at Carl Hoppl's Valley Stream Park Inn on Long Island where my family held one of their reunions.

I come from a big family. I mean it is huge. My mother was the youngest of eleven children. That statistic is typical throughout my family tree. There is a standard joke that has circulated about my grandfather's sexual drive. The normal nightly scenario was that Grandma Pirundini would ask Grandpapa, in Italian, "Dearest . . . do you want to go to sleep, or what?" My Grandfather, hard of hearing, would ask, "WHAT?" Hence . . . they had eleven children!

The relatives would have a reunion every couple of years' and between 250 and 350 people would attend. I hardly knew any of them. There were just too many! Dad did most of the event organizing. It got so big; they used to use the grand ballroom of the Biltmore Hotel, NY. One year, through the efforts of my older brother, Vinny, the affair was at Hoppl's.

Vinny performed there with a terrific five-piece band, under the musical direction of saxophonist Jack Dema. They accompanied a floorshow of various stage acts, playing dance music before and after the show. The place had a fine chef, good service, nice ambiance, and fair prices. For most people, that format made for a delightful evening. But my relatives are not like most people. They loved to argue. And when it came to insulting people, Rodney Dangerfield would come to find out, they were the *masters of the act!*

As the date for the big affair drew near, some of the reunion committee members asked Vinny, "Who is performing in the floor show?" Vinny told them that it was, in fact, three acts. A flamenco dance team was scheduled to open the show, followed by a wonderful vocalist. The closing act was an up-and-coming comedian.

One cousin from Brooklyn asked, "Why do we have to have a singer in the show? We have Cousin Dick who can sing a few numbers!" My cousin Richard Torigi was an accomplished operatic baritone with a long list of credits, including singing at the New York Opera House and playing the understudy to the lead role (played by Robert Weede) in the hit Broadway musical, *The Most Happy Fella.* In the 1950's Dick also performed regularly on an NBC television series out of New York, called *Opera Cameos.*

Vinny proclaimed, "Hey, nobody loves to hear Dick sing any more than I do, but do you expect the club to cancel the scheduled vocalist for the evening? Sometime during the affair, I'll see to it that Dick gets up and does a couple of numbers, too. Okay?"

The disgruntled cousin retorted, "I'm tellin' you, you oughta cancel the singer!"

Another cousin asked, "Who's da comedian?"

Vinny answered, "He's a very funny, up-to-date comedian who will probably be a big-name star real soon. His name is Rodney Dangerfield. He's originally from Babylon." The reply was typical. "How good can he be? WE NEVER HEARD OF HIM!"

The evening arrived. I brought my new bride, Sal, to the affair. The total number of people in Sal's family back in England can be counted on two or three hands, so meeting all of my family would be a unique experience for her. Dinner came and went, then everybody was up and about again. Some danced to the band's great music, while others drank and socialized. Everyone was boisterously laughing and yelling. It was bedlam.

Then with the music stopping and the lights flickering on and off, Vinny stepped to the microphone and announced, "Ladies and Gentlemen . . . kindly find your seats, as Carl Hoppl's will now present its floor show."

This routine had always worked in the past, for other groups, but once again, my family is not like other groups. Vinny must have made the announcement seven or eight times. Finally, my Uncle Nunzio went on the stage and said to Vinny, "Vincenzo, adesso basta. Enougha is enougha. Letta me use a the mika. I get thema quiet for you."

Vinny said, "Sure, Uncle Nunzio . . . GOOD LUCK!"

My uncle said very softly and ultra-sweetly, "Signore, attenzione per favore."

Several relatives noticed him. One even yelled out, "Hey, that's Uncle Nunzio. What's HE doing up there?"

Most of the crowd, however, was still yelling and having a grand old time, while ignoring the old gentleman. Suddenly his voice started to get louder and his face started to get redder, a sure sign that Uncle Nunzio was getting angry. "SENTIMI!" (Listen!) he yelled, but to no avail.

This was now a personal affront to him. You could see the loss of respect in the rapid enlargement of the veins on his forehead and neck. He yelled out to the crowd, "Ti sto avertendo, NON FARMI ARRABIARE!" (I'm warning you, DON'T GET ME ANGRY!) He added as he pointed to one of my cousins, "YOU . . . SIT! . . . QUIET!" She responded with her own threatening hand gesture. Then he bellowed over the microphone, like a raging behemoth, in decibel levels that could be heard a city block away, "STA' ZITTO! . . . SHUTTA UPPA!"

Everyone who was talking immediately stopped and looked up with total shock at Uncle Nunzio. The confused looks on most of their faces implied that they had no idea why he was yelling! He simply returned to his normal soft manner and said, courteously, "Grazie. Thanka you verry mucha." He handed the microphone back to my now smiling brother, and the show began.

The flamenco dancers had to cut down the time of their act for a couple of reasons. For one thing, they had to get back on schedule, because so much time had been wasted in trying to get the show started. For another thing, in the corner of the room a couple of my cousins who thought they were Jose Greco, were mimicking the professionals. Everyone started to divert their attention toward these two up-stagers until finally one of my aunts went over and said, "You two *citrullos* (jerks) are going to stop the show for the rest of us." She actually grabbed one of them by his ear and pulled him to his seat. Everyone laughed of course, but even her good intentions were somewhat aggravating to the dancers, so they simply said, "Thank you very much, ladies and gentlemen. You've been a delightful audience. Good night!"

The vocalist for the show, who was good enough to have recently performed at the Copacabana, in New York, had to endure comments from my cousins, like, "Hey . . . have you ever heard of Richard Torigi?" and "Yeah . . . let Dick sing!" He cut his act short, too.

In between acts, Vinny made a comment to the crowd, assuring them that as soon as the show ended, he would bring Dick up, "But please folks, let's give the rest of these fine entertainers a chance. Everyone, please simmer down."

He then presented the star of the show, Rodney Dangerfield. As Rodney came out, he said to the band, "Tough crowd tonight, hah?" He went into his normal routines, but the crowd was completely out of control. Most of my relatives think they are born comedians anyway, and they heckled Dangerfield throughout his show.

5

Rodney Dangerfield

He handled himself very well. However, some of his routines, although funny, were somewhat risqué, and these upset my Aunt Nancy, who was very religious. In fact, my cousin, her son Albert, now deceased, was a Passionist priest. She was normally one of the few soft-spoken persons in the room, but at this point, she could not restrain herself. What she did next might very well have changed Dangerfield's career theme forever.

Aunt Nancy, atypical of her normal nature, got up and stood right in front of the comedian. While pointing her finger in his face, she scolded him as if he was a misbehaving child. She said, "Young man, you shouldn't tell dirty jokes like that. You should be ashamed of yourself. Don't you know that there are ladies here?"

Everyone heard her very well, and they applauded her as she went back to her seat.

I think that because Dangerfield took it from her without argument or reprisal, he automatically started to get the crowd to become the listening audience they should have been in the first place. Everyone waited intensely for what he would say next. Instead of putting her down, he sidestepped the whole episode with, "Gee . . . *nobody gives me any respect!*" The crowd finally started to laugh, so he ad-libbed further on the "lack of respect" theme.

"I get no respect at all. I took my wife to a tunnel of love, and she told me to wait outside." He got more laughter. He eventually won over the crowd completely and did a whole improvised show on respect or the lack of it.

"With animals, I never had any luck. When I play the horses, I always go broke. Every time I bet, I hear the same thing: 'They're off . . . EXCEPT ONE'!"

Rodney Dangerfield went on to become the big-time star that Vinny had predicted. He never totally cleaned up his act, but he did "find" himself; and his catchphrase slogan "I just get no respect" contributed a lot to his image and his success. I'm not positive, but I think my Aunt Nancy's browbeating might very well have been the inspiration for it all!

Dangerfield's career started blossoming in 1965, and it didn't take long before he began headlining in Las Vegas. He often appeared on *The Ed Sullivan Show, Johnny Carson's Tonight Show* 35 times, and he was a regular on *The Dean Martin Show*.

With a partner, he opened Dangerfield's Comedy Club in the Upper East Side of Manhattan. It was a huge success and was a venue for several *Home Box Office* shows, which promoted many standup comics, including Jerry Seinfeld, Andrew Dice Clay, Roseanne Barr, Jim Carrey, and Jeff Foxworthy.

Dangerfield's 1980 comedy album, *No Respect*, won him a Grammy Award. He also acted in several successful movies including *Caddyshack, Easy Money* and *Back to School*.

Rodney Dangerfield, a stand-up comedian who did it all in show business, died on October 5, 2004, at 82 years of age. He was interred in Westwood Village Memorial Park Cemetery, Los Angeles. His headstone reads, "Rodney Dangerfield . . . There goes the neighborhood."

I'm sure Babylon, Long Island, our shared hometown neighborhood, was proud of him.

Lindsey Nelson

During the late 1960's, Sal and I started working with each other. She sang behind her set of cocktail drums, and I sang harmony parts at the piano. At the same time, the New York Mets were also starting to gel as a professional team. A roster filled with superstars doesn't necessarily guarantee a winning season. I'd rather be on a team filled with nobodies with only a modicum of talent, yet willing to work hard. That was the way it was for Sal and Roger Rossi—and for the Mets—back in the late sixties. The Mets went on to win the World Series in 1969, and Sal and Roger went on . . . to make a good living.

Those early years were a period of metamorphosis for the Mets. They changed from baseball players who were the laughing stock of the league to superstars. Probably the person most cognizant of that transformation was Lindsey Nelson, one of the Mets' broadcasting voices.

Lindsey would finish his twilight and night game broadcasts, and after a considerable drive from Shea Stadium—The Mets original home—he'd occasionally unwind at the Club House in Huntington, where Sal and I performed.

The evening I met him stands out very well in my memory. Sal and I often performed in formal wear. That evening, Sal and I had a difference of opinion on what we should wear. I said to her, as we got dressed, "Honey, I don't want to wear a tuxedo there anymore. I think I just want to wear a sports jacket, with a pair of slacks and a tie."

She inquired, "Why? It's the classy thing for us to go with a tux and cocktail dress."

"I think we can carry this business of being classy too far. The Club House patrons are all dressed casually. If someone comes in with a jacket on, it's a rare occasion, and just a few men wear ties. So why should we dress so formally?"

Sal retorted, "People judge us by the way we dress."

I said, "Yeah, but we're not giving any formal concert there. We're just having a little fun around a piano bar."

Sal won the debate when she suggested that, "we should be dressed BETTER than the patrons. We should stand out in the crowd!" I put my tux on one more time.

We arrived at the Club House, played our first set, and in came Lindsey Nelson. He immediately got everyone's attention because of what he was wearing. It looked like he'd been to thirty separate upholstery shops and asked each for a swatch of their most tasteless and gaudy material. After collecting these various samples, he must have given them to his tailor, saying, "Here . . . make me a sports jacket!"

I looked at Sal and said, "Honey, I don't think my tuxedo is standing out in this crowd anymore!"

Lindsay Nelson was a smart man. He knew exactly what he was doing by wearing such a flashy outfit. For one thing, you could hear everybody talking about his jacket, but their observations included, "That's Lindsey Nelson, the sports announcer, who's wearing that gaudy jacket!" He immediately got recognized everywhere he went. Liberace wore robes and ultra-flashy formal wear, Elvis Presley wore tight pants for his gyrations, Minnie Pearl would wear her various bonnets and hats, and Lindsey Nelson wore his outrageous sports jackets. They were all easily recognizable, and they set fashion statements for others to follow until today, i.e. Elton John's enormous glasses, and Lady Gaga's "whacko" outfits.

He never once tried to overpower you with his vast knowledge of sports, nor did he show any signs of boredom with your lack of that same knowledge. When I got to know him, I found him to be a person with whom it was easy to converse. He, of course, loved to talk about the Mets.

One conversation was especially memorable. At that point, the Mets had already established a very fine pitching staff. They had Tom Seaver and Jerry Koosman, two stalwarts at that position. I commented to Nelson that I thought the Mets were so fortunate to have both aces. He turned to me and said, "That's true, but they have a new guy coming up that I want you to keep an eye on. He has the fastest fastball I've ever seen. If he ever gets his control of it . . . he is going to be nothing less than sensational!"

I asked the legendary announcer, "What's his name?" He answered, "I'm sure that you've never heard of him, but you will. His name is Nolan Ryan."

I watched out for Ryan and, sure enough, he turned out to be a Hall of Fame pitcher. I also observed him develop his control and repertoire of pitches surrounding his unbelievable fastball. Nolan Ryan eventually retired from his pitching career and went on to own The Texas Rangers baseball team. I always had to give Lindsey Nelson the nod for recognizing his greatness way back in 1967.

Lindsey was a television and radio sports announcing icon, a member of the Sportscasters and Sportswriters Hall of Fame, he spent seventeen years announcing for the

New York Mets, and three with the San Francisco Giants. During his 33-year career, on TV, Nelson announced golf, football, and baseball events, including five Sugar Bowls, twenty-six Cotton Bowls, and four Rose Bowls. However, I'll always remember him for being such a warm and congenial raconteur. When he would arrive at The Club House restaurant, the piano bar would come alive with the latest news about the Mets. We'd all get that news, long before most avid sports fans would in their next day's newspaper. He was fun to be with, and yes, seeing him wearing his atrocious sports jackets were fun, too. Whatta guy!

The Flame

Many of my stories include references to a restaurant called The Flame. Here I'll tell my story of The Flame itself. It was the most charming restaurant that I ever been to, or worked at during my career. With our four-piece band, my wife and I performed there for nine years. We never regretted one moment. Every night was exciting. There, we met an endless number of celebrities. Naturally, many of our stories would come from this setting. The Flame was one of a kind.

From our elevated stage in the lounge, we had a panoramic view of the lounge, dining room, and restaurant lobby. We musicians probably knew more of what was going on at any given moment than anyone else in the club, including the hostesses, bartenders, customers, waiters, and waitresses. Especially from our elevated view from the bandstand!

We always knew when a newcomer came through the front doors. The inevitable sequence of facial expressions would soon reveal a novice. First, newcomers would notice the beautiful ambiance of the dining room, its posh motif and settees, the subtle but effective lighting and the varied artwork discreetly displayed throughout that room. Their jaws would drop slightly and their eyebrows would lift, as they tried to soak up this display of eclectic taste. A wry grin would gradually broaden to a wider smile of definite approval.

Then they would turn to their right toward the lounge. This is where the fun really began! We watched faces transform from delight to astonishment. Those expressions sometimes intensified to the point of shock.

The new patrons would first notice the massive oak tree, which emerged from behind the highly polished, copper-top bar and spread its bows across almost the entire lounge and up to the vast boundaries of the cathedral ceiling. The place had a romantic touch about it!

I understand that for a tree to become the extraordinary centerpiece that was the Flame's oak, it must first die and somewhat petrify before removal. The tree was found by the owner of the club, Peter Makris. At immense expense, he had it transported from its native ground in Illinois, and then trunk and limb-by-limb, reassembled in North Palm Beach.

The Flame periodically decorated the tree according to the various moods, themes, and colors characterizing the current season. Apple blossoms in Spring. Multicolored leaves, ala New England in the Fall. Christmas decorating was always cheerfully outstanding. The best decor of all was when America celebrated her bicentennial in 1976. Then, it was laden with an abundance of red, white and blue ornamentation.

"Customer watching" became a favorite pastime of ours at the Flame, and the newcomers were our favorite targets. After the tree, they would soon notice the rest of the lounge. The huge crest ostentatiously perched above the dance floor and stage area. The classically presented piano bar, with its luxuriously comfortable stools. The attractive and elegant outfits that adorned the waitresses and bartenders. Finally, they would notice my band of musicians! We had a great music group. Anywhere else, we would have been noticed first; but here we placed last, after The Flame's decor and charm.

Only after people became acquainted with the lavish presentation of the club would a sense of our talent drift into their consciousness. People would focus their attention on my wife, Sal, and for good reason. Her wonderful lyrical style and sparkling vocal tones have always been attractive indeed. Sal's "doubling" on *cocktail drums*—not a common instrument for someone to be playing in the 70's, not to mention someone with her beauty and stage presence—held that attention.

They would soon notice our talented bassist/trombonist, Michael Burns. Mike was very distinctive in that he played both instruments, additionally providing lead and backup vocals, all with tremendous fervor and musicality. I always referred to him as our *Utility Man*. He had a magnetism about him that made it very difficult for people to look away. He was in total command of his fingertips and vocal harmonies.

Customers would notice our regular drummer and me toward the end of their sensory journey at the Flame, not necessarily, because we had less talent than the rest of the group, but because we were hidden behind our respective instruments. I doubled on synthesizer and vocals, and when Mike would drop his electric bass into his left arm to pick up the trombone for a solo, I would take over his bass part on my synth. When Sal sang a feeling ballad or the band played an upbeat rock or jazz tune, I would favor those arrangements with the strings or horns from that keyboard. Sometimes I'd show off my classical background with more elaborate embellishments on the acoustic grand.

The repertoire, musicality, versatility, instrumental and vocal blends that we collectively and individually exhibited were, with all modesty aside . . . extraordinary. We turned down myriad offers to work at other top clubs and hotels across Florida. Once, we even turned down an offer to perform at New Hampshire's Mount Washington Hotel, for the *Republican Governors Convention!* We turned down all of these offers because we didn't want to tempt the fickle finger of fate. We loved working at the Flame. Why get greedy?

Sometimes, customers would get so wrapped up in the Flames decor, or my group's presentation, that they wouldn't immediately notice whom they happened to be sitting beside. More often than not, that ordinary-looking customer was someone of tremendous prominence and, quite often of national and international celebrity status.

Our opening night at the Flame, I asked the head bartender, Gino Ziretti, "Isn't that the golfer, *Gardner Dickenson,* the winner of *the Doral Open?*"

Gino replied calmly, "Oh yeah, he's here all of the time. You think that's something, you should see some of the people that come into this place. You won't believe it."

Gino was right. I couldn't believe it. It was a regular occurrence for us to be visited by stars from all walks of life. I mean BIG names like, the great crooner and TV personality *Perry Como*, who lived nearby, and television host, *Mike Douglas,* who lived in Fort Lauderdale, but always visited Tequesta. Country singing star, *Tammy Wynette*, another "local," was often there, and so was actor, *George Murphy*. It was the "norm" for us to come to work and, before performing, ask, "Well, who's here tonight?"

We met the great American Olympic gymnast, *Cathy Rigby,* daredevil star *Evil Knievel, Liberace, Mel Tillis,* Speaker of the House of Representatives *Tip O'Neil,* actor *Douglas Fairbanks, Jr., Barbara Eden* and many great golfers—all at the Flame. We once saw newlywed actress

Kate Jackson chasing her groom around The Flame's busy dining room, just like a couple of kids playing tag.

Because the restaurant was the finest in the area, and because owner Peter Makris was an avid golfer, he naturally attracted all of the local golfing professionals, as well as many of the pro tour golfers. Several of the major PGA Tournaments were held at the (former) JDM Country Club, in the next town, just a stone's throw away. So many big names spent considerable time at the Flame. Legends of the game, like *Lee Trevino*, *Arnold Palmer*, *Bob Murphy*, and *Bob Hope*, were among them. They gave the Flame's image and reputation a real boost.

Golf professional Lionel Hebert, who won the 1957 PGA Tournament, would drop by quite often to sit in with my band, on trumpet. He wasn't bad.

Lionel Hebert and Gardner Dickenson

Ken Still wanted to give me golf lessons in exchange for my teaching him how to play the piano.

Don January, Cary Middlecoff, Julius Boros, Dan Sikes, Judy Dickenson...the list went on and on. A total duffer myself, I had my biggest thrill when The Golfer of the Century, Jack Nicklaus came in for dinner with his wife Barbara and their family. This occurred quite often because they lived not six minutes away.

Golf course designers *George Fazio* and his two nephews, *Tom* and *Jim Fazio* were all close to Peter Makris, so they were there all of the time. Tom, one of Peter's best friends, is now considered one of the world's top golf course designers. Golf club and equipment designers Tommy Dorr and Toney Penna likewise were always there.

Insurance magnate Bill Elliot was there, as was another close friend of Peter Makris, William Clayton Ford of Ford Motor Company of America. One time, a small branch from the oak tree accidently fell on Gardner Dickenson. He came in the next day playfully wrapped in bandages and joked that he was "going to sue!"

All of these celebrities and famous sports, music, business and political figures were always more than charming to my band members and me, so to use the word "thrilling" would be an understatement. We were ecstatic! We found ourselves regularly rubbing elbows and nonchalantly conversing with, being requested musical selections by, and, on occasion even drinking with people of this stature. The result was euphoric!

Because of our success at the Flame, Makris put us in several of his other fine restaurants. We found ourselves performing in the Flame restaurants of Tampa, Palm Beach Gardens and on famous Worth Avenue, Palm Beach. We also received contracts for engagements at his Lord Chumley's Pub, and Peter's Private Club, both in Tequesta, Florida. As nice as all of these clubs were, none of them captured the flavor, taste, and mood of The Flame in North Palm Beach.

We had worked for Makris nine years during a thirteen-year period. In 1979, I left to enter into a business partnership with Jess Santamaria. We bought the seventeen-acre, thirty-six room resort called The Royal Inn, in Royal Palm Beach. It had a one-hundred and eighty-seat restaurant and lounge. During the first year, I helped in supervising the operations of both the restaurant and lounge. Sal and I also performed there with bassist, Jim Valley. The venture with Santamaria was very successful and lasted a total of seven years until I finally sold him my shares.

After the first year there, we received an offer to perform in the world-class, five-star, Boca Raton Hotel and Club, in its main dining room. The same dining room had in the past featured such legendary bandleaders as Guy Lombardo, Tony Pastor, and violinist George Liberace, the renowned pianist entertainer's brother. Additionally, people of high stature like Billy Joel, the popular and talented pianist- vocalist - composer would often moor their huge yachts right outside of *The Patio Royale*.

At that time, this glorious facility was ranked in the top thirty hotels of the world, one of only two five-star hotels in Florida! The offer was too good to refuse, so we put together a nice quartet and started to work nightly in the famous Patio Royale. We were there three years, before returning to work for Makris.

However, it happened one night at "the Boca" that the Flame received one of its finest compliments. It came from the general manager, George Roy, and the executive secretary, Dolores Sachs, who later became Mrs. George Roy. Mr. Roy asked me, "Roger, where did you perform prior to the Boca Hotel?"

I answered proudly, "We performed in our own club, the Royal Inn for one year, and prior to that we were at the Flame Restaurant."

"Do you mean The Flame in North Palm Beach? That's our FAVORITE restaurant! We go there quite often on Sunday evenings!"

"Well, that's probably why you didn't know that we worked there. We were always off on Sundays." That compliment, coming from the management of the Boca Raton Hotel & Club, was really saying something!

The Flame was everyone's favorite, yet unfortunately, Makris sold the restaurant. From then on it changed hands several times, and always for the worse. It went from being one of the finest restaurants anywhere, to one of fifty ordinary bars in the county. The new owners immediately removed any evidence of good taste including the gorgeous oak tree and copper bar. What a sin! We had witnessed hundreds of couples meeting each other under that tree, and falling in love right at that bar. We later played for some of those same people at their wedding receptions. The piano bar went next, followed by the posh settees, rich wall cloths and furnishings. They replaced them with wooden benches, and of all things, white ceramic tiles on the walls! It looked like a fish market. You could see the inner pain of former customers when they talked about it. I'll never forget when Sal and I visited the newly installed "restaurant." The new hostess, knowing us, proudly welcomed us and tried to "sell us" the supposed merits of the new place. With moxie, she asked, "So, Sal and Roger, what do you think of our new restaurant?"

Sal and I looked at each other and didn't quite know what to say. We didn't want to cry aloud for the almost sinful way they destroyed our beloved Flame; nor did we want to insult her. So, I just replied the best way I could. With timidity, I answered, "Well, it's not The Flame!" As expected, it didn't make it past 3-months and was put up for sale.

Even when actor *Burt Reynolds* bought the place, it got worse. As an actor, I think Burt Reynolds was terrific. But I think he got some very bad advice when he changed the seafood joint into, of all things, a fifties and sixties style DINER! It had neon lights in the dining room and cheap posters of James Dean, a 57 Chevy, and Elvis on the walls where Makris had formerly displayed classy art pieces, including some Jack Gray oil paintings, at that time valued at $40,000 apiece. It was a nightmare compared to its predecessor, the fishy place; which was a catastrophe compared to the Flame! One by one, all of those places failed. Too many former patrons of the Flame remembered what it had once been.

Gradually, as time moved on and new residents moved from the northern cities to Florida, conversations about The Flame disappeared. The newcomers never knew the jewel we once had there. Peter and Gloria Makris, their former partner Andy Kallas, and bartenders Gino and Bob all eventually died. Recently, I witnessed The Flame's final insult. I drove to its site and found . . . nothing! The building was demolished and removed, and I was viewing an empty lot. My eyes welled.

Tip O'Neill

My trio performed at The Flame on Worth Avenue, Palm Beach, from November 1979 until May 1980. Jimmy Carter was the president, and this country was in big trouble financially. Since he had taken office, the unemployment rate had grown from six to eight percent and was rising by the minute. The poverty rate also rose from 11.4 to 14 percent. Interest rates skyrocketed as did inflation. Average people who made an average pay check found it very hard to dine out. No one was sure if the economy was going to turn for the better or, for the first time since the thirties, take a tailspin into a major depression.

This financial dilemma didn't affect some segments of our society as much as others. One basically unaffected group was the politicians. The president didn't have to worry about collecting his paycheck. He just had to be concerned about getting reelected, two years later, which he resoundingly did not!

The Speaker of the House, Tip O'Neill, was a popular politico from Massachusetts. He was a shoo-in at reelection time. That was a given. It really didn't matter whether the country was in a state of prosperity or depression. So, he didn't have to be too concerned about his personal financial situation. For that reason, I found it interesting to hear him talk about it being everybody's personal responsibility to tighten their belts in such tough times. Shortly after making that statement, he came into the Flame, a very expensive restaurant. He had with him an entourage of twenty-five people. They sat, ate and drank expensive wines for hours on end. It was the turning point of my wife Sal's political transformation, from being a devout Liberal-voting Democrat, to conservatism. She sarcastically said to me, "I can see that the Speaker of the House is really tightening his belt!" I commented that the overweight politician was "actually loosening his belt by several notches!"

In May 1980, my music group ended our engagement at the Flame. We started a three-year stint at the Boca Raton Hotel and Club. We performed in *the Patio Royale* dining room, and occasionally in the Cathedral dining room. It was a world-class hotel in every sense of the word, and a very expensive place to visit.

Not too long after we had started at the prestigious resort, the Speaker came into the Cathedral Dining Room, this time with an entourage of about forty people. My friend, Mickey McGrath, was the maître d' in that room, and he personally served O'Neill. He told me, "Man, they are going through some of the most expensive wines we have like they are water!"

Sal was standing there at the time, so I figured I would only reinforce her recently changed political affiliation with a little sarcasm of my own. I asked Mickey, "Hey Mick, in your estimation, is the Speaker tightening, or loosening his belt?"

He answered with his own appraisal. "Are you kidding? The way he and his party are feasting, I think he removed the belt a long time ago!"

I quipped, "Well, I hope for your sake, he lives up to his name . . . and leaves you a decent *tip*!"

The rest of the story is history. In November 1982, Ronald Reagan beat Jimmy Carter in a landslide. As president, he lowered the unemployment rate from 9.5 percent to 5.2 percent. He lowered the poverty rate from 15 to13 percent, and he lowered the inflation rate by forty-eight percent. He did all of this in spite of a Democratic Congress that, under the guidance of Speaker of the House, Tip O'Neill, fought him tooth and nail.

However, something has to be said about the decorum that took place between them. By contrast to the nasty politics of today, Reagan and O'Neill's relationship was almost "a Buddy System." O'Neill once called Reagan "the most ignorant man who had ever occupied the White

House." Obviously, that was not true, because Jimmy Carter held that distinction. Nevertheless, Reagan retaliated. He made reference to O'Neill's liberal modus operandi of supposedly helping the poor while installing the poor's dependency on government with give-away programs, instead of jobs. He said, "O'Neill is like Pac-Man. He's a round thing that gobbles up (taxpayer) money!" Reagan continued joking by suggesting he'd once received a Valentine's card from O'Neill. He said, "I knew it was from Tip because the heart was bleeding."

Oh, yes, they threw public jabs at each other, but Reagan also wrote in his memoirs that they were friends enjoying cocktails and good humor . . . "after 6PM." O'Neill expounded that "before 6 PM it's all politics!"

Thomas Tip O'Neill, Jr. retired from public life in 1987, almost exactly five years after I changed my political party affiliation from Independent to Republican. He served as Speaker of the House from 1977 until his retirement in 1987. During that span of congressional leadership, he was the only Speaker to serve for five complete and consecutive Congresses. His tenure as Speaker took place during the presidencies of Gerald Ford, Jimmy Carter, and Ronald Reagan.

Ray Bolger

I met Ray Bolger at the Boca Raton Hotel and Club. He was to entertain conventioneers in the Great Hall of the hotel. A true veteran of vaudeville, Bolger in 1926 danced at New York City's famous Palace Theatre, considered the foremost vaudeville theater in the United States. In the 1930's, as a creational inventor of dance movements, Bolger earned many leading roles on Broadway, and ultimately, in film, television and nightclub work.

He sang, danced, and acted for stage and screen, and was mostly known for his portrayal of the Scarecrow in *The Wizard of Oz*. In that all-time classic, he thrilled moviegoers of all ages.

Judy Garland, Ray Bolger and Jack Haley

He came into the main dining room, the Patio Royale, the night before his show. I had the band in that dining room. The maître d' Bob Caston, came up to the bandstand and told me, "Ray Bolger is in the room, Roger. He has invited you to his table when you're done playing."

"I thought I recognized him when he came in. Please tell Mr. Bolger that I would be very honored, and I'll be over on my next break."

When I went to his table, he introduced himself and his piano accompanist, who was his music director. I sat down, they ordered me a cup of coffee, and we talked. I really didn't have much time, and I apologized for the brevity of my visit. "I have one more dance set to play, and I have to finish on time. The hotel likes to get everyone from these dining rooms into the various lounges afterward. If I play past my allotted time, it encroaches upon the other rooms' activities."

"Oh, that's okay, we understand all of that. We have scheduled a rehearsal tomorrow afternoon for tomorrow night's show. Perhaps you'd like to come?"

"Wow, Mr. Bolger, under normal circumstances that would be wonderful. But unfortunately, I have to decline. You see, I have a wedding reception that my band is playing for tomorrow. Gee, I'm starting to sound like Mister Scrooge, and I don't mean to."

"That's quite all right. We know how commitments go. You just have to do them."

"I'll tell you, Mr. Bolger, you're such a giant in the ranks of show business, I would feel very honored if you

27

were to sit in with my band for my next set, and perhaps, sing or dance to a number or two. Could you?"

The famous actor and showman thought for a moment or two and then answered my request. "Well, I would like to very much. You make such great music. But I have a bit of a problem. You see, the convention that hired us for the show tomorrow evening paid us a lot of money for that entertainment. They might be very upset if they were to know I gave it to your guests for nothing tonight.

Do you understand my problem? Eh . . . just give me a second to figure this out." He thought some more. "I'll tell you what, announce me in any manner that you would like, but don't mention me by name. Then, if you could go into one of those nice, society-type of dance beats . . . I'll take it from there."

"Great, but what do you plan on doing?"

"You'll see. Just play a song like *Cheek-to-Cheek, A Fine Romance,* or something like that. I'll handle the rest. Just keep playing until I look up at the bandstand and I signal for you to end it. But above all, do not mention my name!"

"No problem. Gee, it has been a wonderful experience in meeting you both. I wish I could spend more time with you. Please forgive me."

I got my band back on the bandstand and explained to them what was going to take place. I then made my announcement. I said, "Ladies and Gentleman. We feel very honored to have one of America's all-time great actors and showmen in our presence this evening. I was asked not to mention his name, but I'm sure you will recognize who he is because his famous reputation precedes him. Ladies and gentleman, I present to you a show business living legend!"

Ray Bolger - The Straw Man

With that said, I went into one of his favorite songs, *(Once in Love with) Amy.* I was just as surprised as everyone else in the room to watch what he did. He simply got up, walked to the middle of the dance floor, bowed slightly to the guests in the room, and then went over to one of the tables where a middle-aged couple was seated. He extended his hand to the lady at the table, brought her out to the center of the dance floor and danced with her. He then brought her back to her table, pulled out the chair courteously in seating her, and he went on to the next table to repeat the gesture with another lady. He must have danced with a dozen women in total, and always had one or two outstanding dance steps to exhibit, without repeating himself.

It was absolutely delightful. I'm sure that each lady felt like they were some sort of movie star, dancing in one of those romantic movies that came out of the thirties or forties. The dining patrons applauded in appreciation after he sat each one of them down. Ray Bolger finally gave me the signal and I ended my musical arrangement precisely with his last dance step. It was as if we had rehearsed it for hours. The dining guests gave him thunderous applause as he escorted his final partner to her chair. He bowed, this time fully from the waist, and he then turned with one hand pointed toward our bandstand, recognizing our musical accompaniment.

When the applause subsided, and Bolger had returned to his seat, I came close to the line in acknowledging who he really was. I said to him over the microphone, "Sir, you requested that I let you remain anonymous in announcing you, and I will. But I think it is obvious that everyone here tonight knows exactly who you are! Some of the ladies were actually drawing straws . . . in order to dance with you, and you didn't look like any scarecrow to me!" Everyone laughed and then applauded for him again. The whole episode was truly exciting.

I didn't have much time left, so I concluded the evening by inviting everyone to the last dance. I said, "Ladies and Gentlemen, I would like to end our evening with you tonight, by inviting all of you to come to our dance floor for the last dance. This song is one that I'm sure our phantom dancer will reminisce over. It was recorded and sung by a very close friend of his, the late, great Judy Garland. Ladies and gentlemen, from the movie in which they both starred: The Wizard of Oz . . . 'Over the Rainbow'."

Sal went into her rendition and the dance floor became absolutely packed. Sal projected the song beautifully, but then something very bizarre happened. In the middle of the song, our amplifier went totally dead! As I continued to play the song with my right hand, I tried to jiggle the connection from the microphones to the amp with my left hand. It refused to work. I had to finish the song by myself on the piano. When I got done, everyone applauded, but they knew that we were having electronic problems.

Later, when everyone vacated the room, I went to check out the problem. I turned the amp on, and it worked fine. We never had a similar problem with that amplifier, before or after that one time. It was very odd. I continued to use that same amplifier for several years after that episode, without any problems. It went dead just for that song! It was eerie! To this day, my wife honestly believes that it was Judy Garland trying to send her a message from heaven. Sal believes the great singer was telling her, "You might sing very well, Sal, but nobody can sing that song like Judy Garland! . . . NOBODY!"

Several weeks later, I received in the mail an autographed photo of Ray Bolger, with him kicking his foot high above his head. The inscription states, "To Sal and Roger, you are truly delightful. All the best, Ray."

Shelley Winters

While my trio was performing the music for the Sunday brunch at the Boca Raton Hotel & Club, I had the opportunity to meet the famed actress, Shelley Winters. Frank DiGrazia, the maître d, approached me at the piano saying, "Roger, I was told by Shelley Winters to ask you to join her and her party on your next break." I inquired, "Franco, do you mean Shelley Winters . . . the actress?" I inquired.

"Right. That's the one!" he said, grinning. "She's seated at table 11."

"Why sure, Frank. Tell her I'd be pleased to join her and I'll be over there in about . . . ten minutes," I said, looking at my watch.

Shelley Winters was a great actress, who appeared in dozens of films, and on stage and television for over 50 years. She won Academy Awards for *The Diary of Anne Frank*, and *A Patch of Blue* received a Best Actress nomination for *A Place in the Sun*, and Best Supporting Actress for *The Poseidon Adventure*. She also appeared in such films as *The Big Knife, A Double Life, Lolita, The Night of the Hunter, Alfie,* and *Pete's Dragon*.

When I arrived at her table, she was bubbling with as much enthusiasm as I was. She said happily, "Hi! Come on over and join us." She pointed to an empty chair next to her. I went over to the seat, and while I was standing Frank made the introductions.

"Miss Winters, let me present to you, our band leader and pianist, Roger Rossi." She replied with emphasis, "VERY pleased to meet YOU, Mister Rossi."

Academy Award Winner, Shelley Winters

She proceeded to quickly introduce the various people at her table. I didn't catch any of their names. I think it was her birthday, but I'm not certain. I had seen so many of her movies, throughout her long career, that I was simply in a daze.

"Your music is delightful," she said. "Do you perform here all the time?"

"Yes, I do. I've been here now for a couple of years, five and six nights a week and for the Sunday brunches."

I couldn't believe that I was actually talking nonchalantly with this two-time Academy Award Winner. I thought that she additionally should have won for several other movies she was in, too, including her fine role in *The Poseidon Adventure.*

I innocently divulged my excitement. "Gee, it's such a thrill to be able to talk to you. I've enjoyed all of your work immensely." I wasn't trying to come onto her. However, she replied, suggestively, "Well, I'm thrilled too. You're such a fine musician . . . and you're young . . . and very good looking. I'm VERY interested . . . eh, in YOUR work."

Her guests chuckled at her hinted flirtation. Although I've been known to occasionally tease and flirt myself, I wanted her to know that in this instance I was not flirting or teasing. Oh, don't get me wrong. Shelley Winters in her youth was a real beauty to behold, and perhaps at another point in time, and different circumstances, I might very well have flirted back. But this was not that time, nor circumstance, starting with the fact that I'm happily married.

I even mentioned to her, "Gee Shelley, I hope you haven't misunderstood me. I happen to be a real fan, but I also happen to be a married man." I courteously announced this fact, because I didn't want the flirting to get out of hand.

She countered more aggressively with, "Well, that won't necessarily stop ME! I happen to think that married men are the BEST kind!"

Her party now laughed openly and, although I did too, I felt myself starting to turn red. It was now getting evident that although all of this was being said in jest, there was an undercurrent of reality coming through. I really was lost for words. I thought to myself, "She must be joking," and yet, I didn't want to come off like a spoilsport and ruin her poke at humor. I did feel somewhat uncomfortable, so I decided to politely return to the bandstand as soon as I could.

Before I got that chance, somebody either from her party or from the hotel went to take a photo of her. As they set up the pose for the picture and told her to look their way, she abruptly said to them, "Wait a second. Let me get ROGER into this!" That said, she reached over and forcefully pulled me, not only into the camera's sight but close enough to cuddle up to me and nestle her face against mine, as if we were longtime lovers. The photographer snapped the photo and caught me with my eyes agog. Everyone at her table roared with laughter.

Soon, I excused myself and left to perform with my trio. All in all, I thought the whole episode fun. Nobody was hurt by it. The bottom line is that I really enjoyed meeting her, so I didn't mind her sexual repartee.

Later that evening, when my wife Sal showed up at the hotel, to sing the evening sets with my band, I told her about my meeting up with Shelley Winters that day. Sal asked me, "What is she like?"

I told her that she is actually a very down-to-earth person and a lot of fun to be with. Then I described how Shelley had playfully made a pass at me.

"You're kidding!" Sal exclaimed, with her eyebrows raised and a wry grin on her face.

"No, I'm not . . . She actually pulled me into a pose with her, for a photograph."

Sal said, "Oh, my Goodness! I can see it now. When I'm getting my groceries rung up by the cashier at the supermarket, I'm going to see a picture of my husband under a gossip tabloid's headline:
"SHELLEY WINTERS AND HER SECRET LOVER!"

Cornel Wilde

In 1983, Claire Eaton, from the banquet department of "The Boca," called to tell Sal and me that she had free tickets to Lynda Carter's Maybelline Pro-Celebrity Tennis Match, in Deerfield Beach. How could we refuse?

We arrived at the Deer Creek Racquet Club to find our tickets waiting for us at the "Will Call" window. When we found our seats, Claire spotted us in the crowd and came to join us. She said, "It's just about to start. You're in for a treat. You wouldn't believe how nice all of the celebrities were to me last night."

I looked at the program and saw it included some very big names. The announcer introduced the players who all came out in tennis whites holding their racquets. They were David Hasselhoff of *Knight Rider* and *Bay Watch* fame; Leslie Nielsen from *Airplane* and *The Naked Gun* movies; Desmond Wilson of the Redd Foxx T.V. series, *Sanford, and Son*. Of course, the event hostess, Lynda Carter (Wonder Woman) was there. Last, but not least, was actor Cornel Wilde.

They all joked around but really were very good tennis players. I was impressed. Who impressed me the most was the oldest of them all, Wilde. Born in 1912, in Hungary, Cornel was truly multitalented. He was a talented linguist and mimic; a qualifier for the USA fencing team prior to the 1936 Summer Olympics; but instead took a theater role. Some highlights of his illustrious career include being hired as Laurence Olivier's fencing teacher, and then, given a role in his production of *Romeo and Juliet*. Wilde's performance got him a film contract in Hollywood. Later, he played the lead role of Frederic Chopin in *A Song to Remember*, and was nominated for Academy Award's Best Actor. He also starred in *The Greatest Show on Earth*; and *A Thousand and One Nights*. He has a star on Hollywood's *Walk of Fame*.

At the tennis match, the veteran actor was getting on in age, but definitely not in attitude. He was in great physical shape; and just prior to playing his match, he did some warm up exercises that dazzled the crowd, me included. First, he did some normal exercises like stretching, knee bends, and upper-torso rotations. Then he got down on the ground and did a few pushups. The crowd started to cheer lightly. And then . . . he did a few

ONE-ARM pushups! The crowd yelled, applauded and whistled loudly. Then, lying prostrate on the ground, with his outstretched arms ahead of his body as if he were stealing second base, he did pushups! The crowd went wild!

His tennis playing was somewhat stiff and jagged, but he held his own against much younger opponents. All the celebrities put on a real show. It would have been worth it even if we'd had to pay.

When the match ended, Claire excused herself to take care of several chores. She told us to wait for her, for some coffee. We waited as the crowd cleared out. Finally, only Sal and I remained near the tennis court. Suddenly, out of nowhere, Cornel Wilde walked over. He smiled and said, "Hello. I left my gear bag here."

I said, "Hello, Mr. Wilde. You put on a great show out here today. I was impressed."

"Thank you. It was a lot of fun for me, too."

"Where did you learn how to do pushups like that? They were phenomenal!"

He answered humbly, "Oh, I just like to keep myself fit."

Then Sal interrupted and told him, "I just wanted to tell you that I've enjoyed many of your movies but one, in particular, is a favorite of mine. I must have seen *The Naked Prey* three or four times, and every time I've enjoyed it more!"

I echoed Sal's claim, "Oh yeah, that was a great movie!"

"Yes. It's one of my favorites, too!" he concurred,

The film, made in 1966, tells of an African safari guide who gets himself into a bad situation with a warrior tribe. They sent him out alone with nothing on and no weapons. Then they proceed to hunt him for the sport of it! It was truly exciting throughout the movie, and at the end . . . well, I'll let you find out for yourself. Find it on some late-night movie channel.

As Wilde talked, he started to step backward. As he did, he tripped over his own equipment bag. He was going down, and in the worst possible manner, indefensibly backward! Thank God I was there. I followed him down with my hands and arms catching his chest and head just before they violently hit the ground. I stopped the back of his head from hitting the hard tennis court surface, with just a foot remaining between them. I pulled him up level again, and he couldn't thank me enough. He said, "Thank you. Thank you so much. It appears that you're in very good shape yourself."

He was slightly embarrassed by the whole episode, and I guess I couldn't blame him. After all, the man had looked like an Olympic gymnastics champion in the beginning of the event, and he ended up looking (to us) like a horribly uncoordinated klutz only an hour and a half later.

He thanked me again, picked up his bag and left. A short time afterward, Claire Eaton came out and Sal told her, "You wouldn't believe what just happened with Cornel Wilde!" I said unassumingly, "Ah, don't make such a big deal about it... I ONLY SAVED HIS LIFE!"

Gabe Kaplan

In September 1984, Sal and I flew from Miami to Malaga, located on the Costa del Sol coast of Spain. Our journey was long and tiresome because of stopovers in New York and London. In New York, we visited my brothers, Bill and Vinny, and their families. And in London, we spent time with Sal's sister Joyce and her family. Upon arriving in Malaga, we put aside our flight fatigue because we anticipated a short cab ride to our final destination of Marbella (pronounced Mar-bay-ya), Spain.

There we would meet friends Claire and Mickey McGrath for two weeks of golf, beach fun, wining, dining, casino gambling, bullfights, flamenco dance shows, and excursions to places like Casares and Ronda. We had even planned an excursion to Morocco, on the African continent. So, at the Malaga airport, we easily sidestepped our travel weariness, with all this upcoming fun dancing in our minds.

We endured the crowded, mid-sized airport terminal. After customs and immigration interrogation, I cautioned Sal to watch our hand-held luggage, while I got a baggage dolly to retrieve the rest of our gear from the conveyer belt. As I left her, she reminded me, "We have two pieces of luggage, one garment bag and . . . oh, Honey, uh . . . don't forget your golf clubs!" She grinned broadly and I smiled slyly, implying that I caught her little joke. Like sure, I was about to forget my golf clubs! I had probably bored her to death with that one subject, throughout most of our plane flight.

I was able to locate our entire luggage, with one exception . . . my golf clubs! I waited and waited, but to no avail. Slowly the bustling airport's population dwindled until there were only three people in the entire airport. Sal, I and one other person watched the empty conveyor come to an abrupt halt. No one from either the Airport Authority or Iberia Airlines was anywhere to be found. We were on our own.

Sal approached me, asking, "Honey, what's going on? Were you able to get all of our luggage?"

I answered her nervously, "No, Sal. We're missing my clubs, and there's no one around to assist us."

Sal said, "It looks like that man over there has the same problem we have."

Right at that moment, the man turned toward us. Automatically, we started walking toward each other. I said to Sal, "Let me ask him. Maybe he knows what we should do."

"Roger, do you know who that is? That's Gabe Kaplan, the comedian!"

"You mean the guy from the T.V. show, *Welcome Back Cotter?* You know Sal, I believe you're right."

As we got closer and closer and our eyes zeroed in on each other, I said, "Hi . . . You're Gabe Kaplan, aren't you?!"

"Yes, I am," He responded.

41

I introduced us. "Gabe, I'm Roger Rossi and this is my wife Sal. We're kind of in the same business as you are. I'm a musician and bandleader and Sal is my lead vocalist."

"Well, it's nice to meet you both. Have you lost your luggage, too?"

Gabe Kaplan - Welcome Back Cotter

"Yeah, I'm missing my golf clubs, and man, this place IS empty. All I see are a few people out by the taxicab stands. How about you? What are you missing, Gabe?"

"A suitcase. Do you have any ideas what we should do?"

"Eh . . . yeah, I do. I bet you that our lost luggage is down at the bottom of that conveyer belt."

Sal interjected, "That makes sense, but what can we do about that?"

Sizing up Gabe I said, "Well, you're a little bigger than I am, Gabe, so you'd probably have difficulty going down there. It might be easier if I give it a try. It's quite obvious to me that no one from this airport is coming around here for quite some time. I'll go down there. If I locate our stuff, I'll throw it up to you guys, okay?"

Gabe said, "Please be very careful down there. I don't want you hurting yourself."

I started down the conveyer-belt chute, not knowing what to expect. I momentarily had a fearful image of getting mangled and maimed by some machinery. As I entered the secluded area, I was relieved to find only more conveyor belt. At the very bottom of the conveyor, on the floor, were a suitcase and my set of golf clubs. They had simply fallen off the belt. As I traveled further down to retrieve our gear, I realized that it was a smart decision to let me attempt it, rather than Kaplan, as the area was very cramped and my smaller, 5'11" frame could barely make it. I doubt that his bigger dimensions could have fit.

I yelled up to them with glee, "I've got 'em. Here they come."

"Oh, wonderful," he replied, as he reached down to grab them from the top of the chute. I climbed back up and Sal and he helped me out. While I was dusting off the remnants of my small expedition, he exclaimed to me, "Gee that was really nice of you. I can't thank you enough. Where are you folks going from here?"

"We're on our way to Marbella," Sal said.

"Well, that's where I'm going. Why don't we share the same taxicab?"

"All right. That would be nice, "I said.

We got all of our luggage together and moved it out to one of the few remaining taxicab drivers, and I asked the cabbie, "Comprende Ingles, Señor?"

"No, Señor," was the reply.

"How about you, Gabe. Do you speak Spanish?" I asked. He replied with a cordial smile, "No, Señor . . . Nada!"

"Well, I'll try my best."

In my very broken Spanish, which I had learned in high school, I negotiated for the cabbie to take the three of us to our hotels in Marbella for only $7. I thought that it was a fair price because the map had shown the distance from Malaga to Marbella to be very insignificant.

We all got on our way, with Gabe up front with the cabbie and Sal and I in the back seat. As it turned out, the trip lasted at least an hour through mountainous terrain, but the time passed very quickly. We enjoyed talking with this well-seasoned veteran and star of show biz. He was genuinely friendly. We discussed the various comedians we mutually knew. They were all personal friends of his, but I had worked with many of them. People like Ralph Pope, Marty Brill, Dick Capri, Marge Leslie, Jack Eagle, and Frank Mann. We went back and forth with short stories and tales about the show business acts and nightclubs that we both knew of and had worked, in and around the New York area.

Sal changed the subject and told Gabe that contrary to what people had told us for years, I didn't look anything like him. "For a while there, when your television show was really hot, all we heard was that Roger looked like you. They would come to our piano bar, find themselves a seat, and inevitably say, 'Look, the piano player looks just like Cotter.' We didn't even know what they were talking about because we were always working while your show was broadcast. But one night we finally got the chance to see your show, and I guess we saw a resemblance, but to be truthful, up close, I don't think you look at all like each other."

Gabe said, "I don't think we look like each other, do you?"

"Well . . . maybe the noses do," I said jokingly.

Sal said, "Don't get him started on noses, Gabe. He'll never stop!"

"Gabe, I've been told by many different people, at many different points in time, that I look like you, Vic Damone, Rob Reiner (Meathead on *All in the Family*), John Derek, and Gene Hackman. Now, whatever resemblance all of those people have in common with each other is beyond me!"

45

We finally arrived at Gabe's hotel. While the cab driver got his luggage, Gabe said, "You people have been a real treat to meet. I hope you have yourselves a great vacation. And Roger, how much do I owe you, for my part of the taxicab fare?"

"Nah, it's nothing. I've got it, Gabe. It's just been a delight to spend time with you!"

"No, I insist. Please let me pay my part," he said, cordially.

"Gabe, it's no big deal. I'll take care of it, but there is one thing that I would like."

"What's that? . . . Anything! You name it!"

"Maybe we could get the cab driver to take a picture of us. Would that be okay?"

"Certainly!"

We posed together and the cabbie took the photograph. We said our final goodbyes to Gabe and continued to our hotel.

As we arrived, our friends Claire and Mickey waited out front. After hugs, kisses, and handshakes, I began settling up with the cab driver. Mickey conversed with the gentleman in Spanish, while I talked with Claire and Sal. Mickey suddenly interrupted, asking, "Hey Roger, what are you trying to do, stiff the cab driver?"

"What do you mean? The fare was seven dollars and I gave him a U.S. 10. A forty-percent tip is not exactly what I would call stiffing him, would you?"

Mickey, who speaks Spanish fluently and even used to teach it, enlightened me as to what the cab driver's price really was. "No Pal, it's SEVENTY dollars, for the fare, not seven!"

After apologizing to the driver in my broken Spanish, I gave him an additional seventy-five dollars. Mickey explained to him that my Spanish II class in Amityville Memorial High School had obviously not worked for me.

We got on with our vacation, and when we returned home, we had our photographs developed. We were very disappointed that, out of the nine or ten rolls we took, the only picture that didn't turn out was the one of us with Gabe Kaplan. Our faces came out so dark that you just couldn't make out who was who. In retrospect, I guess after all that Gabe and I did look alike (Chuckle).

Recently, I've come to find out that Gabe Kaplan is not only an actor and comedian, but also a professional poker player. Although he's best known for playing the role of Gabe Kotter on the 1970's sitcom, "Welcome Back, Kotter," he has also become known as a poker player, commentator, and co-host for the American Television Channel series "High Stakes Poker" on the *Game Show Network*.

In recalling on our wonderful experience with Gabe, he was truly a gentleman and an interesting personality. However, if you happen to see him before we do, please tell him that he owes us either $42.50 for his half of the cab fare or another photograph!

P.S. Since I purchase the above photo from ImageCollect, and additionally it was an expensive vacation, tell him we'd prefer the cash!

Princess Diana & Prince Charles

The Prince and Princess of Wales visited Wellington, Florida on several occasions. Sal and I used to live in the community, just west of West Palm Beach. It's also the home of one of the world's finest polo grounds, the Palm Beach Polo and Country Club. The Prince loves the sport, and he was very accomplished player.

During an earlier visit of His Royal Highness, I was attempting to cut through a pine tree root that interfered with a sprinkler head in my front yard. Instead, jumping on a spade shovel, I cut right through my sneaker. My injury was serious enough to require fifteen stitches and crutches for two weeks.

Prince Charles-Princess Diana

Arriving at the West Palm Beach hospital, I found it swarming with police. I said to a curious deputy, "Gee, you didn't have to send for so much help. It's just a little cut, no big deal!"

48

Confused, he asked me, "What? . . . What are you talking about?" I said, "Oh nothing. I'm just kidding you. What's going on here? I've never seen so many police officers in one place at the same time."

"Prince Charles. He was playing polo and collapsed from dehydration, or something. You can't get in there right now. You'll have to wait."

"Oh, sure! The Prince needs to get himself a Vitamin B12 shot, and in the meantime, I'm bleeding to death!"

"I thought you just said that your little cut was no big deal!" He had a point. So, I waited. To make matters worse, I never even met the Prince!

However, because we attended many of his polo games, we did get to see him quite a bit. I'll never forget the astonishment of my in-laws, visiting from England when we took them to one such match. My mother-in-law said to us, "I can't believe it. We had to come on the other side of the Atlantic to see him. We never see him back home!"

Sal's sister, Joyce said, "It's amazing. Here we are standing only ten feet away from him. I've never been this close to him!"

Although we never talked with the Prince, we did actually converse briefly with Princess Di. The occasion was a Royal Polo Match, followed by a ball at the Breakers Hotel, in nearby Palm Beach. Both events occurred on November 12, 1985. They were charity events dedicated to raising funds for the United World Colleges. Because the ball that evening conflicted with my performance at Peter's Private Club in Tequesta, I could not attend. The fact that the 5,000- $50,000 per ticket price tag conflicted with my bank account was really just a secondary issue! (Ahem, ahem.)

Several of the local Chamber of Commerce members were asked to man the various concession stands for the polo event that would take place earlier that day. Since I was a past president of the Wellington Rotary Club, a member of the Chamber, and considered one of the local community leaders, my wife Sal and I were two of the volunteers.

Our job was to mix up vats of lemonade, pour them into Styrofoam cups, and hand-carry them into the bleachers to the fans watching the Royal Match. We did this for hours on end in extremely hot weather. Both Sal and I were ready to pass out from heat exhaustion. Besides carrying the trays of lemonade, we had to run across the field, before the matches, between the timeouts and the chukkers. It got to the point that the perspiration would actually cool off our faces from the heat.

As we were mixing lemonade on the service side of a see-through wall, we noticed, through that partition, a sizable entourage descending toward the Royal Box. Suddenly, the Princess of Wales was right in front of us. Stopping to peer through the wall, Diana stood less than five feet away from us. She was absolutely stunning. Di had a unique face. Her eyes were enchanting, her smile warm and pure. I have never seen such perfect skin tones. Simply flawless. She asked us from her elevated position, "What are you doing down there?"

Sal answered her, "Well . . . we're preparing some lemonade for your Royal Highness and some of your guests!"

"Well, thank you. What a lovely gesture! . . . Good day!"

She turned and walked away toward her seat in the polo stadium. Sal and I looked at each other and didn't know what to say. We just smiled, knowing that we had just enjoyed a beautiful and extraordinary moment in our lives. We had spoken with the Princess of Wales, and she initiated the conversation. She was very beautiful . . . and also quite human! Her tragic death stunned us. Sal was born in London, and the Royal Family holds a special place in her heart. Now, one of her all-time favorites is gone, violently swept away. May Princess Diana rest in the peace she could never find here on earth.

Robin Leach

Early in 1985, Sharon Edelman and Mike Abate of the Palms West Chamber of Commerce approached me. Sharon was a director and Mike was the president of the organization, whose membership included most of the top business people from Wellington and Royal Palm Beach.

Sharon said that the Chamber was going to sponsor a holiday parade through Wellington on December 15th. She added that the local Palms West Hospital would sponsor a concert in Royal Palm Beach the evening before. Sharon asked me, "What can you suggest to us and what do you have to offer us for that evening, Roger?"

"Just about anything that you would want, Sharon. Pop music, Dixieland, classical, big band, fifties – sixties - seventies and eighties rock." She said, "Whoa! Stop right there. What do you have to offer in the big band category?"

"Well, I've got a lot of powerhouse-musician friends and we could put on a nice event with a fourteen-piece outfit. I would co-direct it with a good friend, Pat De Rosa. Pat plays all of the saxes and besides having performed at some of the great New York nightclubs, he used to be with the Glenn Miller Band for years. I'll round up the finest available musicians in Palm Beach, Broward, and Dade

Lifestyles of the Rich & Famous

Counties, to fill in the rest of the band. We can feature my wife, Sal on lead vocals, and we'll play Glenn Miller, Duke Ellington, Artie Shaw, Tommy Dorsey, Woody Herman . . . you know, all of the big-band hits from the

30's, 40's and 50's. We can perform for dancing, or in concert, or perhaps a combination of both."

Mike said, "Gee! That sounds like it's just what we want." Sharon agreed.

I told them the price, the contracts were drawn up and signed, and I booked all of the musicians. It would be outdoors, at one of the public parks. On several occasions, I met with the planning committee and tried to get them to understand the importance of securing a local-indoors hall in case of inclement weather. They all voted it down. Sam Lamstein, the mayor of Royal Palm Beach, even joked about it. "I'll tell you what. I'll simply make an official decree, like the king of Camelot. *No bad weather* on December 14th. That will take care of the problem!"

Everyone on the committee laughed. I did not. "You folks can laugh, but this is my business. I know from past experiences that these things happen. If we don't prepare an alternative plan, everything can go right down the drain. I've contracted some of the finest musicians you could find anywhere. They're all solid professionals and they all expect to be paid, whether we have great weather, or it rains, or snows. And I've seen THAT ruin an engagement for us, too. Right here, in Florida!"

"No, your band will get paid, Roger. Don't worry about it. It's not going to snow," Sharon said, laughing.

Toward the end of November, Sal and I decided it would be nice to have a little party at our house, after the holiday concert. Sal asked me, "How many people did you want to invite?"

53

"Hell, I don't know, Sal . . . twenty, maybe twenty-five. Mainly the people on the committee and their spouses. Can you handle that?"

Sal replied confidently, "Sure. That won't be a problem. Why don't we start our guest list, and we'll take it from there."

When we'd finished counting the important people connected with the coordination of the concert, Sal said, "That's not any twenty-five people. We're up to forty-one guests, plus you and I. How are we going to fit them all?"

"Well, Honey, we do have a fairly good sized home, and it IS a cocktail party, not a sit-down dinner, you know. They can roam around the bar area, the living room, and playroom, around the swimming pool and patio. We'll fit them all in."

"Roger, I'll do my best and I'm sure that Lee can help out, too. Oh, my goodness, December 14th . . . That's her birthday!"

I said, "Okay . . . that means we now have forty-four people in attendance, counting our daughter. Hey, it's not everyone that gets a fourteen-piece big band for their daughter's birthday!"

We sent out the invitations for our party. Soon, I received a telephone call from Sharon Edelman. "Roger, I just received your invitation. I think it's great you and Sal are going to host a party that night. Can you stand a few more V.I.P.'s?"

"Gosh, our invite list is ready to explode now, Sharon. Who did you have in mind?"

"Well, for starters, Robin Leach, the host of the television series, *Lifestyles of the Rich and Famous.* He'll be our grand marshal for the holiday parade, the day after your concert. Both he and his producer, Malcolm Boyes, will appear at your concert. Can I invite them for you?"

"Definitely! Anybody else?"

"Yes. I've got some people from *The Globe* who have been very helpful with this whole event. I'd like to invite them, too. It's the publisher and several writers."

I told Sal the guest list had now grown by about five people. "But I don't really think they'll come, so don't worry about it!"

December 14th arrived. Even before I got out of bed, I knew we were in trouble. It was extremely cold, and pouring rain. The day before, the temperature was about 80 degrees and now it was in the 40's, with the worst yet to come. We all tried to cheer ourselves up and decided that it would still be a "go" for the concert. Throughout the day, all the musicians, one by one, called and asked us if we were still playing the concert. I told them to bring their heavy jackets and if they could find an old pair of gloves, to cut off the fingertips. That way they could keep their hands warm, and still be able to play their instruments. I said to them, "The concert officials are still expecting about 2,000 to 3,000 people. You BETTER be there!"

Around two-thirty pm, it stopped raining. Our hopes grew brighter, yet the temperature still dipped. We set up our staging. The soundmen got their tests out of the way. I set up my keyboards, went home, showered, dressed, and returned with Sal for the big night.

We arrived about twenty-five minutes before the downbeat. The temperature was in the 30's, and the open field, where the audience was to sit on beach chairs and beach blankets, was nothing but a sheet of ice from the day's rainfall. There were fewer than 100 people in the audience. Although they were diehard fans of ours, I had to question their sanity. They sat bundled up in blankets. I made an announcement that as long as they were out there listening, and for as long as the musician's lips could hold up, we would perform our scheduled show.

It was COLD! I had to play the keyboard gloved, but my fingers were stiff as a board. Even so, the band impressed everyone, including me. They never once complained, and they played with heart. Again, Pat De Rosa was a real delight to work with. Finally, Sal took off her raincoat and came center stage to perform in a stunning, low-cut gown. She sang out with all the bravado and charm she possessed.

The few people that came were treated to a great sound that night. Well, actually, half a night. We finally had to quit at the intermission. It was much too cold for audience and performers to continue. We finished the evening with a duet that Sal and I sang, called "Blue Moon." Shortly after we finished the arrangement, much to our surprise, Robin Leach showed up on the stage. He complimented the band. He said, "You gentlemen can play anywhere with that great sound. And YOU, Sal Rossi! I can't believe you. Not only do you sing so wonderfully well, but I think that with that dress you're wearing you must have all the courage in the world. Folks, did you know that song originally was called "Red Moon," but they changed the name to "Blue Moon," in honor of the change in Sal's skin color!"

Later we showed up back at our home to find a traffic jam out front. People from the next day's parade showed up and crashed the party. Neighbors, business people from the Chamber all came because they'd heard that Robin Leach was going to be there. We stopped counting after we had reached 85 guests. I told them all, "Sure, come on in. You're always welcome here." I didn't have the heart to turn anyone away.

The mayor arrived with his wife, and he apologized to me. He said meekly, "Roger, we should have listened to you and had the school hall as a backup."

"Mayor, you ought to leave decrees of that nature for Richard Burton to make!"

When Robin Leach and Malcolm Boyes arrived, they hung out at the bar.

Aside from joining in with everyone else to sing a chorus of "Happy Birthday" to our daughter Lee, I really didn't get much more out of Robin for the remainder of the evening, even though he stayed until the very end of the party.

I tried several times, to loosen him up and engage in conversation, but I kept on getting these one and two-word responses.

"So, tell me, Robin, how do you feel about living in the States?"

"It's okay."

(Pause)

"Gee, you've had such great success with your television show. Did you ever imagine that it would be that successful when you first started out?"

"Yes and no."

(Pause)

"Sal said to me tonight that this weather reminds her of London. Does it you?"

"A little."

(Pause . . . yawn)

I remembered that earlier at our concert, he'd used some dry humor with what he'd said about Sal turning blue, so I figured that I'd try some of my own brand of dry humor. I asked, "Robin, you know my wife Sal is originally from London?"

"Really?"

"Yes. I would have thought that you would have noticed that she was British. . . . It was so cold tonight that she sang with a STIFF upper lip!"

The people that were there at the bar, including our bartender, Isis, all doubled up in laughter. All except the famed television host. He simply responded with a deadpan face, "I see."

Malcolm Boyes, by contrast, was bubbly and enthusiastic. He told me that I should bring the key musicians from my band——like my lead trumpet player, drummer, Pat De Rosa and Sal—with me to Hollywood. He said that he'd be happy to set us up with a few concerts to play, and he'd show us all around town. I never took him up on it, but I thought his suggesting was nice. I went to take a picture of him with our daughter Lee and he said, "Sure, but only if I can give her a birthday kiss." He did, and I snapped the photograph.

One of my friends took a picture of Sal and me with Robin. Although it turned out slightly overexposed, it hangs in my office with a caption saying, *"The Lifestyles of the POOR AND UNKNOWN."*

Later, I bumped into Robin Leach when he served as grand marshal for the Grand Opening Parade at Macy's in Palm Beach Gardens, Florida. My jazz band was playing for the event. We had our picture taken with him, but I don't know why. He didn't remember coming to my home, complimenting my wife, watching my big-band concert in the cold weather, nothing. I said, "Robin, you must remember coming to my home in Wellington, back in December. It was after my big-band concert in the freezing weather. Remember?"

"Aaaaaa . . . yes."

(Pause . . . yawn)

Perhaps he was bored with my friends and my modest 5,000 square foot home, which of course pales by comparison to the extravagantly magnificent mansions featured on his T.V. show. Or perhaps he is a boring person in real life. Or perhaps both. Who knows?

Jerry Lewis

Not too many people ask you to join them on their honeymoon. In September 1987, Sal and I stood as matron of honor and best man for Claire and Mickey McGrath. While planning their wedding, they suggested we come with them.

We asked. "Are you out of your minds? It's your honeymoon! You guys should be on your own."

"Yeah, it's our honeymoon all right, but it's also a vacation. We're going to Las Hadas, a resort in Mexico. That's where they filmed the movie "10" with Dudley Moore and Bo Derek! Why don't you come?"

We talked it over and decided to go along.

A couple of days after their wedding, the four of us departed for the famous resort, which was rated in the world's top five. It's still a favorite retreat for many of Hollywood's top movie stars. However, to get there from the airport we had to travel by land for almost an hour in a cargo van with no air conditioning. It was painfully hot! In an effort to get our minds off the heat, we talked a lot.

The McGraths described how many big stars hang out at the resort. The conversation drifted slightly and Sal happened to ask if they had seen any of the *"Jerry Lewis Telethon"* on television.

They said that they had, and we passed the time talking about the annual television show, which raised so many millions of dollars for Muscular Dystrophy research.

"Call security. Jerry Lewis is here"

Finally, our van trip came to an end. We were all soaked with perspiration, and our clothing stuck to our skin. Claire and Sal's hair had gone limp. At the entrance, four beautiful ladies were waiting to greet us as we climbed out of the van.

They wore white dresses of soft fabric. Their hairdos were impeccable.

They were the epitome of freshness. We had arrived out of hell's inferno into the paradise of heaven, and these four ladies were angels. Holding enticing trays of cocktails, they said in rehearsed unison, "Bienvenido a Las Hadas. Welcome!"

We grabbed four drinks and guzzled them as quickly as politeness would permit. Then we looked at each other with shocked faces. I said, "Ugh . . . margaritas!" With the ingredients of tequila, lime, and SALT, it was like pouring chilled acid down our parched throats! I requested, in my broken Spanish, "Señoritas . . . agua por mi amigos! Por favor!" After they brought us our water, we began to feel better.

We checked in at the front desk. There was a small shuttle cart waiting for us at the front entrance. It had our luggage on it, and enough room for the driver to take us to our respective hotel suites, which were really luxurious villas. Soon, our friends called us, asking Sal, "How are your accommodations?"

"Everything's wonderful. The suite is spacious and beautiful!"

"It IS?"

"Oh yes. And how nice of the resort to indulge us with champagne!"

"You got CHAMPAGNE?" Mickey asked.

"Yes, we did. We also have flowers and a bowl of fruit!"

"WHAT? We didn't get any of that stuff here!"

Sal surmised the situation quickly. "Oh, no. I think you have our suite, and we ended up with the wedding suite!"

It was what had happened, but the McGraths insisted that because we were already settled in, we should keep things the way they were. So we ended up with the bridal accommodations. It made us feel like we were on our second honeymoon. Of course, we turned the fruit, flowers, and champagne over to our friends. They shared the champagne with us anyway.

The following evening, we went to one of the formal dining rooms. After we were seated, Claire asked me, "Do you remember who we talked about yesterday, while we came from the airport to the resort?"

"You mean . . . Jerry Lewis?"

"Right! Take a look behind you."

I did. Sure enough, seated at the very next table was the movie and television star, having dinner with a small group. I said, "Wow!" I said. "What a small world."

We were seated next to him several times during our stay, but we really didn't want to bother him. He looked like he was enjoying his time off from what I would guess had been some very hectic preparation for his telethon. We couldn't help but notice him every day on the beach. The resort set him up with his own private cabana. It stood out like a sheik's tent on the sand.

One day, we were returning from the enormous swimming pool, and the comedian was on his way there. As we approached I said, "Hi, Mr. Lewis. That was a terrific telethon this year." He simply smiled and said, "Thank you."

I took it a step further and said, "I'm a musician/bandleader from Florida, and I think you know somebody with whom I've often worked."

"Who's that?"

"Saxophonist, Sam Bidner."

"Oh, Sam has been with me for years. He plays well."

As we were parting I added, "Well, I hope you enjoy your vacation."

"Thank you," he said, continuing to the swimming pool.

We turned to observe him as he walked away. He walked over the long, rope bridge that spanned across the pool. Suddenly, he started clowning around a la his character in the movie *The Jerk*. He acted like he was going to fall off the bridge into the pool while yelling in his inimitable high-pitched voice. "Oh-oh . . . ah . . . Oh my goodness!" He had us in stitches! He brought me back to my early childhood, when I would see him on the Ed Sullivan show with Dean Martin. Man, those guys were hysterically funny. One time I even laughed so hard at those two, I actually wet my pants!

Meeting one of America's all-time great funny men, Jerry Lewis, and watching him nonchalantly clown around, was the highlight of our trip. Come to think of it, that's exactly the word that comes to mind when I think of Jerry Lewis. He's a *trip!*

Alexander Haig

Chuck and Harold's Restaurant is on the corner of Royal Poinciana and County Road, in Palm Beach. It features some wonderful dining and ambiance and used to have live music and dancing nightly. I used to perform there often, filling in for former bandleader Peppi Moreale, whenever he took off and I was available.

I would typically start the evening by counting the rest of the band into a lively riff, which would serve as background music to my welcoming announcements to the patrons of the club. Completing those greetings, I would segue into a light jazz tune, and then finally settle into some softer, dining music. That was the normal opening format, and my announcements were always more or less the same. That is, except for one particular evening in 1991.

I led the rest of the band into our intro riff; then I said, "Good evening, ladies and gentlemen. Welcome to Chuck and Harold's."

As I was talking and playing, I noticed (retired) General Alexander Haig sitting nearby. Haig served as White House Chief of Staff under Presidents Richard Nixon and Gerald Ford. At one time, he was the second-highest ranking officer in the Army, and Supreme Allied Commander of Europe, commanding all U.S. and NATO forces in Europe. He truly had an illustrious life and military career; a recipient of the Distinguished Service Cross, the Silver Star with Oak-Leaf Cluster, and the Purple Heart.

I recalled a few years earlier, when General Haig was Secretary of State for Ronald Reagan, he once created a slight image problem with the media.

It happened in 1981, when a would-be assassin shot the president, severely injuring him. Immediately following that dastardly attack, confusion and hysteria filled the airwaves. Television and radio stations around the country, and I presume the world, buzzed like beehives. They were all racing to "scoop" their competitors with various versions of the breaking story.

News bulletins interrupted all of the scheduled programs with updates of the incident, trying to keep the populace abreast of what happened.

One T.V. reporter even patched into the White House telephone system in an attempt to fill in details for his broadcast. Alexander Haig answered, and trying to quell any thoughts of that attempted assassination being of broader and more severe magnitude (i.e., a coup or an invasion), said softly but emphatically, "As of now, I'm in control here, in the White House."

The media, who stirred up quite a furor over the whole thing, misinterpreted it. Some suggested that Haig had made a Freudian slip, and was asserting his true aspirations of becoming President. The Democrats, and some Republicans who had their own presidential aspirations aligned themselves with the media, while the remainder of the G.O.P. naturally responded, 'Poppycock!' In any event, I'm sure that Alexander Haig eventually regretted his choice of words. He certainly never lived it down.

I've always been a fan of General Haig. Yet, I just couldn't resist spicing up my opening greetings. I continued, "I'm Roger Rossi, and I'm filling in for Peppi Moreale, who's on vacation . . . and you might say that . . . eh . . . as of now, I'm in control here . . . at Chuck and Harold's!"

I'm sure that the general thought that I was some sort of wise-ass. Nonetheless, he laughed along with everyone else. He even got up to dance to our music. Additionally, he applauded us. I felt quite honored!

Later, Alexander Haig did unsuccessfully run for president. Who knows? Maybe it WAS a Freudian slip!

John Kennedy, Jr.

At Chuck and Harold's in Palm Beach, you just never knew who was sitting next to you. Some people showed up for dinner in very casual attire, while others dined in business suits. Then again, because the world-famous Breakers Hotel is just a stone's throw away, some people came over after attending a charity ball, dressed in formal tuxedos and gowns. One night we played dance music to a group of twelve formally attired men who danced with . . . each other. Most evenings, the bulk of patrons were the local lounge lizards. Some were tourists from around the world, while others were celebrities. You never knew what to expect.

I vividly recall one Monday evening as I played with the house band, filling in for the regular bandleader. It was in November 1991, just a few weeks before William Kennedy Smith went on trial in West Palm Beach. Palm Beach had started to scurry with activity.

Smith, a member of the Kennedy clan, was being tried for rape. The whole area was bustling with reporters from around the globe. They all knew that various Kennedy family members were going to be around to support the young medical student.

When I came to work that evening in the bar, the large television, as usual, was broadcasting some sports information for the upcoming *Monday Night Football* game. Because the television's sound was always turned off and the bar area was slightly removed from the main dining area where the band performed, it never really bothered anybody. People came into the bar, sipped their beer, enjoyed the game, and never interfered with any dining customers who wanted to hear the band.

It was especially nice for us musicians to watch T.V. during our breaks. We would find any available seats. Of course, if the staff needed those seats for customers, we would vacate them and stand until others became free. After viewing part of the game, we would return to the dining room to play dance music.

Suddenly, that Monday night, a tremendous ruckus arose in the front bar area. While we performed, we conversed among ourselves, trying to figure out what the commotion was all about. We could hear everyone cheering, so the bassist, Phil Scarfone, said, "Somebody must've scored a touchdown."

"No, I don't think it's that at all," I said. "I can see some very bright lights reflecting off the mirrors in there. I bet someone is getting a speeding ticket, and I'm seeing police lights."

"Yeah, you're probably right. Or maybe it's an accident that happened right out front."

We continued playing and forgot all about it. On our next break, we again headed toward the bar to check the score. My original seat was occupied. I thought first, it was my son Roger sitting there. I said to myself, "What is Roger doing here? He must be planning to play a joke on me by acting incognito." I was all set to grab him affectionately in a wrestling-type headlock. Nearing the young lad, I realized that it wasn't my son at all. It was some other young man sitting there watching the game.

I joked to one of the waiters who knew I had been sitting there, "Hey Tom, that guy has some nerve sitting in my seat!"

The waiter chuckled. "Roger, do you know who that is?"

I looked the guy over, scrutinizing his face more thoroughly. "He looks awfully familiar, but no, I don't know. Who is he?"

Tom smiled broadly. "That's John Kennedy, Jr.!"

"Well, so it is," Man, for a second I thought he was my son. Now I know what those lights were reflecting off the mirrors. They were from the local television stations, weren't they?"

"Yes."

"Look, Tom, just tell him that it's all right. . . . He can stay in my seat!"

The waiter laughed, and as I passed by the late president's son to seize another available chair, I asked him, "Excuse me, but do you happen to know what the score is?"

He answered politely, "No, I'm sorry, I don't. I just started watching the game."

"Okay, thanks anyway."

As I walked away from the famous young gentleman, I thought of all the things that might have happened had I got him into that headlock playfully intended for my son. Bodyguards might have jumped me. National and international photographers and reporters, still hanging around the club for a possible story, would have had a heyday. How about some of those supermarket-type tabloids? I can see the headlines now. . . .

PIANIST ATTACKS JOHN JOHN
BERSERK MAN MUGS PRESIDENT'S
SON FOR SEAT IN TV BAR

Later, in July 16, 1999, the world was shocked when John F. Kennedy, Jr. died in a plane crash near Martha's Vineyard, Massachusetts. JFK Jr., often referred to as John-John, was an American lawyer, journalist, and magazine publisher, and the only surviving son of President John F. Kennedy.

He was young, handsome, charismatic and a creative gentleman. However, for me, in November 1991, he was also a regular guy watching a Monday night football game at a T.V. bar.

John Patrick

I met the great author, John Patrick, while my wife Sal and I performed at Heritage Park in Delray Beach. John, a resident there, wrote such fabulous plays and screenplays as *Teahouse of the August Moon, Three Coins in the Fountain, High Society, The Curious Savage, Love is a Many Splendored Thing* and *The Hasty Heart*. To simply have him in our audience would have been an honor in itself. To have him applauding endlessly and enthusiastically, as he did after each selection, was no less than heartwarming.

After our performance, he invited us to join him for dinner, which we regrettably had to decline due to a previous commitment. We did however, talk for more than an hour with the famous playwright. John was already 89 years old, but he was as vibrant and alert as could be. He complimented our performance and said to Sal and me, "I wish that I had known you both when I was younger. I would have helped your careers. I would have had you in one of the movies that I wrote, for sure!"

I said, "Hmmm, that would have been very nice."

Shortly after our meeting, he celebrated his ninetieth birthday. Unfortunately, once again, we could not make the celebration because we were performing elsewhere. When we did return to perform at Heritage Park again, I called John several times to invite him to our show. I left message after message and received no replies. I could not understand why he was ignoring us, especially when he had been so wonderful to us only a few months earlier. I later found out that he had entered into a terrible state of depression.

About a month passed, and we were shocked by the news of his suicide. The loss of John Patrick was the loss of a great man with a great mind. More importantly for us, it was the loss of a man with a warm and congenial heart.

Donald Trump

In November 1999, with my 4-piece band, *"Roger Rossi and Class Action,"* I played a Palm Beach dinner-dance for a charity group called *Friends of Abused Children.* The event, held at The Palm Beach Shores Resort, was to honor their "Child Advocate of the Year," Dorothy A. Sullivan. Donald Trump was the "surprise" guest speaker.

After I piano soloed for cocktail hour, my band joined me to play dance music. We played a few songs when Jeanette Cassin, a Co-Chairperson for the event, approached me. She asked, "Roger, are you aware that Donald Trump is going to say a few words?"

"Yes, I was told."

"Would it be possible for him to use one of your microphones?"

"Oh, sure. Absolutely."

"Thank you, and would it also be possible for you to play some fanfare music, after I welcome him to the stage?"

"Yes, I could do that, too. When did you plan on doing this?"

"In about two minutes."

Ms. Cassin left the stage, giving me enough time to plan a proper fanfare. As I looked toward the back of the room I noticed Donald with Melania. I'm not sure if she was still his girlfriend, or if by that time had become Mrs. Trump. Either way, they certainly are a beautiful couple.

I had to get focused, and think quickly about what I was going to play for his fanfare. Then, *BINGO*, it hit me.

I don't know how many of my readers remember, but all the way back in the middle of the 1980's, there was a political group in America that wanted to draft Donald Trump to run for the Presidency of the United States. He mentioned it numerous times during election years. He would say, "I'm thinking about running for president!" He said it time and again. However, when it would get closer to the moment of truth, and the Media would "pin him down" asking, "Mr. Trump, are you going to (in fact) run for president?" He would always decline saying, "No, not at this time."

Now, everyone that truly knows me, also knows that I have a rather warped sense of humor. It's been with me ever since I first started playing shows with comedians. So, what surfaced from those memories was to always think with a sense of "weirdness." Weirdness can often be funny. The shock of it all throws people off their "norm" and they ultimately . . . laugh!! Just think of the great comedian Jerry Lewis. When he would act weird, he would send his audiences into frantic hilarity.

I decided to play a piece composed in 1812 by James Sanderson, and played by brass bands in welcoming Presidents from George Washington to present day. It's called, "Hail to the Chief." But, my weird humor came into play not only because Donald Trump wasn't (yet) a president, so it was shocking for the audience to hear it played; but also because of the way I presented and played it. I didn't tell my lead-vocalist wife Sal or band members what I was going to do.

I first pressed the button on my keyboard selecting one of the raunchiest rock-guitar sounds I could find. Then, I put an extreme amount of reverb (echo) into the amplifier. To top it off, I played the reverent piece using dissonant chords, making the music sound slightly out of tune. Most people find dissonance to be abominable. They might squint their eyes shut, and cover their ears with their hands because to them, the dissonance would sound so harsh.

So, here's what happened. Jeanette Cassin came back on stage, and taking the available microphone in hand, she proudly announced, "And now, ladies and gentlemen, it gives me great pride in presenting our surprise guest speaker: Palm Beach's one and only Donald Trump!"

I played my obscene sounds with the reverence and bravado that you might expect in presenting Washington, Lincoln, Truman or Reagan! It was with total chutzpah!!

The unsuspecting crowd, Sal and my band members, all went into hysterics, joined immediately by Jeanette

Cassin and almost simultaneously by the caught-off-guard audience. Additionally, Donald Trump, who like me has a serious side to him but obviously also a great sense of humor, approached the stage fronting a broad grin.

He took hold of my provided microphone, and while looking at me, declared as expected, "No, I'm not doing that at this time."

Nodding affirmatively, I smiled back, but thought to myself, "Hmm, it seems to me I've heard those words before." That encounter with Donald Trump took place in November 1999, 16 years before he actually decided to run.

Shortly afterwards I received a very nice letter from Jeanette Cassin which I've posted for your perusal at the end of this story.

To my delight, in 2015, *The Donald* finally declared his presidential candidacy. Hardly anyone gave him a chance in hell to go any further than a few weeks or months, but he proved them all wrong when he not only became the front runner for the Republican Party, but ultimately that Party's Nominee.

In the November 2016 elections, Trump overcame all odds by stating repeatedly, "I'm going to make America great again!" He was elected our 45th president. May God bless America, and President Trump's sorely needed leadership!

Interestingly, I have a personal note to offer to my readers. Because Trump was inaugurated president in 2017, I personally (and proudly) can lay claim to the fact that I was the VERY FIRST musician to ever play *Hail to the Chief* for President Donald J. Trump, but oddly enough, that took place 17 years before he took office!!

Donald Trump and Melania

of Abused Children, Inc.

222 Lakeview Ave., Ste. 160-209 • West Palm Beach, FL 33401

(561) 659-5005

Mr. Roger Rossi
1872 Autumnwood Way
Palm City, FL 34990

Dear Roger,   November 29, 1999

It was a true pleasure to work with you to bring our "Child Advocate of the Year" dinner, honoring Dorothy A. Sullivan, together. Your piano accompaniment during our cocktail hour set the perfect mood for our guests.

You adapted beautifully as our evening progressed with a surprise visit from Donald Trump, our honorary chair, as well as working with the dance troupe La Mystique.

Our photos demonstrate the fun had dancing to your music, which you varied to please our entire audience. There were very few people in their chairs during your performance! I very much appreciate your flexibility during the evening and will recommend you as our band for our 2000 dinner.

Many thanks from myself and Friends of Abused Children, Inc.

Sincerely,

Jeanette Cassin

Jeanette Cassin
1999 Board Secretary and Co-Chair for "Child Advocate of the Year" Dinner-Dance

The Personalities

PART TWO: The Vocalists

Dorothy Collins
Tommy Desmond
Johnny Mathis
Gene Stridel
Tennessee Ernie Ford
Vaughn Monroe
Tony Bennett
The Shangri-Las
Julius La Rosa
Perry Como
Vic Damone
Mel Tillis
The Ink Spots
Melissa Manchester

Roger Rossi

Dorothy Collins

I come from a very musical family. My father Vincent started his musical career as a concert violinist educated at the Royal Conservatory of Bellini, in Palermo, Italy. Later, he received his Masters from Columbia University. After the Great Depression interrupted his classical career, he worked with the great jazz violinist Joe Venuti and for five years with vocalist Kate Smith. My mother Eva, whose voice was at least equal to Smith's, took relief from the humdrum of raising her six children, by playing guitar and mandolin duets with Dad. Mom finally insisted Dad had to get "a real job" and spend more time at home. He ended his promising music career by working for the Musicians Union, Local 802, in New York City.

My brother Vince, an accomplished pianist and part-time trombonist, also received a couple of music degrees. Sister Eve and brothers Bob, Bill and Paul collectively studied saxophone, clarinet, violin, voice, trumpet, and piano. I took up the piano in 1951 and, later, bassoon. With so many music students practicing under one roof, the cacophony of sound was often followed by brief arguments about individual practice time. Sometimes those spats were settled by practicing duets together. Occasionally I sidestepped the problem by joining my waiting pals out front. We had installed a basketball backboard on a telephone pole and friends Buddy Passela, Johnny Werner, and even three girls, Cathy McCauley, Mary Ann Teleisha and Jackie Franklin, always had a game going.

We also had neighbors who were musicians, famous ones. In the fifties, there was a television show that probably had every music lover in the land tuning in. It was The Lucky Strike Hit Parade. That show, a forerunner to such shows as Dick Clark's "American Bandstand" and The Casey Kasem Show, was just about as big a production as there was.

The format had performers counting down the top music hits of the week. They counted from number ten down to number one. Unlike Clark and Kasem, who would spin recordings of their hits of the week, the handful of stars on the Lucky Strike Hit Parade actually performed those hits live.

Two of those stars were vocalist Dorothy Collins and bandleader, Raymond Scott. Dorothy and Raymond lived about six or seven houses away from our Lee Avenue home in Babylon. They came to our house on several occasions, joining my parents for cocktails and dinner. Scott became friends with Dad, who by that time was an executive with the musicians' union.

Originally, when we all moved into the area, the population was small. In time, the community grew, and we children had a problem with interrupting traffic. We, of course, felt that the cars were interrupting us! What did we know about streets being built for automobiles? We were just a bunch of kids trying to have a little fun. There was no facility in which we could play ball, so we had to be creative. We'd play stick ball, kick the can, running bases and of course, basketball, out on the street. It's too bad kids don't play games like that today. There were no costs for the equipment, and it kept us out of trouble. Most drivers would break up our game by simply driving right through without hesitation. They'd yell at us, "Get the hell out of the way!" We'd have to immediately jump aside because they'd stop ONLY if just about to hit us.

Raymond Scott and Dorothy Collins, by comparison, used to exercise saintly patience. It seemed like they actually enjoyed our brief interference. They'd stop their car, giving us more than enough room and time to finish our immediate play. When we were done, they'd applaud us as we'd let them by. We got to like them so much that we would wave and yell greetings to them as they passed. We knew that they were big television stars, but we also knew them in a way that the rest of America never saw them, as down-to-earth people. Then we would see them on their TV show that weekend, as the star performers they both were. Years later, Dorothy was a regular on the Allen Funt T.V. hit, (Smile! You're On) Candid Camera.

I get together a couple of times a year with my longest known friend Buddy, and his wife Josephine. I've not seen Cathy, Jackie, Johnny, or Mary Ann in over forty-five years. However, speaking for all of them, I don't think we could ever forget how nice Dorothy Collins and Raymond Scott were to a bunch of ordinary teenagers who lived down the block!

Tommy Desmond

On the evening of January 4, 1959, at the Highland Hotel in Massena, New York, I officially agreed to work as a piano accompanist for Tommy Desmond. I'm not 100 percent sure the agreement was legal and binding. It was scrawled and signed by Tommy and me without benefit of any witnesses. Furthermore, we were both stone drunk at the time.

That evening was special, marking the completion of my eight-month engagement with my trio. Furthermore, it was the end of Tommy's two-week entertainment contract there, as the headliner. Additionally, it was a triple birthday—mine, Tommy's and drummer Bob Andrew's. Needless to say, the place was jammed with friends of the band and of Tommy. They came in to celebrate with us. We must have had three dozen empty cocktail glasses sitting on the piano. Most of those drinks were the customers' way of telling us, "Thanks, and good luck!" Most of those drinks were purchased by the ladies in the place.

By my nineteenth birthday, I had unintentionally gained a reputation of being a ladies' man. I had lots of girlfriends in high school and in my brief time at music school. However, if girls didn't initiate any sexual advances, I was too shy to try.

I remember a high school chum giving me his spin on how to make sexual advances with girls. His advice was that upon encountering and shaking hands with them, I should use my index finger to vigorously scratch the

inside palm of their hand. He told me that if interested, the girl would signal me back by caressing my hand with her thumb. The very first time I attempted this technique with a young girl, instead of caressing my hand in return, she looked me square in the eye, and said, "Don't peck like a chicken; ask like a man!" I turned as red as a beet quickly beat it out of there, and never tried that ever again.

Tommy Desmond

At the Highland Hotel, it was quite different, as Bob Andrews and Tommy Desmond taught me the ropes to sexual encountering. However, undoubtedly my best tutoring came from our bassist Marty Weinberg, with whom I shared an apartment. Marty was and is literally a sexual expert. After receiving his Bachelor's degree from St. Lawrence University, Master's from the University of Massachusetts, and Ph.D. in sociology from Northwestern University, he became Assistant Professor at Rutgers University; then served as a senior research sociologist at the Kinsey Institute; and received the International Distinguished Scientific Achievement Award from the Society for the Scientific Study of Sexuality. Now in 2016, as a professor of sociology at Indiana University Bloomington; a charter member of the International Academy of Sex Research, Marty is consider one of the world's greatest experts on sex, having written a dozen or more books on the subject.

Yes, being the youngest man in the band, I learned a lot from these well-seasoned "sexperts," and because of our combined prowess, the Highland Hotel was always filled with the fairer sex. Bob, Marty and I were single, while Tommy was married. That shortcoming didn't bother Tommy when he came to town. Between the four of us, we must have gone out with half the ladies in the Massena area; all of the good-looking ones, at least.

Toward the end of the evening, Tommy pulled me aside and asked, "Hey man, now that you're finishing up here, what are your plans?"

"I'm not really sure, Tommy. I thought that I'd go back to my hometown on Long Island, and perhaps try to round up some work in the Big Apple. What are your plans?"

"I'm going to need a piano accompanist, and man, I like the way you accompany me! Are you interested?"

I would have done almost anything to be Tommy Desmond's piano accompanist. In retrospect, he was one of the greatest entertainers and vocalists I have ever heard. I've been to concerts by Frank Sinatra. I've seen and heard the best vocalists in the world. Tommy was as good as anyone. He sang a style that was a cross between Nat King Cole and Johnny Mathis. He had the entertaining qualities of a Sammy Davis, Jr. Yet, he also had the smoothness, charm, and warmth of a Perry Como.

Added to all of those attributes were his physical properties. He was a very good-looking black gentleman who had boxed professionally. He had the exact dimensions of young Cassius Clay! He was six feet three inches tall and weighed two hundred and twenty-five pounds. His boxing record was very good (20-1), but he was knocked out in his last fight, and just didn't like it. He once showed me pictures of an exhibition bout he fought in Montreal against the great Archie Moore.

Wrapped around all of those qualities and talents was an obsession with his expensive and classy wardrobe. In those days, he wore tailor-made suits and tuxedos that cost him five and six hundred dollars apiece. When he came on stage, everyone watched and listened to him with bated breath. He was a force that could not be dismissed. If there ever was a vocalist who had a great chance at making the big-time ranks of show business, Tommy was that person. I have no doubt that even with those show-business superstars I just mentioned on the same stage. Tommy Desmond would have stolen the show. No wonder he made such a hit with the ladies.

I told Tommy, "Yes, I'm interested. How much are you prepared to pay and where do you plan on working?"

The salary he mentioned was fine, and he said, "We're going to open at Three Rivers."

It was natural for me to presume Tommy was referring to the club in Syracuse, New York, only 145 miles south of Massena, called the Three Rivers Inn. That club featured nothing but big-time stars like Sammy Davis, Liberace, Dean Martin and Jerry Lewis. I told Tommy, "That would be acceptable."

He said to me, "Well, I'll tell you what. I'll quickly type up an agreement for us, with all the facts. We'll let that hold us until we get it all down on a Musician's Union contract. Okay?"

I agreed. Then I returned to the bandstand to finish my last dance set, while he disappeared to take care of his small chore. The performance done, I made it over to the bar where Tommy now sat with three or four adoring ladies. He said to the bartender, slurring in his half-drunken state, "Give ush a drink. Roger and I are shelebrating our birthdays and our new partnersship!"

He gave me the agreement papers. I scrutinized them the best I could. My vision was now blurred, my brain was vegetating, and my right ear was being nibbled by some gorgeous blonde I had never seen before. In reading the agreement, I saw my name, Tommy Desmond's name, my salary and Three Rivers, all listed properly. I signed both copies. Tommy also signed both and gave one to me. We toasted each other. I don't know her name, but the blonde drove me home and stayed the night. Why? I don't know. I was useless!

The next day, my head throbbing, I decided to look over our new agreement. I started to peruse it. In the middle of the document, my eyes opened VERY wide. I read my name, Tommy's name, my established salary and everything seemed fine. But then it hit me. Tommy and I were to start working together at a place called the Club Des Forges, in THREE RIVERS, QUEBEC! That's how I ended up in Canada for three years.

Things actually went pretty well working with Tommy Desmond. We appeared at the smaller clubs throughout Quebec. We did some small city television and radio promotion for our gigs. Everywhere we went, the clientele and club owners applauded his hiring me as accompanist. However, there were occasional exceptions. Several black entertainers asked Tommy, "We have a lot of black piano players in town, man. Why are you using that white boy?"

They knew I was within earshot of their prejudiced remarks. I felt very good when Tommy defended me with, "It's simple, man. I've heard those guys play piano. Even hired some. . . . Nobody plays like Roger! Noooobody!"

We decided to enter a T.V. talent show, the Canadian Talent Search. We won first prize, which mainly brought us notoriety. The show aired throughout Vermont and Quebec. It attracted some backers, who became our managers. They were Joe Azaria and Larry Fine, the publisher, and editor of a celebrity, gossip-supermarket tabloid called Midnight, which became the main competitor to the National Inquirer. Midnight eventually was bought out and became Globe. When Azaria and Fine ran it, they had enough clout to get us booked in some good rooms. We started working places like The Faisan Bleu, The Chateau Saint Rose, and The El Morocco, all in the Montreal area.

I remember the El Morocco engagement as if it were last night. The club had a history of using big-name entertainment. The week before we arrived, it had featured the legendary drummer Louis Bellson, and his wife the renowned Pearl Bailey. We were asked to replace the scheduled recording star Brook Benton, who had taken ill. They replaced everyone in his show but couldn't get an M.C. At rehearsal with the band, they asked me. Big mistake! I was never so nervous and flustered in my whole nineteen years. Stage fright can be devastating! If it had happened anywhere else but a big time, famous place like the El Morocco, it might not have been so bad. Surely my knees would not have shaken as violently at "Joe's Bar." In front of all those sophisticated people, the El Morocco stage felt like 6.8 on the Richter scale. I never realized I had a speech impediment until that night. Coincidently, I've never had one since! My brain went totally lame.

Several knowledgeable people, including Tommy and the club's bandleader, coaxed me and coached me. "Look, Roger, it's easy. The band will play some opening music. While the music is being played, you trot onto the stage and pick up the microphone. The band will stop playing when you start talking. All you have to say is, "Good evening ladies and gentlemen. The El Morocco proudly presents . . ." and then you say the name of the opening dance act. Got it?"

I nodded half-heartedly.

We finished rehearsing, and while having dinner I practiced my opening lines. That evening, the moment of truth came. The club's lights dimmed, the band played its riff, and I jogged to center stage while a spotlight tracked me. As planned, the band stopped playing and the drummer started his roll. At that point, it was like Vladimer Horowitz had just finished playing the Star Spangled Banner and the T.V. broadcast went off the air. Nothingness! Tommy told me later that I never got past 'G-g-g-good . . . evening . . . eh . . . ladies and gen-gen-gentlemum . . . Eh . . . gentlemum.' After that, I started to laugh quietly. I felt drunk, yet, hadn't touched a drop that night, until later! My laughter wavered from louder to softer to louder. I stood on that famous stage, clutching the microphone with one hand and covering my mouth with the other, hysterically laughing like a blithering idiot. And yet, I was so stupefied, I could not walk off. I simply laughed.

Tommy, trying to help me, yelled out from backstage, "Roger, welcome the people here."

I peered toward the stage's curtain, and asked Tommy, over the hand-held mike, "Where?"

He responded angrily, "Just welcome them, man!"

I turned to the audience, and said, "You're welcome!" Again, I went into hysterics.

Finally, the bandleader introduced the opening act and gave the downbeat for the band. They didn't need a cane to yank me off stage. The spotlights focused on the dance act. I stood alone in the dark. Thank God for darkness. It covered my redness!

I dejectedly went backstage and apologized to everyone. Tommy comforted me by saying, "Don't worry about it, man. You should've seen me the first time. I was worse." I knew he was lying, but it made me feel better. I felt even better when he later gave me recognition in the middle of his show. He said, "Folks, that young man at the piano is only nineteen years old. I've had several accompanists during my career, and he's the best . . . Roger Rossi." Everyone in the place gave me thunderous applause. Then he said, "Of course, tomorrow we need to find a new Master of Ceremonies, but Roger will be my piano accompanist for as long as he wants the job!"

I felt an even stronger kinship with Tommy after that. I settled down and became a real asset for him. Eventually, my accompanist position grew into a musical directorship. From the piano bench, I conducted the various bands with whom we worked. Not only were we a musical team, we became great friends. Long before the T.V. show All in the Family poked fun at racial situations, Tommy and I did. This, of course, was before people got so insanely sensitive, and "politically correct." One time he referred to my curly hair by calling me Roger "Spaghetti-head" Rossi.

The next night, I got even. It was opening night at a club in Montreal. When I first saw Tommy, I shook his hand and said ceremoniously, "Congratulations Tommy. You've finally made the big time!"

Bewildered, he asked, "What do you mean?"

"Didn't you see it, man? You had to see it when you came into the club!" With absolute bewilderment, he once again asked me, "See WHAT? Roger, what are you talking about?"

I said to him, "Tommy, they have your name in neon lights . . . out front!" Now he was really getting excited. I could see it all over his face.

"Where? . . . I didn't see a thing."

I took him outside and pointed across the street to a delicatessen's billboard. In huge, blinking neon lights the billboard advertised:

"S M O K E D   M E A T ! S M O K E D   M E A T !"

So, I had my nickname, and now Tommy had his.

Tommy had a great sense of humor and timing. I recall when we played a benefit with several other entertainers including my future wife Sal and her singing partner Jill Walker called, The Walker Sisters. The show was for the inmates at the Saint Vincent de Paul Penitentiary in Montreal. Tommy, who once served prison time in the states during his earlier years, could truly relate to those inmates at Saint Vincent's. He got them all singing an island song, a la Harry Belafonte.

Belafonte used to tell various sections of his audience, "Okay, now only the ladies sing!" Later, "Now, all the men over forty!" And, "Women over eighty!" Of course, the avid singers in the audience went completely silent. Then, he would announce, "Now, only women thirty-nine or younger." Every lady in the audience bellowed out with great loudness.

Tommy did the same routine, with one variation. When it came to the chorus, he brought the house down with, "Okay, MURDERERS ONLY, SING!" Later, "All right, ONLY BANKROBBERS!" Then, "Alright, "Let's hear it from . . . THE COUNTERFEITERS!"

Those guys couldn't sing a note; they were too busy laughing! As usual, they wouldn't let him off the stage without encore after encore. Tommy got that same reaction everywhere we performed!

Eventually, we recorded a single at the R.C.A. Victor studios, titled I Want a Girl. It was an updated version of the Roaring Twenties hit. The recording was released on the EMC Label. It helped us get recognized across Canada. We started getting bookings in some of the great hotels and clubs in Toronto, Ottawa, Hamilton, Niagara Falls, and London.

One week we opened the same show at the Chateau Saint Rose that singer, Tommy Edwards headlined. Edwards had a number one 1958 hit, "It's All in the Game." Edwards had the hit, but Tommy Desmond, who acted more as the M.C., stole the show. Even the management approached us afterward, saying they had made a mistake. They should have put Desmond in the star spot. It was a letdown to hear Edwards sing after Desmond!

We were also doing some of the better coast-to-coast television shows. Several times, we were on the Canadian equivalent of The Merv Griffin Show, or The Tonight Show. On April 4, 1960, Tommy was featured on that show with actress-dancer Gloria De Haven and the legendary drummer, Gene Krupa. It aired immediately before the Academy Awards Presentation. Tommy made a hit that night, and Ben Hur won the Oscar.

Somewhere in the middle of all that activity, I met Sal. For me, it was love at first sight. For Sal, it took a little longer. She was so different than all of the "ladies" I had previously known. She was a REAL lady, and I found that all of my usual lines didn't work on her. It took a while before she realized those lines were a facade. She made me change, gradually undoing Marty Weinberg's and Tommy's "tutoring." However, Sal knew I was working with a great entertainer, and she never objected.

Tommy, on the other hand, never changed. Things turned worse almost overnight. He was very heavily into alcohol including an insane mixture of green chartreuse and vodka, along with Quaaludes, hashish, marijuana, and various pills ingested day and night. He tried to introduce that garbage to me, but I never fell for it. It all caught up to him.

Too many times, as we went to work at a top club somewhere, I would have to drive from our home-based Montreal to our destination, while he'd try to resuscitate himself from the poisoning he'd put his body through the night before. When we arrived at that club, I'd have to rehearse the band by myself, as he was still flying high. One day we even went to the wrong club in the wrong city, because he had misread the dates on the contract. We were in Quebec City when we were really supposed to be at a club in Toronto.

All this time, he constantly fought with his wife, because of the other women he always had around him. She was no angel, either. I just tried to keep myself out of it. It was difficult because he would lie to her, then ask me to verify the lie.

He had all the qualities needed to make it big, except one. He lacked personal discipline. I finally stopped working with Tommy and started working with vocalist Gene Stridel.

About six months after leaving Tommy, I received a call from a mutual friend in Montreal. He said that Tommy had gotten very high one night, ignored a stop sign and driven his car under an eighteen-wheeler transport truck. He was almost decapitated. Tommy Desmond, one of the greatest talents I've ever known, was dead at thirty-one years of age. If I had not left him, I would have been in his car that night. He was on his way to a gig! It's a damned shame. If he had done the right things in life, we could have been headlining in Las Vegas, and throughout the world.

Johnny Mathis

In 1960, Tommy Desmond and I performed in an intimate Montreal lounge, the Venus De Milo. It was on Saint Catherine Street, right in the heart of the city. A baby grand piano sat on a cute stage. Tommy would perch on a stool and sing his torch songs. The room was always busy, for two basic reasons. One, it always featured very good entertainment, and two, it was a small room.

It was a perfect place for us to hone in on our musical skills, and to work on new arrangements. This way, when we worked in other clubs that featured orchestras with which we worked, we were quite prepared. Tommy and I both liked performing there. The place attracted a lot of young couples. Because there was no dance floor, we could always emphasize love ballads. Tommy Desmond had a broad spectrum of songs in his repertoire, but he loved to do the songs that Nat King Cole and Johnny Mathis recorded. Actually, his voice sounded close to both of those vocal superstars.

One evening, a young man sat by himself in the crowd, obviously enjoying our musical presentation and style. He heartily applauded every song. He listened to every single note we played and sang with such dedication that, even when the waitress delivered his cocktails, he did not turn from observing us. After we had finished our last set, he approached us. After introducing himself as an American by the name of Paul Green, he gave Tommy his business card, telling us he was Johnny Mathis' stage manager.

Paul said, "The two of you are really wonderful performers. I know that Johnny would love to meet you!"

Tommy replied, "Thank you. We'd like to meet him, too."

"Well, that won't be too much of a problem. He's performing every night this week at Her Majesty's Theater. Just tell me what show you'd like to attend, and I'll get you free tickets. After his show, I'll introduce you to him backstage."

Tommy thanked him and said Sunday was our night off.

"That will be Johnny's last night. Then we have to head back to the States." As he talked, he wrote a little reminder on a small pad. "I promise there will be two tickets waiting for you at the "Will Call" window, in the front lobby. Included in the envelope will be my personal directions to where we can all meet when the show finishes. Okay?'

When Tommy and I finished performing Saturday evening, he received a telephone call and came back and told me that something very important had come up. He couldn't make the Mathis concert the following evening. "I'm sorry, man, but I just can't make it. Why don't you take Sal with you?"

As we hurried into the front lobby Sunday evening, Sal was ecstatic. She said, "I can't believe this is actually happening. I'm going to finally see Johnny Mathis performing . . . live!"

As we headed toward "Will Call" I said, "Well, don't get your hopes up too high. We don't have the tickets in our hands yet."

"Please tell me that you're teasing me. We will get in, won't we?"

"I'm teasing you, Sal. I actually brought along enough money to pay for our own tickets just in case Johnny Mathis' stage manager forgot us."

"Oh, thank you, Honey. This means so much to me!"

"Yeah, but then again, maybe the tickets aren't there. And who knows, maybe the show is sold out. What do we do then?"

The lady behind the "Will Call" window presented me with the envelope. I concluded the tease by opening the envelope very slowly, peeking inside and then announcing, "Ah SHUCKS . . . The tickets are in here!"

As promised, Paul Green had also included a note: Glad you could make it. At intermission time, watch the stage door at the left of the stage. I'll come out and look for you.

I'll only have a minute, so be sure to watch for me. (Signed) Paul.

Sal and I got our programs, found our seats and soon the show began. It started out with a cute puppet show that everybody enjoyed. Next came a dance troupe called the Herme Pan Dancers. They were terrific. Then Johnny Mathis entered. He sang many of his top hits from the fifties, songs many of us grew up with. They were the songs we had danced to, with our teenage puppy loves. Songs like "A Certain Smile," "The Twelfth of Never," "It's Not for Me to Say," and "Wonderful! Wonderful!" He also sang some special material, and one song, in particular, I thought unique, called "Keep It Simple."

At intermission, Sal and I watched the stage door. Sure enough, Paul Green came out. I conveyed Tommy's apologies and Paul told us where to meet him after the show for an introduction to the star. Sal was overjoyed. "Oh, thank you. That would fulfill a lifelong dream!"

We found our seats again, and the show continued along the same concept, but in a different order. The Hermes Pan Dancers came out first and did a number. When they finished, the famous vocalist came out and joined them in a routine that revolved around a cheerleader theme. Johnny danced with them while dribbling a basketball and they cheered as if it were a college ball game with musical cheerleaders. It was very clever and very entertaining. The puppeteers came out and did a skit. Then Johnny finished up by singing some more big hits: "Chances Are," "Venus," "Misty" and one of my all-time favorites, "When Sunny Gets Blue." Sal was in seventh heaven!

Then the whole troupe came out for the finale, then their final bows. Each group took its bows. First the puppeteers group, which got very good applause. Then the Herme Pan Dancers, who received great applause. Then Johnny came out and almost brought the house down with thunderous applause. Young girls were screaming like the Bobbysoxers for Frank Sinatra back in the forties. The curtains came down behind his exit. The crowd jumped up, screaming for curtain call after curtain call. The whole show came out together. They stood there in a line facing the audience and bowed together to receive the ovation. The audience would still not let up. People yelled, "Bravo" while others whistled loudly. The energized teenaged girls screamed their brains out.

Sal was ready to cry from the joy of seeing such a great performance by such a fabulous singer. I was also quite moved by the show, and of course by Johnny's great voice. His breath control and phrasing were the very best I had ever heard.

But then something happened that was unusual, to say the least! Johnny stood on the extreme left side of the stage, next to the puppeteers. One of the members of the group was holding a rose used in one of the puppet skits. The guy holding the flower elaborately stepped out of the group line and walked up to present the rose to Johnny. Johnny giggled, as did the audience.

But then Johnny walked to the far-right side of the stage, completely passing all the members of his show, and presented the rose to one of the male dancers from the Herme Pan Troupe. They stood there giggling together as the final curtain came down.

Sal looked at me stunned and confused. "What was THAT all about?" I just shook my head, as shocked as she.

Twenty minutes later Paul Green escorted us back to Johnny's personal dressing room. We could hear the teenaged girls screaming at the top of their lungs, just outside the backstage exit doors. "JOHN-nee, JOHN-nee. We want JOHN-nee."

As we entered, we were taken aback by the transformation in his appearance. The sides of his hair were now oiled and pulled back, and the top of his hair was teased into a pompadour high above his forehead.

His clothing was peculiar. It was downright feminine. His shirt was more like a girl's blouse made of chiffon, frilly in the front and on the cuffs and almost transparent throughout. He was wearing ultra-tight pants. This was not the Johnny Mathis we had just seen performing, nor the same man we often watched on television. It was a totally different person!

Neither Sal nor I commented, nor even suggested our inner thoughts. The earlier rose presentation on stage was now clear to us.

We simply smiled as Paul first introduced me. "Johnny, I would like you to meet a very fine pianist. This is Roger Rossi."

Mathis extended his hand. It felt as if I was holding a young girl's gentle hand, like a caress, not a handshake. He said, "I heard that you are very accomplished."

I answered, "Thank you very much. I thought your show was fantastic. Please let me introduce my fiancée to you. This is Sal Lacey."

Mathis looked at Sal for a moment and shook her hand, but turned toward me again as he spoke. "Pleased to meet you," he said, as his eyes roamed the span of my body.

As we continued to talk, he never looked at Sal again, whether she was talking to him or he to her. He would not take his eyes off me, or my body. He was definitely trying to flirt with me. It was to the point of being downright embarrassing. This icon of love-ballad singers, who had probably turned on millions of women by the flutter of his vocal chords, appeared behind the scenes to be blatantly homosexual.

By this time Sal had gone through several emotional reactions. Initially, we were both suspicious by his actions on stage with the rose and the male dancer. Then, she was deflated and disappointed that a vocal star with whom she'd fallen in love from a distance was not even interested in looking at her. NOW, she was quickly becoming perturbed by his obvious attempt at flirtation WITH HER BOYFRIEND!

She became so aggravated with him, she simply clammed up without a further word. I guess Sal thought that if he wasn't going to bother looking at her; why continue the facade by conversing with him. In our naiveté, we had presumed that he was straight. The transformation we witnessed firsthand was a shock, then it was an awkward embarrassment. It became apparent that we weren't really the best of guests for him, so our visit was short-lived. He said politely, "Well it was nice meeting both of you. I must go now, as my limousine is waiting."

We left his dressing room and started toward the stage door. The group of young girls was still waiting for him on the other side of the exit door. They were still screaming at very high decibels. I said to Sal, "Let's watch to see how he is attacked by all of these young and naive girls."

"Naive, all right; like I was. I doubt very much whether he'll give them even a moment of his time. As a man, he's such a disappointment!"

As the young hopefuls continued yelling their chant, a garage type door discreetly opened over on the other side of the building's backstage area. A beautiful limousine backed up and the male dancer who had earlier received Mathis' rose, got into the back seat. Soon, the famous singer joined him. They cuddled up next to each other and drove off.

In the meantime, from the other side of the building, the girls who had no idea that their singing idol had already departed, continued to chant, "JOHN-nee, JOHN-nee. . . . We want JOHN-nee." Their singsong chorus was heard by nobody except the remaining members of the stage crew. With the echo of their voices growing fainter and fainter, we vacated the premises, feeling sorry for them.

From time to time, we will still listen to a Johnny Mathis recording, because we still think he is a great singer. But somehow something is now missing. For one thing, Sal and I know that he is definitely not singing his love ballads to HER!

Gene Stridel

Gene, a native of the West Indies, was born Gene Strider. He originally sang lead vocals with a touring United States Air Force troupe that entertained at U.S. airbases around the world. Later, he changed his name and started singing professionally. Shortly after Gene settled in Vermont with his family, I came into his life.

We met when I was the piano accompanist for Tommy Desmond. Stridel came into a club where Tommy and I performed. Tommy asked him if he'd like to "sit in." When he accepted, we performed as if we'd been working with each other for years. The audience went wild over how well he sang and our tremendous rapport together. He had great breath control and a special phrasing ability a la Johnny Mathis. After performing a few selections, he told me, "Man, you're the finest piano accompanist I've ever worked with." He later said, "Roger, I know that you're Tommy's accompanist. I wouldn't want to interfere with that, but nothing lasts forever. If you ever find yourself out of a gig, you have a standing invitation to call me. I'd love to work with you." About a year and a half later, when things were not going so well with Tommy. I accepted Gene's offer.

Arriving at what would be our base of operations, Burlington, Gene showed me all around the town. Burlington was the largest city in Vermont, but I always thought of it as a town. Between thirty-five and forty thousand people lived there. After performing for three years in places like Montreal, Quebec City and Toronto, it felt more homey to me. For one thing, practically everyone knew each other. Well, at least they all knew Gene. He was a local "star."

As I met the various club owners, musicians, and restaurant patrons, it gradually became apparent that all these people knew me, too. Prior to my arrival, Gene had a huge article put into the Vermont Sunday News, all about me, my past credits and about our upcoming engagement at the very popular "Baggy Knees" nightclub in nearby Stowe, Vermont. I hadn't known any of this until I finally met Gene's business manager, Norman Herberg. He said, "Roger, I'm really happy to meet you. I know you and your trio will do a great job at the Baggy

Knees next week, and I loved that article about you in the Sunday News."

Roger (22 years of age) and MGM Recording Artist Gene Stridel.
Courtesy of WWLP-TV, Channel 22, Springfield, MA

I asked Gene, "What article? . . . What trio? . . . What is the Baggy Knees?"

Gene smiled. "We've got our work cut out for us. I lined up some really fine musicians for us to rehearse. We start rehearsals tomorrow."

After I found an apartment, Gene and I did get to work. We rehearsed the musicians that would form my trio. Then we opened at the Knees, a 200-year-old reconverted barn. The club was an ideal room in which to break in our new group. We eventually changed and upgraded the musicians, and rehearsed some more. In fact, except for the brief interruption of my wedding to Sal, it seemed like all we did was rehearse and perform. Eventually, Gene and I were performing at the best places Burlington had to offer, like The Top Hat, The Fez, and The Gilded Cage.

Herberg and the places he booked us were all good for us on a local level. But we needed to make some changes in order to push our careers up a notch. Norman also knew this, and through his efforts, we met Hermie Dressel. Hermie was involved with Mercury Records. He also managed the great big-band leader, Woody Herman. Hermie Dressel made a special trip to Burlington to meet us. Eventually, a management team was set up with Herberg taking care of the local bookings, in between the bigger dates that Dressel got us elsewhere.

Hermie Dressel had the right connections and know-how that Gene needed on a national basis. Initially, because of my youth, he opposed my staying on as Gene's music accompanist and director. He figured that at twenty-one, nobody is a music director for a projected recording star. Hermie finally heard me piano soloing and accompanying Gene. He told me, "Congratulations. You will probably be the youngest music director any major recording star has ever had, and I highly approve."

Immediately, Hermie got us some really classy bookings. Some of the top nightclubs, supper clubs, hotels and resorts (in places like Boston, Springfield, Albany, Saratoga, and the Catskills) were becoming our stage. Gene and I were always doing interviews for radio, television, and newspaper columns. We had a trial run at one of the (now, "former") Schine Hotels. Immediately, all of the Schine Hotels across the country were asking to book us. Because we didn't want to travel too far from Burlington and our families, we turned down offers from Schine hotels outside of New York and New England.

We followed big name people everywhere we performed. Our typical itinerary would be a six or eight-week stint at the Schine Queensbury Hotel in Glens Falls. Then we'd follow the great jazz pianist, Teddy Wilson, into the Schine Inn at Chicopee, Massachusetts for a four or six-week stand. Then, two weeks at the famous Concord Hotel in Monticello, New York, to appear on the same bill with comedian Buddy Hackett. The following week, we were at the Schine Hotel in Massena, New York. We often worked a great room in Schenectady, New York, called Mike Roth's. They always featured great jazz legends there. We preceded musical giants like Bobby Hackett, Coleman Hawkins, Morgana King, Teddy Wilson, Carmen McRae, or composer-pianist-vocalist Freddy Cole, Nat's talented brother.

Throughout that time, we were booked through Woodrow Music, Inc. Woody Herman's personal music, and theatrical booking agency. Hermie was "keeping it in the family," so to speak. We would occasionally stop in to see Herman perform, and on several occasions, he honored us by coming by to hear us. He'd always bring with him some of his band members, so, naturally, this was a double thrill for me. I thought they were all consummate jazz players.

Hermie was working hard on Gene's career. He finally landed a record contract for him with Verve, a subsidiary of MGM Records. "One More Fool and One More Broken Heart" was released and getting very good play on the radio, especially in the areas where we had bookings. We were ecstatic when on April 11, 1962, Variety, a tabloid considered by most to be the Bible of the music industry, picked Gene's release as one of the "Top Singles of the Week." It held that rank among releases by such heavyweight performers as Steve Lawrence, Dinah Washington, The Marcels, Pat Boone, Don Shirley, Duane Eddy and Betty Carter. After that, we performed to "standing room only" audiences everywhere we were booked. Many new fans seemed to sense that they were witnessing the beginning of Gene's stardom.

Things were happening very quickly. To be truthful, the next turns of event are still a little hazy in my mind, because I never got into the business end of Gene's life. One day, Gene said to me, "Roger, I want you to know that I've made some changes with my managers."

"Like what, Gene?"

"My contract has been changed to a group out of Springfield, Massachusetts. Norman Herberg is out of the picture completely. Hermie is going to handle a great deal of the promotion and bookings. We're going to travel with a road manager from now on, a woman named Madeleine Turner. That's all that I can tell you right now."

I always felt terrible about Herberg. He got Gene started, and was the one who initiated the search for a co-manager, bringing Dressel in. Now these other people were in and Herberg was out. Nobody ever said that show business was fair.

All of these new people in our lives seemed to have connections with organized crime, based in Rhode Island. Very quickly we started working a totally different nightclub and hotel circuit. Hermie wasn't given the free hand he had in the past. As a result, we didn't go through Woodrow Music anymore, but directly through Gene's new managers, who had their own booking agency.

We played rooms that had a different type of clientele. The customers were wearing ultra-expensive jewelry and had huge tabs, yet talked tough and cheap. The entertainers we followed were different, too. Although not so jazz oriented, they were all big-name headliners.

Moneywise, it was a step up, for sure. Gene's new handlers were always very polite. Business was usually conducted with soft-spoken voices, but I wasn't sure I liked the change.

About the time all of these professional and business changes took place my wife announced that she was expecting our first child. I didn't like the idea of Sal and our baby subjected to touring conditions, nor did I want to leave them both behind. Although I felt Gene Stridel stood a great chance of making the big time, my marriage and fatherhood were far more important to me.

Additionally, between accompanying Tommy Desmond and then Gene Stridel, I had been on the road for nearly seven years. I was pretty tired of living out of a suitcase. Furthermore, I wasn't too crazy about working for Gene's new management team. This was a perfect time for us to make the split.

Still, leaving Gene was not easy. We had become good friends. He had led my bridal party as Best Man and we frequently got together socially with him and his wife, Mary Jane. We knew we would miss them both. I gave my notice, and Sal and I left for my native Long Island when she was in her third or fourth month of pregnancy. I found work, performing locally and teaching part-time to try to make up the difference in pay I lost from not working with Gene.

One night I caught him on a coast-to-coast television showcase. Gene sang a couple of songs. He sounded great, as he always did, and it was obviously starting to pay off for him. That was the last time I saw Gene. Soon after, he sang on a nationally promoted chewing gum commercial for Wrigley's Spearmint Gum. It was playing on every radio station throughout the country, almost every hour. I'd turn on the radio when driving; and there was Gene singing, "Hi ho, hey hey, chew your little troubles away!"

Years later, after Sal and I had moved our family of three children along with our German shepherd, "Paka," to Palm Beach County, Gene called me. He asked if I'd like to work with him again. He was going to open at the Fountainbleu Hotel in Miami. I declined, telling him I was working with another very talented vocalist, my wife. He wished us well and suggested that we could all get together for Christmas that year. Mary Jane and he had divorced but were still friends, and she would be coming down to Florida for a visit.

He also told me that he no longer was backed by The Mob. He broke their agreement when he could.

It had been about ten years since we had all seen each other, so I was really looking forward to it. It never happened. Shortly after we spoke, Gene died in a "freakish" drowning accident in Fort Lauderdale.

[See more in "The Gangsters" section – The Raymond Patriaca Crime Family]

Tennessee Ernie Ford

There were many television shows in the fifties and sixties that featured Top-40 music as a theme. They were gigantically popular, and the viewing audiences could not get enough of them. Every network was competing with its own version of music performers and hosts. Perry Como and Dinah Shore were great singing hosts for their shows, and on The Arthur Godfrey Show, Godfrey sang, played an instrument, did comedy and also featured other fine performers. Jackie Gleason and Milton Berle were geared toward comedy on their shows, but they also included musical interests. Ed Sullivan did none of those things himself, but as a master of ceremonies on his show, he introduced new musical talent to the world. On The Lucky Strike Hit Parade, there were several musical hosts, and their objective was to call the attention of the world to the songs that were making it as the top ten favorites across America. Later on, The Steve Allen Tonight Show did most of the above.

During this early period in American television, there was one more show that also made it big, but with just a slightly altered style. It was The Tennessee Ernie Ford Show.

The host's inimitable down-home-country attitude won over viewing audiences throughout America. It didn't matter if the viewers were "city slickers" from New York and Boston, or country folks watching his show from the suburbs of Nashville. Everyone loved Tennessee Ernie Ford. He was talented, warm-hearted, unaffected, humorous and, most of all, entertaining. His sincerity was the first thing that got you. Then, one by one, the rest of his attributes followed. He was country music's answer to Perry Como. Ford's hit recording of Sixteen Tons is still considered one of the great classics of country music. Both he and Como projected an inner warmth and sincerity, and it rubbed off onto their shows' presentations.

In the early fall of 1961, I performed nightly with Gene Stridel at a lounge in Burlington called The Gilded Cage. It was small and intimate, a perfect place for Gene and me to break in and perfect new arrangements for my trio. The audiences in the Cage were always enthusiastic, devoted fans. The room barely sat forty people, and most of the time all seats were taken. We liked the room a lot, including its staff, owners Sarah and Nick Pappas, and clientele. As a matter of fact, only a few months earlier, Sal and I had enjoyed our wedding reception in that room and the adjoining restaurant.

Dining in the restaurant one evening, Ernie Ford and his manager happened to hear our performance. That evening, a midweek night, Gene and I were without benefit of my trio, who worked with us on weekends. Tennessee Ernie inquired about who they were hearing. Instead of going back to their rooms at the Vermont Hotel next door, they opted to come into our lounge to listen. They stayed for the entire evening . . . and then some!

In that intimate room, Gene and I could converse with most of the patrons without using a microphone, although Gene did use one to sing. Gene simply said, "My goodness, what an honor to have you with us tonight!" Everyone immediately recognized the great television and recording star and put down their cocktails to applaud.

Tennessee Ernie said softly, "Thank you. We were just having a great dinner in the next room, and we heard your wonderful music. Please don't stop. We came in to hear both of you!"

Gene and I went into our best stuff, and we received nothing but ovations from the audience, especially from the famous singer and his manager. We didn't really know any country music, but that didn't matter. The country star was musically well-rounded and appreciative of everything we did. We finally took a break, after giving what amounted to a concert of more than an hour.

Gene and I went to their table, and they got up to greet us with such enthusiasm, it was almost embarrassing. "You both are fabulous. Please join us for a cocktail."

They were asking us so many questions about ourselves. They wanted to know, where we were originally from, how long had we been working together, and what were our plans for the future. We never did ask them why they were passing through Vermont and where they were going. We never found out either.

In the middle of our conversation, Gene's manager, Norman Herberg, came into the club. We immediately introduced him to Ernie and his manager. We had to leave the three of them so that we could return to the bandstand for our final set of the evening. Before we left the table, however, the famous gentleman suggested that he didn't want the evening to end. He said, "Did you say this will be your last set? Shucks."

Norman immediately picked up on the innuendo, and suggested, "Well, if you'd like, we could all go over to my home for a nightcap. What do you think?"

Gene said, "That'll be great!"

I nodded approvingly and Tennessee Ernie asked, "Are you sure that we're not putting you out?"

Norman said assuredly, "Absolutely not. It would be our great pleasure to have you as our guests!" He then suggested that Gene and I call up our wives and invite them, too. "Let's have a party," he suggested.

I pulled Norman on the side, and said to him, "Norman, my younger brother Paul is visiting with us."

"Bring him, too. I'd love to meet him!"

Gene and I postponed our final performance by about five minutes as we called home. Sal finally awakened to answer.

"Honey, freshen yourself up and put on a nice casual outfit. I'll be there to pick you up in about an hour. I have a special surprise for you."

"What is it?"

"If I were to tell you . . . it wouldn't be a surprise, would it? By the way, tell my brother to put on a nice pair of slacks and sweater, because I want him to come, too."

About an hour later, I picked them up, and they were just bubbling with questions. "Where are we going? What's happening? What's the surprise?"

"Well, we've been invited to Norman and Pat Herberg's home for an impromptu cocktail party. We are going to be a small group, the Herbergs, the Stridels, the three of us, and . . . a very special television and recording star, and his manager."

"Who? Who is it? Please tell us. The suspense is killing us."

I said with a wide grin, "Tennessee Ernie Ford!"

Both of their jaws dropped wide open. My brother Paul, who looked like he was in a state of shock, said, "My God . . . you mean the Pea Picker himself? Wow, that IS big!"

When we got to the Herbergs' residence, both Sal and Paul were very eager to get inside to meet the TV star. The Herbergs sat us in a circle in their living room, and we had the celebrity to ourselves. We must have conversed and joked with each other for a good three hours. The thing I primarily remember about him was how accommodating he was. He was the epitome of good manners, warmth, and sincerity, and he made each of us feel important.

I also remember that he had some very good advice for Norman Herberg. He said, "You have to get these two fine performers into the bigger cities. Not that there's anything wrong with Burlington. It is truly a wonderful place, and I wouldn't mind living here myself. But if you want them to make it into the big time, you have to get bookings in New York, Chicago, and L.A. The way that Gene sings, he's good enough to become a major recording artist, and Roger can be right there with him, as his piano accompanist. They just have to get the proper exposure." Norman did take his advice, and we started up the ladder of success because of it.

We never saw Tennessee Ernie Ford again. He died in 1991. I will never forget how down-to-earth and friendly he was on that fall evening up in Burlington, Vermont.

SOME ADDED NOTES: Tennessee Ernie Ford study classical music and voice at the Cincinnati Conservatory of Music. After serving in World War II, he worked as a radio announcer, and soon recorded on the Capitol Records label. He released his first gospel album, Hymns, in 1956, but his signature song was "Sixteen Tons." He hosted his own TV show, The Ford Show from 1956 to 1961. His nickname was "The Ol' Pea-Picker" because he often used the phrase, "Bless your pea-pickin' heart!"

Ford was awarded three stars on the Hollywood Walk of Fame; one for radio, one for records, and one for television. He was also awarded the Presidential Medal of Freedom in 1984 and in 1990 was inducted into the Country Music Hall of Fame.

He died on October 17, 1991, shortly after having dinner with President George H.W. Bush.

Vaughn Monroe

I met Vaughn Monroe in April 1962. Gene Stridel and I were performing at the Schine Inn, in Chicopee, Massachusetts, and I heard that the great singer was performing at the Red Barn, in nearby Springfield. I had to go over there to meet this popular and famous recording star, who happened to be a longtime friend of my family. The way that he became a family friend was testimony to the man himself.

In 1946, my older brother, Vinny came down with polio. We lived in Brooklyn at the time. I was six years old, but I recall how devastated my whole family was. Vinny, sixteen was told by his doctors that he would be paralyzed for life, from waist to toes. They said, "Young man, you just better get used to the fact that you'll never be able to walk again!"

Roger at six years old in Brooklyn

After eighteen months of rehabilitation in a hospital, he proved them wrong. He was able to accomplish this task because he was one of the most stubborn and bullheaded human beings I've ever known. I know my families' bloodlines originate from Sicily and Modena, Italy. But I think somehow, Vinny inherited a touch of Calabrese blood. He was what we Italians playfully refer to as "testa duro" (hard head)! Thank God.

Vinny's normal daily agenda, while in the hospital, was to work out with the parallel bars for three to four hours. Gradually, the deadened legs his upper body was dragging came back to life. Toward the end of his rehabilitation, the hospital would let him go home for a couple of days with his family. I remember the symbols of his slow but steady progress, how he graduated from a wheelchair to crutches, to walking canes, and finally to only one cane. Years later, he threw that away, too!

I'm told that Vinny went into that hospital with his biceps the size of his wrists. He came out, a year and a half later, with arms bigger than his legs. Call it determination, or if you prefer, bullheadedness, but because of it, whatever it was, he could walk again, albeit, with a limp, but never the invalid his doctors predicted he'd be.

There's something that Vinny found out about physically overcoming a disability. The mind must win the first battle. Two things kept Vinny's optimism and spirits high. One was the piano the hospital moved into his ward so he could continue his music studies. The other was the ever-present benevolence and kindness of Vaughn Monroe.

The very popular RCA recording star knew my father from the musicians' union in New York. My father was on the executive board of that union for many years. He helped Vaughn Monroe as he did many people. My father had a knack for straightening out a multitude of problems. He would talk with the performing artist, with the musicians, with the hiring establishment, and bingo, a contract was established, and everyone was happy.

Monroe never forgot. When he heard that Vinny was laid up in the hospital, he went to visit him. He arrived with a brand-new RCA Victor 45 RPM phonograph under one arm and a stacked bundle of Vaughn Monroe's recorded albums under the other. He did an awful lot of spirit rising for Vinny. All the doctors, nurses, and patients in that hospital witnessed the recording star visiting Vinny. Soon the entire hospital knew him. Monroe cheered my brother with wonderful words of encouragement. It was just the medicine that Vinny needed.

Vaughn Monroe followed up that visit with several others. One time, he even sang a song for Vinny's ward, with Vinny accompanying him on the piano. The nurses would place the young pianist on a rolling table, then roll him to the piano. Vinny played lying flat on his stomach!

It was precisely the inspiration my brother needed. Before you knew it, he was making such progress he sat in a chair and practiced all by himself. He got better, both physically and musically. The only time I would see him was when he came home for a visit. Every time, he was obviously stronger and better. I remember walking proudly around the block with him and two of my other brothers, Bill and Bob. Vinny did it himself, with just the help of his canes. Our neighbors from 72nd Street in Bay Ridge, Brooklyn, applauded as we walked by. He was getting better.

Vinny was eventually featured, at nineteen, with his high school orchestra, in Babylon, Long Island. The music director, Dudley Mairs, conducted the concert, and Vinny played Grieg's A Minor Piano Concerto. I remember that well. Man, he was something else! Much of this success could be traced back to Vaughn Monroe's help in sparking Vinny's determination.

Later, when Vinny went on to advanced music studies at Fredonia State, I inherited the phonograph player and all of the recording stars' albums. I played everyone, every day. My family never got tired of hearing "Racing with the Moon," "Dance Ballerina, Dance," "There I've Said it Again," "Ghost Riders in the Sky," and "It Seems Like Old Times." Later on, I saved up my own money to buy Monroe's hit recording of "Let it Snow! Let it Snow!"

We all loved the guy and his music, but in a much different way than his millions of fans did. For the Rossitto family, there was an added dimension to Vaughn Monroe. He was more than a singing star. He was a humanitarian!

It was approximately fifteen years after Vinny had left the hospital when I went backstage at the Red Barn, to meet Vaughn Monroe. I felt funny knocking on his dressing room door. I could hear that he had several people in there. I did anyway. He opened the door and asked, "Hello. Can I help you?"

I answered, using my given name, "I'm sorry to bother you, Sir, but my name is Roger Rossitto."

"Rossitto? You're not related to Vince Rossitto, from New York, are you?"

"Yes, he's my father."

A broad smile came over his face. "How's your Mom and Dad, and your brother Vinny?"

I answered, "They're all fine. Thank you."

He welcomed me in, introduced me to the people in the room, ordered me something to drink, and fired question after question at me. "What's your brother doing these days. I heard he went into the music business? I haven't seen your father in close to a year now. What's he up to? What are you doing in Springfield?" He was genuinely interested in me, my family, my brother's welfare and successes. It was hard to believe that I was candidly speaking with such a giant in the recording field. We must have talked for a good forty-five minutes. I enjoyed every second of it.

Toward the end of Vaughn Monroe's days, he lived with his wife Marian at The Yacht and Country Club Stuart, Florida, where they were members. My band performs there regularly. He died in 1973. Later, after a successful career as a music educator and professional pianist, my brother Vinny also passed away.

CREDITS AND ACCOMPLISHMENTS

Vaughn Monroe recorded for RCA Victor's Bluebird label. As a vocalist, he was an American icon, but also played trumpet in his own big band. He hosted The Vaughn Monroe Show on CBS Television in the early 1950's, and also appeared on Bonanza, the Mike Douglas show, The Ed Sullivan Show, Texaco Star Theatre, the Jackie Gleason Show, The Tonight Show starring Johnny Carson, and Dick Clark's American Bandstand.

He was an actor and has two stars on Hollywood's Walk of Fame – one for singing, and one for acting.

Tony Bennett

In early 1963, I met Johnny Bennedetto, Jr. at The Ebb Tide, a club in the Roosevelt Motel in East Meadow, Long Island. John is the older brother of the famous singer. He was a fine vocalist in his own right. As a matter of fact, I was told that he was supposed to be the singer in the Benedetto family. He had formally studied voice, and so, every time that Tony would go to sing, his parents would tell him, "No, no. Johnny is the singer in this family, not you!" As it turned out, Tony went on to make musical history as one of America's greatest contributors to pop music and Johnny did very well with a string of beauty salons on Long Island.

Nevertheless, Johnny's business success did not erase his desire to sing. So he often sat in with the band I worked in, the Gino Rondi Trio. I had recently finished seven years on the road, as a piano accompanist to both Gene Stridel, and Tommy Desmond. I guess I made Johnny feel comfortable to the point that he tried singing professionally.

Mr. Tony Bennett

Later, I saw an advertisement in a Long Island newspaper, mentioning his engagement at one of the finer clubs, the Casa Seville. It read Johnny Bennett, Tony's brother, singing nightly! I considered it a bit of a put down on Johnny's individual talent. He certainly could stand on his own! I never got the chance to stop by and catch his act, but I know it was good.

Early in 1967, I was booked into a famous nightclub called the Living Room, in Manhattan. The engagement as piano accompanist to very funny comedian Marge Leslie lasted about two weeks before I resigned. It was much too far for me for me to travel every night from my Patchogue, Long Island, home. Marge opened the show, and vocalist David Allen closed it. The gig was wonderful. It was a real joy to work with Marge, and the place always had big-time showbiz people. In that two-week period, I met Bobby Short, Erroll Garner, Jack Leonard (the comedian), London Lee, Rodney Dangerfield, Shirley Jones, and Jack Cassidy.

One night, I looked up from the piano keyboard to see Tony Bennett. He was seated with another fine vocalist, recording artist, Sylvia Sims.

When I finished playing the floorshow, I took the liberty of going over to meet him, one of the few times I've done that with a celebrity. I leaned over, smiled and asked, "Excuse me, Sir, but aren't you Johnny Bennett's brother?"

He looked up and smiled, answering, "Yes, I am. Do you know him?"

"Yes, I do. He often sat in with me piano accompanying him at the club I worked, on Long Island."

The famous singer stood up, offered his hand, and asked my name. I answered, and he invited me to join them. We conversed during my entire break of about forty-five minutes. Sylvia Sims was not talking too much because Tony and I were. Every time I started to get up and leave, he asked me another question, either about me or about his brother John. I didn't really want to crash their party, so I finally excused myself.

As I walked away, I realized I had just enjoyed one of the greatest moments in my life. Meeting Tony Bennett a great legend of song and a fine painter, too—does not happen to many people in this world. I felt privileged!

The Shangri-Las

In the sixties, I played the piano on several of the Shangri-Las' hit recordings including their big hit, "Leader of the Pack." I have mixed emotions on this subject.

To begin with, I come from a classical music background. My early goal in life was to be a concert pianist. I studied the classics seriously for hours on end, every day. I became good enough to win the prestigious Music Lovers Club Scholarship, in competition against the finest of career-minded music students on Long Island. I loved Chopin, Beethoven, Bach, Haydn, and Mozart, to name a few. And although my hands are much too small to "master" most Russian-composer works, I did play several of Rachmaninoff's beautiful compositions.

In my teenage years, I became interested in the creative genius of such jazz giants as Duke Ellington, Art Tatum, Ella Fitzgerald, Mel Torme and Oscar Peterson. I found myself constantly attending concerts to hear jazz, symphony orchestras, and classical artists.

Because of my background, I can't get too impressed with any piece of "music" that unnecessarily centers its composition around the sound of a motorcycle revving its engine, leaving a strip of rubber on asphalt and eventually crashing. This cacophony of abhorrent sounds is the focal point of "Leader of the Pack," and I find it an assault on my hearing.

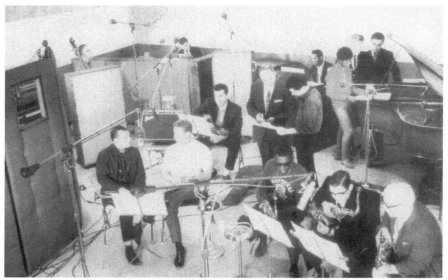

STAFF AT ULTRASONIC RECORDING STUDIOS
Roger Rossi at Piano

"Leader of the Pack," co-written by Ellie Greenwich, George "Shadow" Morton, and Jeff Barry, was recorded at Ultrasonic Recording Studios, in Hempstead, Long Island. Although the instrumental part was recorded at a separate time from the vocal part, I met the Shangri-Las on several occasions. The group consisted of two sets of sisters, Betty and Mary Weiss and twin sisters Marge and Mary Ann Ganser. Every time I encountered them, they acted like a bunch of giddy imbeciles. Later, Marge Ganser died of an accidental drug overdose.

The reason I ever got involved in the first place has to be attributed to my friendship with Amityville High School chum, bassist-guitarist Charlie Brockner, who introduced me to Bill Stahl, the owner of Ultrasonic from 1962 to 1980. Because Stahl had set Ultrasonic up with excellent equipment and acoustics, it became a hotbed for big name groups and performers to have their sessions. They eventually recorded The Doobie Brothers; Tower of Power; Fleetwood Mac; Hall and Oates; The Marshall Tucker Band; Peter Frampton and Billy Joel. I played for many other recording dates there and eventually became their Staff Pianist. Naturally, when the date for recording "Leader of the Pack" was booked, the studio recommended me. I was offered the booking, took it and played it.

Throughout the session, I was nothing less than cooperative and helpful to producer Morton, who quite truthfully seemed to be floundering. I know that as lousy as the song was, it actually sounded much better because of my efforts and those of the sound engineers Brookes Arthur, and another Amityville friend, celebrated engineer, composer, musician, Rod McBrien, now deceased. The year was 1964.

When I arrived home, Sal greeted me with, "How did your recording date go, Honey?"

"Sal," I answered grumpily, "I wish you didn't ask me that question. It was a total fiasco. The song was a simplistic piece of tripe. There were no written arrangements, so we had to listen to a simplistic demo recording, and then try to assimilate and improve upon what we heard. The whole session could have been done in one tenth of the time if the producer knew what he was doing. Most of the time, I had to tell HIM what to do, and what would sound better on the piano and guitar parts. The musicianship was very poor. Can you believe? It took sixty-three recording takes."

Sal replied, "WHAT?!"

Most recording dates have the music written out. Therefore, two, three and sometimes four or five takes suffice. If the producer is exceptionally meticulous, or if things are exceptionally out of whack, it might even go into seven or eight takes but sixty-three is utterly absurd.

"I'm telling you, Sal," I continued, "if that piece of garbage is ever accepted by a recording company, much less released, I should quit the business! I know that my piano teacher, Mary Findley Ades, God rest her beautiful soul, will turn in her grave!"

I guess I should have quit the music business. It was not only accepted and released, but rose to the very top of the pop charts. It reached number one on the Billboard charts November 28, 1964, by knocking "Baby Love," the Supremes' big hit from first into second place.

"Leader of the Pack" was Billboard's number one for only a week, but it was number one on several other charts for as long as ten weeks. Because of the song's storyline (girl meets boy, her parents disapprove, he dies in motorcycle accident), BBC radio banned it. Despite the ban, it reached number eleven in the United Kingdom. It has been re-released and is marketed as a classic to this day. It has sold millions of copies! Additionally, it was later recorded by several other big-name artists, including Bette Midler, Twisted Sister, Dan Fogelberg, and even Alvin and the Chipmunks.

I was paid the standard, low-rated musicians' union scale, which at the time was something like $45. Because none of the musicians' names ever went on the recording label, we were never entitled to any royalties. We were to receive only "residuals," with payments received, policed, and dispersed by the musicians' union, one of the very reasons why I ultimately quit that union! For the first year or two, I received three or four meaningless checks; and then, they stopped until I complained about it to the Federation of Musicians, about three years ago, I received another four or five meaningless checks. Every time a check arrived, I would sarcastically bellow, "Whoop-ti-do!" When reading further about the Shangri-Las, I found that they also felt they were totally "ripped off" by the recording company.

When I played piano on a Janis Ian song called "Letter to Jon," I didn't receive ANY residuals. None whatsoever! It was hard for me to believe that nobody in the whole country played it on the jukebox. It was on the flipside to a big hit of hers, called "Society's Child."

For my part in "Leader of the Pack," through all the years since, I've made approximately $600, including residuals. That was my "total take" for time, energy, and (exploited) talent spent on this all-time . . . "classic."

To add insult to financial injury, I bumped into its producer, George Morton, very soon after the song reached number 1. He was leaving a Manhattan restaurant as I entered. He wore dark sunglasses, his jacket over his shoulders like some Hollywood movie star. He had two young women holding on to his arms. I said to him, "Hey, Shadow. Howya doin?"

He retorted, "Do I know you?"

"Well, you should. I'm Roger Rossi. I played piano on your recording of "Leader of the Pack'."

He chuckled, turned his back on me, and walked away. I swear I never wanted to kick the living crap out of anyone as much as I wanted to at that moment. I think you could've fried an egg on the back of my neck.

I saw him once more at the grand opening of a new recording studio on Long Island. I brought my wife and parents. I'll never forget my mother's reaction when she saw George Morton. He once again wore his dark sunglasses, although the sun had set hours earlier. My mother said, "My goodness, that gentleman must be some sort of recording star. Look at all the pictures they're taking of him. Do you know him?"

"Yes, Mom. That's George Morton. I've done some recording work for him. . . . Eh, by the way, why don't you start counting how many shots that the photographer is taking of him. I've already counted at least 50."

"I don't understand," my mother said.

"Just count them, Mom. Sip your wine; eat your cheese and count."

Clickety, click, click, click, click, click. The photographer went at rapid-fire speed and we all quietly counted. "1, 2, 3, 4, 5, 6, 7 . . . 8, 9, 10. . . ." A minute later, he was still at it. "78, 79, 80 . . . 81, 82, 83."

About that time, my wife said to my parents, "That must be some GREAT photographer. He NEVER has to change film!"

My mother, who still didn't quite get it, asked, "Why is that?"

"Because he probably doesn't even have any film in his camera, Mom. Yes, George probably hired him to shoot a few shots of him, but I bet that he also instructed him to continue to look like he's taking pictures when all he's doing is clicking his strobe light. It makes everyone in the place focus their attention on George Morton, so, like you, they think he's a recording star."

My mother became slightly annoyed as the photographic hoopla continued while we talked. By now, we'd reached the approximate count of "188, 189, 190, 191. . . ."

"That means he's really a small person, trying to act big and important," my mother said.

"You know, Mom, I came to that same realization when I bumped into him at a New York restaurant not too long ago."

A few months after "Leader of the Pack" made it to the top of every music survey list, another music group, The Detergents, recorded a song meant as a spoof to "Leader of the Pack." They did almost everything the same, including an almost exact duplication of my piano part. The main exception was in the lyrics. Their recording was called "Leader of the Laundromat." It also became a hit and even reached number nineteen on the Top Forty List. At the very end of their recording, one of the Detergents asked, "Who is that banging on the piano?" That's the way the song ended.

They were playing both hits, on every radio station across America, practically every five minutes. I was tempted to call the top stations in New York and say to them, "HEY…that's ROGER ROSSI who's banging on the damn piano!"

Thirty years later, in 1994, Sal and I got away for a long-awaited, much-deserved, two-week vacation to my ancestral home, Italy. In Venice, I suggested we visit its one disco nightclub, El Saud. After our long trek through half of Venice's delightful byways, Sal didn't need coaxing.

We found our seats at the very small bar up front, which seated maybe six people. Because it was still afternoon, we never did see the disco dance area, which I presume was in the back. But that was all right with us. At that moment, we were mainly hot and thirsty.

The bartender was an attractive young lady of perhaps thirty years. She spoke only Italian. I struggled with my broken Italian to order our cocktails. Much to our surprise and pleasure, she got the order right. We sipped our drinks and enjoyed the ambiance of the club. We listened to some taped fifties and sixties American rock 'n roll hits. The bartender wanted to make us feel welcome, so she tried to start up a conversation with me. She asked me, in

Italian, what part of America we came from. I replied, "Florida   Palm Beach, Florida."

She smiled and sighed, "Ahhhhhh!" Then she asked me what I did for a job.

I replied, "Musica. Sono pianista professionale (I'm a professional pianist) . . . eh . . . mi moglie una vocalista (my wife's a vocalist). . . . Como se dice, cantare? (How do you say, Singer? Capisci?"

She put up with my stumbling over her beautiful language as she smiled broadly and said "Si, capito!"

A very strange thing took place at that exact moment. While we talked, "Leader of the Pack" started playing. I pointed to the speaker system and tried to explain to her that the piano playing she was hearing at that moment, was in fact, mine.

She smiled and nodded, "Si." I knew that she didn't understand. I tried again. She continued to smile warmly and to nod.

A young lady seated a few chairs from my wife was listening and asked, "I don't think she understands you. Are you saying that you played the piano on that recording of "Leader of the Pack?"

I smiled and said to her, "Oh, you're American…. Yes, that's right. I played piano on some of the Shangri-Las hits, including this one."

She said with excitement, "Oh . . . wow! Let me tell her for you."

She talked to the bartender in very fluent Italian as Sal and I looked on. Suddenly, the bartender got sooooo excited. Talking a mile-a-minute to the bilingual customer, she looked directly at me, her eyes and her smile widening. Then she ran out and brought in two more employees from the back of the club. While she talked to them, she gestured toward me. There they stood facing us, eyes agog, broadly grinning, and talking rapid Italian. I did not understand a word.

Our helpful translator explained to me, "At first, she didn't quite understand what you meant. Now, she thinks that you're a recording star!"

I thought to myself, 'has the whole world gone crazy?'

Sal put both her arms around me and said to the translator, "Well in my book, he IS a star!"

I said, "Thanks, Honey." Then I paused and added, "Yeah, maybe I'm a star in some books . . . but unfortunately . . . that doesn't include our BANK book!"

Julius La Rosa

For almost half a year, from late 1970 through April 1971, Sal and I performed at The Dolphin restaurant in Miller Place, Long Island. The restaurant was managed by Kay Petrone.

Around that time, we met and became good friends with Ed and Jean Brown. Jean was an amateur singer with a nice voice. She occasionally sat in with us. Ed was a veteran broadcast announcer. He had a great speaking and announcing voice. More importantly, he was gifted with a great mind and vocabulary. He used to announce the news on a very big radio station in New York City, WNEW, which broadcast on both the AM and FM frequencies. The same station regularly scheduled the Julius La Rosa Show.

One evening in February 1971, Sal and I met Julius La Rosa.

The Browns kept promising they would bring the famous singer in to meet us. The couple had dinner with La Rosa, then the three adjourned to the piano bar, where we were introduced.

Soon, we invited Jean Brown up to sing a number or two. She accepted and sang a beautiful selection from The Yearlings, called "Why Did I Choose You?" That show only ran for three performances, but the song is delightful.

As she finished her last note, I quietly asked her if it would be apropos for me to invite La Rosa up to sing. She said, "Absolutely! He'd love to."

I leaned in toward the great singer and, without the microphone, I quietly asked him, "Mr. La Rosa, it would be a great thrill for me and everyone here if you were to sing a song or two. You're certainly welcome to if you'd like."

"To be truthful, I've had a bit to drink tonight. But if you can put up with my slurring of words and speech impediments . . . sure, I'd love to!" Everybody at the piano bar laughed, because it was obvious that he was not drunk, just slightly high.

When I handed him the microphone, I asked him what he would want to sing. He thought for a moment, and then asked us what we knew. I answered, "Well, we have a fairly big repertoire. Please do what you feel comfortable with."

Somebody seated at the piano bar suggested that he sing "My Funny Valentine." Valentine's Day had been just a week earlier, so it was a perfect choice. He accepted the request, I found a key for him, and he started to sing.

Everything was going fine until we got about ten or twelve measures into the song. He started to forget the words. This is a problem that occurs at least once in the life of just about every vocalist. It has happened to every singer I know. For some people, like me, it happens a lot!

A few years earlier, Sal and I were in the audience and had witnessed the taping of a Steve Lawrence and Eydie Gorme Television Special. The director must have stopped the tape a dozen times because Eydie kept forgetting the words. And she was totally sober. It happens!

Sal knew the words to My Funny Valentine. She lowered her head so that none of the audience could see her prompting Julius, and he went on like the great pro he is, without being detected by anyone. The audience never knew! They yelled out, "Sing another!" and "More. We want more!"

I said, "Please Mr. La Rosa, sing us another one."

"I'd be happy to!" he replied. He sang us a beautiful song that I did not know (and had to fake) called "Pieces of Dreams," written by composer Michel Legrand only a year earlier. The audience absolutely loved him, and Sal and I felt very honored to have him sing with us. In spite of the pleading by the audience to sing some more, he declined. He went back to his chair at the piano bar, and everybody ganged around him for autographs and handshaking. We decided that it was the perfect time for us to take a break.

I went to the regular bar and ordered a drink from Mike, the bartender. As I relaxed with the beverage, Vera, a waitress, came over to Mike and me, and said, "That Julius La Rosa has a great voice, but he also has a dirty mouth!"

I asked her what she meant. She said that every second word out of his mouth was the (expletive). I was shocked, and said honestly, "I wasn't aware of it. I know that he's had a little too much to drink! He's probably just too relaxed, and doesn't realize he's in mixed company!"

Mike, who had a strange sense of humor, said, "He probably figures that because he's a singing star, he has the right to talk any way he wants. You watch how I'll straighten him out. I'm gonna bring him down a peg or two!"

"What are you going to do?" I asked.

"Oh, you'll see. You'll get a kick out of this!"

I really did not want a fight, nor an insulting situation. After all, I felt somewhat responsible for Julius La Rosa's presence there in the first place. So I stayed close to the action, not knowing what the bartender had in mind. He approached La Rosa with a pen and piece of paper in hand. He asked, "Excuse me, Mr. La Rosa. Would it be possible for you to give me an autograph?"

139

Julie obliged with, "Sure, what the (expletive)" He signed the autograph, handed it back to Mike, and returned to his conversation.

Mike interrupted him again. "Excuse me, Mr. La Rosa. Would it be possible for me to get another autograph?" La Rosa nodded affirmatively and proceeded to scribble out his signature again, on a second piece of paper. He finished, gave the second one to Mike, and again tried to return to his conversation. Once again Mike interrupted him. "Excuse me, Mr. La Rosa. Would I be pushing my luck if I were to ask you for just one more autograph?"

The famous singer said, "(expletive) no! I'll be happy to." He signed the third autograph.

As he returned the paper, Mike said, "Thank you. Thank you very much."

"You're very welcome. But let me ask you a question. What the (expletive) did you want three autographs for?"

The bartender said, "Well you see, I have a hobby and it is to save autographs. Occasionally, I make trades with other people who save autographs, too. I figure that with three Julius La Rosa autographs, I might be able to get one Jimmy Roselli autograph!"

Mike walked back to the bar, and without responding, the famous singer left shortly thereafter. I felt badly on two counts. It was wrong for him to use such profane language. Yet, I don't think that insulting him was the proper way to curb it. A simple, "Please, could you refrain . . ." would have sufficed.

Julius La Rosa later sent us an autographed record album, and on it was Pieces of Dreams. It was beautiful! He signed it: To Sal and Roger, it was a lot of fun. Thank you and Saluti. Julie.

I love Jimmy Roselli's voice, and I bet that Julius La Rosa does, too. But there really is no comparing of the two voices. Jimmy is one of the best Italian-American voices this country has to offer. But Julius La Rosa also has one of the best crooning voices I have ever heard. Unfortunately, in my opinion, neither ever reached the great level of popularity to match his respective talent.

La Rosa, a Navy veteran, took the nation by storm when he started singing on Arthur Godfrey's television show, back in the fifties. He recorded only one big hit, "Eh, Cumpari," and even that was not indicative of his true talent. I wish he had recorded and received the proper promotion for songs like some of those Frank Sinatra or Tony Bennett recorded.

I once saw Julius La Rosa perform with a full orchestra on the Jerry Lewis Telethon. That evening, he was as good as anyone I've ever heard. And I mean Sinatra, Damone, Bennett . . . anyone. I think that he was probably America's most underrated vocalist. That is a shame. Sometimes I'll mention his name to young people. Most don't have the slightest clue as to who he is, but then again, many don't know who Sinatra was either. In any event, WE know who Julius La Rosa is. It was our great pleasure when he sat in with us one evening back in 1971. Additionally, I think Mike was a lousy bartender!

Perry Como

We've had the good fortune to perform for singing legend Perry Como several times. One time in particular, when he was dining with his wife Roselle at Lord Chumley's Pub

Perry Como

in Tequesta, stands out in my mind. Perry stopped for a moment to listen to us, smiling in recognition. He waved "hello" to us, before turning into the men's room. Soon, he returned to the front of our stage and listened for quite some time.

He clapped vigorously although we hadn't yet finished our arrangement.

A middle-aged woman was seated between Como and the exit to the dining room.

As he backed up, he tripped on her foot and basically collided with her. You would not believe the angry, detestable sneer that appeared on her face. She looked ready to rip him apart, limb by limb. Every natural line in her aging face became a deep crevice. Perry Como, a consummate and very handsome gentleman, immediately turned to apologize. She was all set to give him a tongue-lashing, when it suddenly dawned on her, exactly who had bumped her. I've never witnessed a miracle, but the transformation of that woman's face came close to one! All frown lines immediately vanished, as if some great plastic surgeon had just done a $50,000 facelift on her. What a smile she showed. She went from witch to angel, immediately. I don't read lips, but I'll swear she said to him, "Ohhhhh Per-ry . . . it's you! YOU can stumble into me . . . ANYTIME! Please . . . DO IT AGAIN!"

Another incident deserves retelling at length.

For ten straight years, Peter Makris, owner of The Flame, kicked off the South Florida "season" with his Annual Flame Golf Tournament. It usually took place in early November, and always sold out.

Played at one of the many prestigious golf courses in the area, the format was very popular. It resulted in bragging rights to most players, friends of Makris and patrons of The Flame. Throughout the tournament, the comradery flowed abundantly. So did the cocktails, during play, and each evening back at the club. Everyone had a great time. For the Flame, it was the true beginning of the season. Businesswise, it gave the place a big shot in the arm. Every year Makris presented a local charity with the proceeds, always a very sizable check. It was a no-lose situation for all involved.

One year, an invitation was extended to Perry Como, an occasional patron of the Flame. Perry Como had a smooth vocal style and was one of the most successful pop vocalists of the 20th century. His recording and television successes ran from the 1940s into the 1980's, were highlighted with many gold-record awards, and his own popular, weekly television show. Perry, who lived in nearby Jupiter Island, was an avid golfer. When Makris invited him, and he heard it was a classy event that benefitted some local charities, He accepted, replying "Sure. Why not!"

It was going to be a great day to have some fun and just plain hit the ball! Most of the other golfers were busy with their own game, so Perry was relatively unbothered. He played the tournament with Peter as his partner, and a pair of Makris' close friends, Andy Kallas and the great golf course designer Tom Fazio.

Meanwhile, out on the course, several Flame waitresses, who staffed the event, circulated around the links on golf carts, distributing refreshments. One of these servers was The Flame's ever-popular Joann.

She stood six feet tall, perfectly proportioned, and very attractive. Joann accentuated her height by wearing high-heeled shoes and styling her hair up. Joann literally looked down on all of the lady customers at the club, and most of the men, too.

Four other characteristics of Joann were even bigger than her height. They were her heart, simplicity, humor, and mouth. Her mouth was not crude. It was just LOUD! It was so loud that it would cut right through the crowd's noise, the musicians' volume, everything. Whenever you heard her laughing loudly, it became contagious. Before you knew it, the whole club was laughing, although only a few people knew why they were laughing. You were in for a fun night as her customer.

Out on the golf course, while Joann cheerfully drove her refreshment cart, Como, Makris, Kallas and Fazio started to play the course, with a fair-sized entourage of enthusiastic spectators. The golfers played the first couple of holes very well. Everyone was in awe of how good Perry could hit the ball. He hit a golf ball very much the way he sang, talked, and did everything else in his life . . . very relaxed. He concentrated hard in his preparation and address of the ball, but then hit it with ease and nonchalance. His total swing was so slow that you could probably time it from beginning to end using a calendar.

PGA legendary golfer Gardner Dickinson once told me that, playing around with Perry, he was almost exasperated by how slowly Perry swung his club. He finally said to Como, with as much restraint as he could muster, "HIT the damn ball!" Of course, Gardner also told me, "However, it was amazing how well Perry scored; so I guess one can't argue with success."

On the third or fourth hole, it finally happened. Perry concentrated on his shot to the green. The gallery, which had grown, silently awaited his backswing. In the meantime, bubbly, happy-go-lucky Joann drove her cart toward them; unaware of who was surrounded by the silent group of admiring fans. Soon, she found herself only ten feet from where Como gradually started his slow backswing. At that moment, she inoffensively bellowed, "PER-RY CO-MO?!"

Anyone who has ever played golf will attest that there is probably only one thing more difficult than stopping your backswing in progress, and that is to exhibit patience, control and etiquette with the cause of the interruption! Yet, Perry reacted to this abrupt disturbance with the patience of a saint. He asked, "WHAT? . . . My goodness! . . . Ah, what is it, dear?"

The spectators, most of whom already knew Joann, responded with uncontrollable laughter. Peter joined in; then, finally Perry started to laugh, too.

The laughter did not change Joann's reaction. She continued, in a flood of high-speed verbiage, "My God, Mister Como. You're my favorite singer. I have all of your recordings. . . . "It's Impossible," "And I Love You So." I've got them all and I've seen all of your television specials." She briefly gulped a breath of air and continued. "And . . . oh, I just love the way that you sing."

Once again, the crowd went into an uproar. Perry coolly smiled and said, "Well, thank you. And what is YOUR name?"

"Joann, and no kidding, Mr. Como, I'm your number one fan. I just adore you. You have no idea how much!"

Perry smiled understandingly, and said, "Well, thank you, Joann. That is really nice of you! Now you do understand that I've got to make this golf shot, or I'm going to hold up the rest of the tournament, don't you?"

Joann, momentarily jogged back into reality, stuttered, "Oh . . . oh, yes. . . . Oh, I'm so sorry Mr. Como. I didn't mean to interrupt your game."

Perry reassured her before hitting his ball, "No, that's okay. You were fine, Joann."

Joann didn't stop, though. Makris had to put an end to it by sending Joann away. He then explained to Perry, "Joann is one of our waitresses at the club. She really is a nice kid, but sometimes she gets a little carried away. I hope she wasn't too much of a bother for you."

Perry said, "No, she was actually a lot of fun!" However, being the devout golfer he was, I'm sure all he really wanted to do for the remainder of the day was to play his game. I'm also sure he expected the other shoe to drop at any moment. It happened later that evening, at the restaurant.

That evening, my band went to the club expecting a special night. We knew from previous experiences with the Flame Tournament that it would mean "standing room only" in our lounge. It was busy under normal circumstances. Add to that the tournament dinner and a possible appearance by the legendary crooner, and . . . voila! A packed house! Those who showed up anticipating an extraordinary evening were rewarded beyond their dreams.

Once my group began to perform, the crowd was so enthusiastic; they just would not let us off the stage. It was request after request, and we fulfilled them all. We were really hot that night, and the audience was with us all the way. We played our first set for a straight hour and a half before we decided to take a break. Even then, most of the patrons were disappointed with our temporary departure. It was just one of those nights. If I didn't know better, I'd have sworn that the crowd came in expressly to see US!

As we walked off the stage, I didn't get ten feet before I noticed Peter Makris making his way through the mob. I smiled and greeted him. "Hi, Peter. Is that Perry Como behind you?"

In all nine years that I worked for Makris, he never watched the time clock, in reference to our performances and rest periods. He never had to. We were very conscientious and fair about it. Peter replied with the only demand he ever made to me. I'm sure he wanted to show us off to his celebrity guest. He replied with, "Yeah . . . GET TO WORK!"

Having just entered the club, he didn't know that we had, just one minute earlier, finished performing twice as long as we should have. I said to him, "Okay, you got it!"

To my band members who were trying to follow me through the crowd, I said, "Come on. You guys have had a long enough break. Let's get back to work!" Their faces registered shock until I explained that we would give a command performance for the boss and a couple of his friends, including Perry Como. They understood, so we got back on stage and went into another hour's worth of music. Peter had reserved a table up front. Unfortunately, after his group was seated, Como had his back to our stage. Yet, throughout our performance, he constantly turned around to view us, always applauding heartily after each song. He made us feel important. I will never forget that.

The crowd was also very nice that evening. The sound level was much lower than you would have expected from an audience that size. It was almost like we were giving a concert, instead of playing in a lounge. We gave them our best stuff, and they reciprocated with thunderous applause, song after song after song.

When Sal finished singing the song (There's Got to be) "A Morning After," she brought the house down. But so, did Perry Como! As he turned to vigorously applaud, Joann was bringing a cocktail tray to their table. It held at least six drinks. When Perry turned to once again applaud, he inadvertently hit the tray of drinks, which overturned onto him. Perry took the whole load on his head. He got drenched, head to toe. Beer, scotch and soda, wine, Margaritas . . . everything.

He jumped up and yelled the kind of response you might hear from a person falling from a five-story window, "YAAIIEEEEEE!" It had to be one of the worst sounds to ever come from that man's beautiful vocal cords. Then he looked up to see Joann standing there with the empty tray in her hand. He reacted even louder, with an agonized wail that came from a daylong suppression of justifiable outbursts. "It's . . . YOU!"

Everyone in the lounge went into rib-splitting laughter.

Joann tried to save the situation, removing his waterlogged jacket and drying him off with towels. I knew there was no way we were going to continue performing with this chaos, so we took a break.

My group had a final laugh recalling the irony that Perry was accidently showered as we finished the song, "The Morning After," from the movie, The Poseidon Adventure. That plot took place on a luxury cruise ship. The female vocalist in the ship's band just finished singing that song when a tidal wave capsized the ship. It was like what we had just witnessed at The Flame, with the tray of drinks turning upside down when Sal finished singing the same song. We joked, "Maybe we should consider hiring Joann. She could do special effects for the customers, just to make our music more realistic!" Perry Como never played in The Flame Tournament again. Hmmmm . . . I wonder why?

On a personal note, my former son-in-law Albert, and his brother Gaspar worked as attending nurses for Como to the day he died. Two weeks prior to his death, I felt very privileged to be with the vocal icon, sharing a brief but wonderful moment reminiscing. I'll never forget how he concluded our chat offering his right hand for a handshake, but then warmly extended both his hands to embrace mine.

My daughter Lee related to me that towards the last part of Perry's life, he often confused her for his daughter Terri, and he'd just start talking to Lee about things she knew nothing about. Lee felt his words to her made him happy and in a comfort zone, so, she just listened.

One night, Albert, Lee, and Perry had just finished dinner at a restaurant and approaching their car, Perry asked Lee, "Will you sit with me?" She graciously accepted and they sat in the back seat while Albert chauffeured. Lee told me, the vocal star "tightly took my hand, and whispered, 'I miss your Mom.'" Then, he breathed deeply and closed his eyes, obviously to recall his wife Roselle's image.

Perry and Roselle Como were married 65 years until her sudden death in 1998. It was reported he was devastated by her loss. Later, on May 12, 2001, they were joined in death when Perry Como died at his Jupiter, Florida home.

Vic Damone

Long considered a singer's singer by most knowledgeable musicians and vocalists, Vic Damone epitomized all that any singer would want to sound like. Vic Damone didn't take a back seat to any of the top singers, especially when it came to strictly vocal abilities. It has been said by many, that he had "the best set of (vocal) pipes in the business!" In the early 80's, we had the honor of meeting the great pop singer at the Boca Raton Hotel and Club.

He came for dinner in the Patio Royale dining room, where my band played six nights a week. His wife a lovely young Texan joined him. Also with him was his piano accompanist and music director, Norm Geller, a very talented gentleman whom I'd met many years earlier, in New York City. They were all in the hotel for a week's worth of recreation, relaxation and some last-minute rehearsing for Damone's upcoming concert, scheduled for the following week in England, with the London Symphony.

Sal and Roger with Vic Damone

Damone had a low handicap in golf, and their daily routine included playing eighteen or more holes, enjoying the amenities of the hotel and Boca Raton, then dinner and cocktails to our music in the dining room. Later, Damone and Geller would patiently wait for the dining patrons to exit so they could use the grand piano (that I played) for their rehearsal.

One evening during their stay, this routine was interrupted when Vic Damone instructed the maitre d'hotel to invite me to their table. I told the maitre d' that I would be happy to join them as soon as I finished performing. About twenty minutes later, I approached their table, alone.

"Good evening, Mr. Damone. I'm Roger Rossi."

"I'm very pleased to meet you. We've been enjoying your music all week. Please join us for a cocktail."

Damone introduced his wife and Norman, and then we talked. I told him how much a fan I'd been for years. I even related a story of many years earlier. In the 60's, at The Sans Suis San on Long Island, a club where he performed, I was mistakenly identified as being related to him. I had arrived from my gig at the Carl Hoppl's Valley Stream Park Inn. Too late to see the show, I sat at the bar, where I could hear Damone singing in the main room. The young couple next to me were whispering and looking me over.

I overheard the young lady say, "He must be related to Vic Damone. He looks just like him." I knew they were talking about me. In my younger, pre-mustache days, many people told me that. Finally, the young lady turned to me. "Excuse me. Are you related to Vic Damone?"

I explained to Vic Damone that I just could not resist the temptation to "play the role" with the young couple. I answered her, "Yes, I am. . . . He's my father! . . . I'm RICK Damone!"

She turned back to her escort and said with excitement, "I just knew it. He's Vic's son, Rick Damone."

I don't think that a half a minute went by and the show inside ended. The crowd was applauding, whistling loudly and yelling "More," while the band played its "chaser" music and the M.C. said over the microphone, "Ladies and Gentlemen, Vic Damone. Wasn't he fabulous?" I continued my story for Damone, "And then, wouldn't you know it. You came out of the main room and started to walk right toward me and this young couple to whom I had just told a playful, bold-faced lie. I said to myself, 'Uh-oh, if Vic Damone doesn't somehow acknowledge me, this young lady is going to know I'm a total fraud!"

"Mr. Damone, you walked right by me, and I said in typical musicians' jargon, 'Hey, Dad!' I almost fell off of my barstool when you answered me with, 'Hi Son!' The young couple was impressed for sure. I wiped the sweat off of my brow."

Vic laughed at my story, telling me he had worked at the Sans Suis San several times, and remembered the club very well. "But I don't remember seeing my son there!" We all had a good chuckle over my story.

I found Vic to be the kind of person with whom it was easy to converse. He was cordial, interesting, and honestly interested in what you had to say. We continued talking about many things. For one thing, he complained to me about the pianos in the hotel.

"Roger, what do you think of the piano you're playing on, in this room?"

"Actually, the piano is a fine piano, Vic. It's the piano tuner that should be thrown out. I think HE'S DEAF!"

"It's atrocious. For a hotel of this caliber, it certainly is unbecoming."

"I don't know what to do, Vic. Every professional pianist who works here complains about every piano here. And yet, nobody in management does anything to change it. Maybe you could mention it to some of the powers that be. Perhaps that would help. In the meantime, I wish you could come to my home to rehearse. I have a beautiful Kawai grand, sitting in my living room, perfectly in tune."

I never expected that he would accept my invitation, but he did. He later declined, when I told him that we lived almost an hour's drive away.

He invited me to his table every evening from then on, for the remainder of his stay. At the Boca Hotel, only the bandleaders were permitted to mingle with the guests. For all other band members, it was an absolute no-no. It did not make any difference that the lead singer was my wife. However, Frank the maitre d' told me, "Mr. Damone has insisted that we break hotel policy, and allow your wife to join you at his table!"

"Gosh, Franco, I don't want to be in a bad situation with the hotel. Are you sure it's okay?"

"Yes, Dolores Sachs, the Executive Secretary, has permitted it."

"REALLY?" I couldn't have been more shocked.

Dolores Sachs, dining a few tables away from the Damone table, had a way about her that made all of her underlings' cringe . . . whether you had done something wrong, or not! She could raise her eyebrows to astronomical heights, stretching her neck above and beyond normal anatomical limits, thereby elevating her head high above all others in the room. She would then turn, periscope fashion, to zero in on the target of the moment. When my wife strolled with me toward Vic Damone's table, she became Sachs's target! Even though Sachs had approved the action, it was obvious she'd have preferred that I decline Vic Damone's cordial invitation, keeping hotel policy undisturbed. But there was nothing she could do except stare, and bite her lower lip!

At Vic's table, Sal asked, "Mr. Damone, can I ask you a question? It's kind of personal!"

He replied warmly, "Sure, what is it?"

"Well, every night that you have come here for dinner, I couldn't help but to notice the small picnic-type basket you've carried."

I interjected, "Yeah Vic, tell us all. . . . Have you been sneaking food out of this dining room every night?"

Everyone at the table laughed as Sal play-punched me on the arm. She then coaxed him more seriously, "Come on, Vic. What DO you have in the basket?"

He covered his lips with his index finger pointing upward, as he whispered, "Shhhh." He opened the basket partially, but enough for Sal and me to peer in. Our jaws dropped. Inside was a tiny dog, the kind that never gets big. He told us the name of the breed, but in the excitement of the moment, I forgot. He said to us, "I just couldn't leave my little baby behind, so I keep her in this case. She has more than enough room inside and plenty of air. Because she hears us and knows that we're near, she doesn't make a fuss." We had ourselves a real laugh over that one.

On the way home that night, Sal asked if I had noticed Dolores Sachs peering at us, from her table. I retorted, "Yeah, I saw her. We've got a dog dining at one table, and a giraffe at another. 'Sorry to inform you, but we're performing in a five-star ZOO!'"

That was our last year at the hotel. It was a year highlighted by two events. One was the presence of one of the world's greatest vocalists, Vic Damone. The other took place shortly after Mr. Damone departed for London.

The hotel's general manager asked me, "Roger, I heard that the Patio Royale's piano is out of tune. Is it true?"

I smiled.

Mel Tillis

While performing at Peter's Private Club in Tequesta, Florida, Sal and I occasionally spoke with some nice people from Pahokee, Ed Wilder and his wife Barbara. The Wilders traveled at least ninety miles round trip to enjoy our music and Peter's classy food and service. Ed was a close friend of another Pahokee gentleman, country music singing star Mel Tillis.

One evening, the Wilders brought Mel in for dinner. We were on the bandstand when they arrived. Almost everyone in the club looked up from their dinner plates to notice who was wearing the fancy Western attire. We heard some patrons in the vicinity of our bandstand whisper, "Hey, that's Mel Tillis!"

Although many cowboys and country folks never take off their hats, not even in finer restaurants, both Ed and Mel checked theirs at the front door. Ed would never want to offend anyone. However, they still had one slight problem confronting them. The club's dress code called for jackets and ties. They both wore jackets. As a matter of fact, Mel's was something to behold. But he was not wearing a tie. He accepted one from the club and put it on to affectionate chuckles at his table. The tie that Sandy, the club manager, selected was a perfect match to his outfit. I doubt one could spend all day at a great haberdashery and come up with a better match. The colors coordinated, the fabric was just right, and the design actually enhanced his Western outfit.

Tillis and the Wilders got settled in, ordered their cocktails and received their menus. Soon, Ed came over to the bandstand to say hello and invite us to join them when we took a break. We, of course, heartily accepted.

We continued performing for about twenty minutes. We couldn't help but notice something very strange happening at their table. Calling Sandy back, Mel Tillis removed the tie. Sandy took it and briefly went to the back of the club, returning with another tie. The famous singer put on the new one, in spite of the fact that it was a horrible match. It was so bad he could have won an award for the "WORST DRESSED" of the year. Our curiosity got the best of us, so we took our break and went to their table.

Mel Tillis' recordings, "Send Me Down to Tucson," "Ruby Don't Take Your Love to Town" (which he personally wrote), "Honky Tonkin'," and my favorite, "Coca Cola Cowboy," were top hits on the country music charts. Mel Tillis has appeared regularly on network television and in concert. He's a confirmed big-name star. Yet, he has accomplished all of this in spite of a speech impediment. He stutters. I have been told it often affects very intelligent people. Their thinking process moves along so quickly that their speech apparatus can't keep up.

Singing, on the other hand, is almost never affected by stuttering. The thinking process of selecting words in song is already done by the lyricist who composed the song. Mel Tillis and other vocalists recite already chosen words. Of course, Mel does it with his inimitable tonal quality and phrasing ability. Tillis does not have any handicap when he is singing.

Quite often, he'll relax his audience by poking jokes at his speech problem, even highlighting it in his act. He has included it in T.V. ads, where retakes or digital electronic devices could have easily removed it.

Upon meeting Sal and me, the singing star said, "It's a a a . . . real pleasure to . . . hear you buba both . . . performing. You sound really . . . wa wa wonderful together."

Ed said to us, "Why don't you both pull up a chair and have a drink with us?" We did. Somewhere along in our conversation, Sal questioned Mel, and his answer touched our funny bone. Even Mel laughed at what came out of his mouth.

Sal asked him, "Could you tell me something, Mr. Tillis? When you arrived, the club gave you a tie, and it perfectly matched your jacket and pants. The color and the design all looked wonderful together. Why did you swap it for a tie that, quite honestly, doesn't look as good?"

Mel replied, "Well, I noticed the first one had bu-bu-bu . . . BEAN SOUP, all over it!" We all laughed. Since then, when dining out, I will occasionally recall with fondness the evening we met Mel Tillis, by my gleefully ordering some . . . bu-bu-bu bean soup!"

The Ink Spots

The Ink Spots originally formed by Deek Watson, one of their singers. The group recorded some blockbuster hits and became a mainstay in the music business after a royal performance at Buckingham Palace. Bill Kenney, the original lead singer, was replaced by Jim Nabbie in 1945. Some of their hits from the thirties and forties still hold sales records. Songs like "If I Didn't Care," "I Don't Want to Set the World on Fire" and "To Each His Own" will live forever in the hearts of fans all over the world. Jim Nabbie eventually trademarked the name, Ink Spots.

Sal & Roger with the Ink Spots

I met the lead singer for the Ink Spots at a supper club called Taboo, in Palm Beach. I'd really gone to see some friends who performed there, bandleader-pianist Bobby Swiadon and his bassist, Jim Valley, who had worked with us years earlier. Arriving, I was disappointed to find the band finished for the evening. Bobby had already gone home. Jim Valley said aloud, "Well, look who's here, one of my favorite pianists, Roger Rossi!"

He brought me over to where Jim Nabbie was seated, and he did the introductions. "Jim, I want you to meet one of the finest pianists you could find anywhere, Roger

161

Rossi. Roger, this is Jim Nabbie, the lead singer for the Ink Spots."

Nabbie introduced me to his manager, Milli Lilley, from Fort Lauderdale, and we talked for a while. Coincidently, he knew my best man, Columbia recording artist Gene Stridel.

A while later, some people at the next table interrupted our conversation by asking us, "Why don't the two of you get up and do a few numbers for us?"

I declined. "Oh no, this is Bobby Swiadon's gig. I wouldn't think of using his piano without him requesting it."

Jim Valley jumped into the conversation, "No, Roger.

Bobby wouldn't mind it at all. I'm sure everyone here would love to hear you and Jim do a few songs together. What do you say?"

"Well, if you don't think I'd be stepping beyond my professional boundary line, it would be fine with me. How about you, Jim?"

Nabbie said, "I'd love to. If you were Gene Stridel's music director, you must be good.

Just a couple of tunes, though, okay?"

Everyone in the general vicinity applauded as we got up on stage.

Jim asked me if I knew a particular song, and I told him, "Yes, I do. What key do you sing it in?"

"I'm not sure. It's been a while since I sang it. Try B flat." I did and he nodded.

He sang the first chorus really nicely, and then he offered the next chorus for me to solo. As I did, I asked him, "How's the key? It sounds a little low to me. Is it?"

"Yes, it is just a slight bit too low."

"Okay. You can jump in at the bridge of the song (the middle section of the song). When you finish that, be ready for a key change up to C flat."

"Wonderful!"

When I finished my piano solo, he took over at the bridge. Then, I modulated up one key. We finished the song to thunderous applause. The audience could tell that they were witnessing two professionals working together under the most impromptu of situations, having just met each other. He suggested, "Let's do another one. But I'm not too sure of the keys for many of the songs in my repertoire."

"Don't worry about that, Jim. I think I know your vocal range now. If the key I put you in happens to be a little too low or high, just give me a hand signal. I'll raise it or lower it for you first chance I get, okay?"

"Yes. Roger, you play some kinda piano!" We did a few more songs and no one in the audience wanted to leave. In fact, some more patrons came in, sat down, and enjoyed the spontaneous concert. We took requests and performed medleys of songs. After every song's arrangement, Nabbie gestured for the audience to include me in their applause. Several times, he shook his head while smiling; suggesting that what he was hearing from the piano was unbelievable.

163

When we finally left the stage, much to the dismay of the appreciative audience, I looked at my watch. We had performed for almost an hour. I shook Nabbie's hand and said, "You sing great, Jim."

He returned the compliment. "Well, the accompaniment you provided was big-time stuff. You play great piano!"

Jim Valley concluded the evening by telling me, "You haven't lost your touch!"

About a year later, I called Milli Lilley. I told her that I was performing at a private supper club in Tequesta, Florida, called Peter's. I related to her that, on my recommendation, the club was interested in featuring the Ink Spots for a Monday evening show in January 1985. Milli told me the price for the legendary four-piece vocal group and asked if I would play the accompaniment for the show? I assured her I would, with the help of my trio, which included my bassist-trombonist, and my wife Sal on cocktail drums. She told me that if Jim and I put on a show half as good as the one that we did together in Palm Beach, the private club was in for a real treat.

When Peter's sent flyers to its members, the event immediately sold out. So many members were not able to book their reservations in time that the club booked the show for an additional Tuesday night performance. As Milli Lilley predicted, we knocked them dead! I booked the same show for the club the next two years. The Ink Spots were always sold out way in advance, and always musically and monetarily achieved success for everyone involved. Here it was forty years after their heyday, and their fans still remembered them well.

Later, as president of the Wellington Rotary Club, I helped raise funds for various Rotary projects by featuring Jim Nabbie and his legendary group. Again, it was such a huge success that we booked an additional performance the following night.

Sal and I opened the show with Sy Pryweller, professor of music at Palm Beach Community College, on drums and trumpet, and Al Greenstein on acoustic bass. Al, who had worked long-term gigs with Lionel Hampton and, additionally with the Sammy Spear Orchestra on The Jackie Gleason Show, had also backed greats like Tony Bennett, Frank Sinatra and Sammy Davis, Jr.

Sal and I sang some of our special arrangements like "Fabulous Places" from Doctor Doolittle, and Harold Arlen's "That Old Black Magic." I finished our featured segment of the show, with a piano medley solo I had arranged, which included Harold Arlen's "Over the Rainbow," and a jazz rendition of "I'm Always Chasing Rainbows" (an adaptation from the Frederic Chopin classic Fantasie Impromptu). I finished the medley with actual highlight parts from the Chopin piece.

The Ink Spots were then introduced, and they came center stage to join us. They performed their hit songs for more than an hour. They featured Jim Nabbie, of course, and additionally Sonny Hatchett, King Drake and… on bass vocals and narrations…Harold Winley. The audience clamored with approval. After almost every number, Jim Nabbie gestured toward my band to share the applause.

They did encore after encore. The audience would not let them off of the stage.

After the show, we had them and some of our close friends who were in the audience, to our home for cocktails.

A local, nonprofit organization, the Performing Arts League, requested that we do the same show for them. We accepted their invitation and it was the most successful concert that they ever had. That was the last concert we performed with the famous vocal group.

I never saw Jim Nabbie again. Years later, while on vacation with Sal in Italy, I read in one of the Italian newspapers that Jim had died.

Melissa Manchester

I received a telephone call from my friend, Al Greenstein, in February of 1990. Al, a fine bassist, also plays an excellent game of pool. We often got together with our other musician friends, jazz pianist Al Castellano, piano player, and entertainer Tony Sanso and jazz drummer Vinny DiRoma. Al opened with, "Hey Roger, I need you to run a gig for me. I'm contracting for a big convention at the Breakers Hotel in Palm Beach. It's on Wednesday, April 25th, in the evening. Are you available?"

"Yeah, Al, I am. Whatcha got?"

"Well, the conventioneers get a choice of one of three shows. They can see Maureen McGovern, Melissa Manchester or Ben Vereen. All three will perform simultaneously in three separate rooms at the Breakers. I need you to open one of the shows with a six-piece band. You're mainly going to warm up the audience. When you're done, you can watch the show. The bread is very good. What do you think? You can pick whichever show you want to open."

I quickly assessed that, although all three performers were great, we'd prefer to see Melissa Manchester. I told

Melissa Manchester at The Breaker's Hotel

Al and he said, "Fine. You'll open for Melissa Manchester in the Venetian Ballroom. I'm confirming the date with you right now, but I'll send you a written confirmation shortly. Just call me when you've booked all of your musicians."

At about five-thirty pm, the day of the concert, Sal and I started to shuttle our equipment into the Venetian Ballroom. I approached the maitre d'. "Excuse me, sir. I'm Roger Rossi, bandleader for the opening group. Where exactly did you want us to set up our equipment?"

"Walk this way."

167

I followed the man to the side of the room. He pointed to a space approximately five feet by six. The area was surrounded by dining tables, which were set up for the audience. Without another word, he started to walk away. I asked him, in total disbelief, "That's it?" The man arrogantly turned and nodded affirmatively one time. I immediately took a dislike to his pompous attitude. Keeping my cool, I said, "I don't think you understand, sir. I'm performing with a six-piece band. You're providing me with space that it would be difficult for a duo."

"Well, that's all the room we can give you," he insisted. Would you like me to tell a table of ten guests that we have no room for them because we had to accommodate the band?"

I retorted, "No, Sir. Simply tell me your name! This way when the people who have booked this convention ask me why I sent four of my band members' home, I can explain to them that it was you, who provided only enough space for a duo. . . . I'm sure they'll understand!"

I've seen many service people who think that because they work in a famous place like the Breakers, they are the reason for that fame. The Breakers at that point was no longer rated a five-star hotel by the Mobil Travel Guide. I felt that this jerk's attitude was part of the problem!

This guy, who earlier couldn't say but three words, suddenly started to rant and rave like a raging maniac. "You musicians are really something. You show up right before you're to perform and you want everybody to jump for you! I'll immediately get a crew of busboys out here, just for you. They have NOTHING better to do at this time. I have nothing better to do at this time. We'll drop everything, and we'll all bow down to your demands. Will that be satisfactory . . . SIR?"

Now it was my turn. "Are you quite finished?" I asked. He didn't answer, and he started to walk away. I went up to him and got right into his face. We stared into each other's eyes.

I said emphatically, "Wait a second. Don't you walk away from me like a coward. I know that you're trying to come on like some sort of big deal in front of your crew here, but that's not going to cut it with me! You just made a bold statement and your facts are all wrong. I'm here with my band ready to set up our equipment two hours before we're to start performing. That's enough time by anybody's standards. Secondly, it is not my fault that you didn't read your preparation list thoroughly enough to see that we're six pieces. And if you don't know by now how much room a six-piece group needs to set up their instruments, amplifiers, and speakers . . . then you shouldn't be working here, you pompous imbecile! . . . Now either you give me the room that my band needs or I'm going directly to Tom Wicky, the general manager!"

I saw that he did not want any part of a *mano a mano* confrontation with me. I just brushed him aside and got on with moving in the rest of my equipment. I knew he had to give us more room, and he did! My bassist, Dave Tomasello, quietly said to me, "Bravo! It's about time that somebody put that jerk in his place!"

The rest of the band arrived and started to assemble their instruments off on the side, while the maitre d' gestapo got his busboys to move some of the tables. They accomplished the total task in no more than five minutes, easily leaving more than enough room for all of the audience. As the crew of busboys did their job, they all smiled cordially toward us. One of them winked at me, while another held his right hand discreetly up in front of his body. His index finger and thumb were touching each other in a sign of support for my verbal retaliation. He said to me, "You did good. He's an a-hole!" I nodded and got on with my work.

We still didn't have quite enough room for comfort, but we made do with what we had. Sy Pryweller, my drummer, had a cramped style in playing, as did I. Steve Ahern and Cody Allan had limited space to set their trumpet, sax, and flute down; but I made them use their instruments so much throughout the gig, that it didn't matter. The real problem was that I had to return the monitor speakers to the van. There just wasn't enough room for them. So it meant that we had to hear ourselves directly from the main speakers and that is never a good situation. It's especially difficult for the vocal renditions.

After quickly setting up, we were just about to test the sound system. The piano tuner for the hotel started tuning the concert grand that Melissa's piano accompanist and music director would use for the show. I approached the tuner, asking him if we could have two minutes to test and he said politely, "Sure. That's no problem!"

As we tested the equipment, one of Melissa's sound engineers for the show was nice enough to help us. He really knew what he was doing. He yelled out to me from the middle of the room, "You have a touch of feedback. I think that it's the 8K band on your equalizer. Lower it just a bit." I did and he said, "Let me hear your mike. It needs a touch more bass. Excellent! Now how about the lead vocalist." Sal tested her mike and he said, "Yeah perfect, except you all need a little more reverb. That's it! You sound good!"

I thanked him. He said, "Oh, I was happy to help. By the way, when Melissa starts her show, you're welcome to come backstage if you'd like. I can only fit two of you back there because it's a little crowded with equipment. But perhaps you and your wife would like to sit and watch it all from up close."

I gleefully accepted and thought, "You see, there ARE some nice people in this world!"

We opened our part of the program with a wide variety of music, as the audience came in, sat, and dined. We received a respectable amount of applause. I thought the band sounded very good, especially in the confined space. We performed almost an hour and a half straight. Then we got the signal to end our segment, as Melissa's show was about to begin. I shut off our sound system, and the band went to the back of the room. Sal and I went backstage.

When we arrived, we received a wave from our new friend and his partner. They were both running the on-site sound for the show. Another guy was also running part of it from the back of the room. We were immediately enthralled by the massive soundboard they were in charge of. It was much larger than those in most recording studios.

Melissa started singing many of her hits. I can only imagine a heavenly angel sounding like that. She sang, *Don't Cry Out Loud*, *You Should Hear How She Talks about You*, *Midnight Blue*, and *Come in from the Rain*, our favorites for many years. We were impressed, not only with her but with the overall sound. It was really fabulous. I asked one of the sound engineers, "What kind of microphone is she using?"

"She has three Sinnhiezers placed throughout the stage and one that is wireless. They're really expensive mikes!"

Sal asked jokingly, "You mean they cost more than our $125 Shure SM58's?"

He laughed. "Your Shures are good mikes, but hers are the best. They run about three thousand a piece!"

Sal said, "Gee, it would be an enormous thrill just to say three words into them. Testing . . . one, two. . . . No less to sing into them. What a luxury!"

The monitor speakers that were on the stage for Melissa and the seven-piece band backing her were overwhelming. Each member of the band had at least one. Melissa Manchester had four that were placed in a semicircle in the front of the stage. Additionally, she had two bigger ones that were placed on each side of the stage, another one in front of the piano, and two extra for the pianist.

We counted 126 assorted spot lights set up overhead, on the outskirts of the stage front. Each one had a separate control and could be turned up and down with a group of lights or, for that matter, all at once. Two lighting and electrical engineers were in charge of it all. The thing that baffled our minds was that this was not a theater. It was a hotel ballroom. Her setup crew had converted it into a theater.

It started to dawn on me. Melissa Manchester had this huge stage to perform with her seven-piece band. They had sixteen monitors and all of the fabulous lighting, microphones, equipment, and crew they could possibly need. In contrast, we didn't have any monitors. We were trying to perform to that same audience in an area that would be barely large enough to fit two of her band members . . . and we had to argue with the maitre d' to get the space that we did!

Later, Sal and I personally lugged our equipment out of the hotel and loaded it into our van. Meanwhile, a beautiful stretch limousine waited for Melissa Manchester. That's when the dawning reached its climax. Stardom certainly has its benefits!

Roger Rossi

PART THREE: *The Tough Guys*

A Tough Guy? Not Really!
George Raft
Joe Louis
Rocky Graziano
Tami Mauriello
Jimmy Hoffa
The Palumbos

Roger Rossi

A Tough Guy? Not Really!

As an adult, I've had five very violent street fights. Fortunately, my record stands at 5-0. All five were by KO's, three were technicals. In every incident, the other guy started the fight.

I never ran from anyone, which is rather amazing. I make my living from the use of my hands at the piano keyboard, considered by most a gentle occupation. I do believe that if things are worked out verbally, everyone involved benefits.

However, when the other guy starts pushing, shoving and throwing punches, or as in one situation, attacks you with a butcher knife along with three cohorts, while screaming, "I'm gonna (expletive) kill you," you sometimes have no recourse but to rise to the occasion, get tough and fight back. It's called self-preservation. Miraculously, the outcome was always the same. My attackers needed medical attention, and I emerged basically unscathed.

The first time, I was a freshman at Potsdam College's Crane School of Music. I chased a student of nearby Clarkson College who had stolen something of mine. I caught up with him, of all places, on the front lawn of my college president! It was late at night. I was able to see him well enough in the moonlight to tackle him. We fought, while I presume the president slept. With a flurry of lefts and rights, I very quickly put the other college student into his own slumber.

My friends, who finally caught up with us, said to me, "My God, Roger . . . you've killed him. He's dead!" I answered nonchalantly, "Nah, he's faking. Let me show you." I kicked the thief in the ribs, expecting to get a groan out of him. The silence was not broken. We fled from the scene in panic. We were still kids in men's bodies. I found out the following day that he was brought to the Clarkson infirmary to finish his nap. But he did survive.

On a January 1968, evening, on the way home from playing at a restaurant in Centerport, Long Island, I decided on a nightcap. I entered Charlie's Place, a neighborhood bar in nearby Smithtown.

I found an empty stool at the bar, sat and ordered a beer. Moments later, while the owner was pouring my beverage, he asked, "You're still working at Glynn's Inn, aren't you? It's a very classy place."

"Yeah, it's really nice performing there. The owner wants me in tuxedo weeknights, and a dinner jacket on weekends. They treat me like a gentleman, the pay and tips are good, so what more could I want?" While we talked "shop," the customers on both sides of me eavesdropped.

Soon, the guy two stools to my right loudly announced to his wife, who was next to me, "Come on, Babe, let's go. I've heard enough of this bull (expletive)."

While I sipped my beer and ignored him, I couldn't help but notice "Babe" struggling with her overcoat. I helped her while her left arm found its sleeve. She thanked me.

He told me, "Keep your hands away from my wife."

I explained, "I didn't mean anything by it. Just trying to be a gentleman."

"A gentleman doesn't help a lady unless he's asked to," he retorted.

"No. A gentleman should always help a lady," I insisted.

Now, he bellowed. "Oh, yeah? A gentleman kicks the (expletive) out of another gentleman."

I guess I should have kept my mouth shut, but I just couldn't. I snorted back, "Look, I didn't come in here looking for a fight . . . but, I'm not trembling either."

Now standing, he backed away from the bar and crashed his stool to the ground. He yelled, "You better be trembling, you son-of-a-bitch. I'm gonna kick your (expletive) ass in." I taunted him. "Oh, boy, I'm really scared."

He put up his fists in a combat stance and stated, "Come on, I'm ready."

I said sideways to his wife, "He's ready. You better take him home."

He pushed his wife out of the way as he roared, "Let me at him. I gonna kill 'em."

I stood up while grabbing my beer bottle by its neck. I timed my shot perfectly, just as in the movies. The beer bottle landed on his head and unraveled a zippered trail of blood across his forehead. Much to my dismay, it only stunned him. I stood there thinking he was going to hit the floor. They always did in the movies! However, he was still standing. The broken glass had also lacerated my hand and two fingers, one of them rapidly spurting blood. Now I was angry!

He threw his first punch which missed my dodging head. It was the closest he came to hurting me, but it angered me more. I counter attacked from every possible angle. A severe right uppercut found its mark in his left ribcage. I followed with a left hook to his right temple.

He charged into me, trying to clinch. I parried and shoved him reeling into a set table and chairs. Then I fiercely punished him with a barrage of rights, left jabs and hooks. He finally grabbed me and we wrestled to the floor. Managing to stay on top, I continued my assault, striking him with rapid shots.

It took three or four men to pull me off. "All right, he's had enough. You don't want to kill him!" one said.

The guy was a bloody mess, both from my pounding fists and my bleeding hand. The place looked as if a cyclone had hit it, with tables, chairs, and stools scattered throughout. Charlie, the owner, brought me into the men's room, cleaned and bandaged my cut hand while warning me that someone had called the police. "You better leave through the back door before they arrive. I don't want you to get in trouble over this guy."

I apologized to Charlie and left.

The next evening, at Glynn's, I performed cautiously, trying to avoid using two tender right-hand fingers. My bruised knuckles looked worse than they felt. Afterward, I went to Charlie's to apologize again. Entering, I spotted Charlie at the right side of the crowded, rectangular bar. I said, "I'm very sorry for what happened here last night, Charlie. I'm sure I must owe you for furniture. Please assess the damages and bill me."

"Roger," he said, "You don't owe me a thing. Not even an apology. I'm so proud of you. That guy comes here every night, has a few drinks and then picks a fight with anyone he can.

You're the first one that not only stood up to him but gave him a taste of his own medicine. You were beautiful."

"Is he here tonight?"

"Yes, he is. I'd introduce you, and sober he'd shake your hand saying, 'Hey, you're a better man than I,' but he's already tanked up and waiting for the bell to start the first round."

"Charlie, who is he? I don't know what he even looks like." I looked around.

"He's on the other side of the bar. Roger, you can't miss him. Just look for the big guy with all the facial bandages"

I looked to the other side of the bar and focused on a man, 6'3", or 6'4", Band-Aids covering his nose, chin, right cheek, and a strip across his zippered forehead. He looked like a professional heavyweight boxer, recovering from a Joe Louis fight. I stood up. "Gee, Charlie, if I knew he was THAT big, I never would have backtalked him last night!"

I must admit that in both incidents, I was later upset with my own behavior. That was not the way I felt with my final fight in 1972. I have to admit I honestly tried to kill my attacker. If put in the same situation again, I probably would react exactly the same way. That's why I call it my "final" fight. My rage was so intense that I realize there is such a thing as temporary insanity! Since that incident, I have gone out of my way to avoid confrontation. I just don't like the person or thing into which I transform.

We were on the Long Island "distressway" going to a July 4th gig. Two couples, in separate cars, showing early signs of "road rage" kept cutting us off. One woman even waved a butcher knife out the window. We tried to get away, zigzagging through holiday-jammed traffic at speeds of up to 85 mph. Finally, they caused an accident with all three cars. One of theirs, a beautiful Corvette, was totaled. Their other car also serious damage.

Amazingly, my car had only minor scratches. The guy from the Corvette was in a state of shock seeing his car destroyed. The woman from the other car came at us with the butcher knife. Clearly, she knew how to use it—holding it with a combat grip a la Marines. I had to parry and shift repeatedly to avoid her attempted stabs. I told the shell-shocked Corvette owner, "You better take that knife away from her, or I'm gonna jam it down her throat!"

He did, and I thought it was over. It wasn't.

The guy with her came from nowhere and cold-cocked me with a left hook to my cheekbone. I barely saw it coming. His hand must have had a sharp ring on it. It ripped my flesh right off the way a scallop knife would, leaving a tremendous scar on my face, that stayed with me for months.

Absolutely enraged, I grabbed the guy's right arm as he tried to hit me again, and caught him with a right to his left ear. I immediately followed with a barrage of lefts and rights. I literally tried to kill him.

He attempted to pivot under me, to lift me off the ground. Instead, he pushed me against the front grill of a car caught in the massive traffic jam we had caused with the accident and ensuing combat. He tried to weaken me with a couple of body shots, but I was so caught up in the moment that I didn't feel the punches until later when it was all over.

Mercilessly and methodically, I beat him into oblivion. As he went down to his knees, I was so insane that I continued my assault with vicious lefts and rights. Finally, I kneed him in the face. I don't think he even knew. I believe he was already out to lunch.

I finally reunited with my stunned wife. She asked me, looking at the unconscious man lying in the middle lane of the expressway, "How is he?"

I said with conviction, "I hope the son-of-a-bitch is dead." Soon, a summoned ambulance arrived and took him to the hospital for a five-day visit. He had, among his injuries, multiple bruises, and lacerations to his face and body and a fractured skull.

I should have gone into the hospital myself for my bruised knee and cheekbone. However, the police put the damper on that when they arrested ME! When they saw the damage that I had wrought on this jerk, they put my hands behind me, handcuffed me and hauled me off to the police station.

I told them that they were arresting the wrong guy. The other people had started it and I was simply defending my wife and myself. They didn't believe me.

I pleaded with them to search for the knife. I said, "That guy who owns the Corvette had it last. He might have thrown it somewhere. Please, search for it."

"Yeah, sure. We'll look for it." They put me in the squad car's back seat.

While they took me away, Sal happened to notice a guy who was driving by. Like me, he also had on a tuxedo, and musical equipment in the back of his station wagon. She called out to him, "Hey, you witnessed the whole thing, didn't you?" He nodded, "Yes."

Sal continued, "Look, we're musicians ourselves. We were on our way to our job when this all happened. Please, tell the police what you saw!"

The guy replied, "Hey, lady, I'm late for my gig already. Forget it!" He drove off.

Down at the police station, they kept me cuffed for more than an hour, while they interrogated me, Gestapo style. Five or six huge cops stood around me, firing questions at me. It was as if I would be beaten up, or executed if I said the wrong thing.

"Do you realize how uncomfortable these handcuffs are? Could you please remove them?" I asked.

"YOU SHUT UP! We're the ones that ask the questions here."

"Gee, you guys must be real brave. Every one of you must outweigh me by at least 80 pounds. There's only one door in this room. What do you think, that if you take off these cuffs, I'm going to beat-up all of you big, brave policemen and then escape? I demand that you either make a formal arrest and book me; or remove these handcuffs immediately and release me."

Just about then, another cop entered and whispered in the ear of the policeman in charge. He told him that I had an unsolicited witness who had seen the whole thing from beginning to end. This witness had come out of the crowd, taking time to corroborate my side of the story. He went out of his way, while a fellow musician wouldn't even bother. The cop in charge looked dejected and told me I could go.

I was almost as upset and enraged with him as I was with the scum I had laid out on the expressway.

Infuriated, I said, "That's it? You mean to tell me that I don't even get an apology for your keeping me in handcuffs for more than an hour while you let those vicious criminals go loose?"

He snorted. "All right, 'We're sorry. Now you can go!"

He turned away from me, in order to make his words the final say. However, I had the final say with, "Gee, Officer, before I go, I would like you to know that as a citizen of this country, I feel very secure and protected from all those bad criminals out there, especially with YOU in charge!" Then I left.

Out front stood Sal, eyes red. I purposely ignored the lit cigarette in her hand, representing a break of her promise, four years earlier, that she would never smoke again. I figured that she had been through just as much hell as had I.

A deputy soon showed up at our doorstep. He served me a summons to court. The guy I had put in the hospital had filed a whole pile of trumped-up charges against me. I filed countercharges against him. About a year later, there was a hearing. When my unsolicited witness came forth to testify on my behalf, it became obvious that I had the upper hand.

My lawyer advised that we could probably get a guilty verdict against him when it was all settled, but it would cost more in legal fees. He explained that New York had recently enacted a law: If a person was convicted of a minor crime, he would automatically be exempt from serving time. Incarceration would not occur unless he was arrested again within three years. In other words, this lunatic could be found guilty, costing me another $1,500, and not serve a minute's time, as long as he kept his nose clean for three years. Our justice system is truly wonderful . . . and fair, too!

We told the lawyer to move for dismissal because we didn't have the additional money. All charges were dropped. That was the turning point in our decision to move to Florida. At one time, we had thought about moving to Arizona, because it was even further away from New York. We finally opted for Florida, because it had the tranquility of the ocean.

Before we left, we took our unsolicited witness and his wife to lunch. We were not permitted to talk to them until the hearing was finished. We exchanged pleasantries and expressed our deep gratitude to him for being willing to testify on behalf of two people he didn't even know. We couldn't thank him enough.

I finally asked, "It would have been so much easier for you to do just like everyone else, to ignore the whole situation and simply drive off. Why did you come forward, the way that you did?"

He told us that a couple of years earlier, he and his pregnant wife were returning from a trip to Southampton, Long Island. They decided to stop at a diner, get some coffee and use the bathroom facilities. After finding seats and ordering, his wife went to the bathroom. When she returned, she found four guys beating up her husband. They stepped on and crushed his eyeglasses so that he couldn't even see them. When she came to his aid, yelling out to the rest of the patrons and employees, these thugs beat her up too, causing her to lose her baby. A full house of customers ignored their pleas for help. When the police arrived, nobody in the place would even acknowledge

187

having seen it happen! Not the customers, not the employees, NOBODY!

He told me, "Roger, I saw what was happening to you that day. I realized that we were seeing a deja vu of what had happened to us. Thank goodness you were tough enough to fight your attackers off the way that you did. But when the police took you away, and nobody would say anything to them . . . well, that's when I decided I wasn't going to let the same thing happen to you."

I have thought many times, about how fortunate I was that he happened to be there on that particular day, at that exact moment. Nobody else, except my wife, would have verified my story. I could very easily have ended up with a criminal conviction. I think about the enormous financial expense a conviction of that nature could have entailed. The costs for my attorney, a civil suit for all my attacker's medical expenses, the mental strain, etcetera . . . and I close my eyes and thank God that this stranger came out of the crowd and stood up to be counted!

I've also reflected on how fortunate it was for me, that at the moment of truth, I rose to the occasion and got tough. Otherwise, both my wife and I could have very easily ended up statistics, injured or dead.

Am I a tough guy, you ask? I mean, really tough? The answer is no! Emphatically, NO! Just fortunate. VERY fortunate!

Now, forty-five years later, I'm happy to say that Florida has been wonderful for my family and me. I have also kept my personal promise in avoiding confrontation and physical combat. I simply smile and say to myself, "That's for young guys. . . . Not me!"

George Raft

In the fall of 1967, I performed at a wonderful eatery in Manhattan, Les Champs.

In the dining room, good service, strolling violinists and accordionists complemented the fine cuisine. I performed in the lounge. I performed in the lounge.

There, the format was continual, alternating pianists. The ambiance was quite classy and charming throughout. It was patronized by the *creme de la creme* of the finance and sports worlds, and by people who made their careers from the arts. It was not uncommon for one of the patrons to burst into a beautiful aria from *La Boheme* or Faust, singing it with all the gusto, correct pronunciations, timbre, and pitch that you might expect from a performance at "The Met." I honestly believe some were Met artists.

The establishment also attracted many tough guys. Some were legitimate, others not quite so legit. I met only the law-abiding ones, but I always sensed the other type were there although they never got out of line. Most of the customers at Les Champs were reserved, yet also congenial and cordial. George Raft was reserved!

When I met the movie star, I realized right then and there that in his movies, like *Scarface and Each Dawn I Die,* he wasn't exactly "acting."

Tough Guy George Raft with Mae West

I don't think George Raft was ever considered a great actor, one who can play just about any role with comfort, ease, and believability. Dustin Hoffman is a great character actor. So are Anthony Hopkins, Mel Gibson, and probably the greatest of all was Sir Laurence Olivier! These people could portray a gentle priest or a soft-spoken college professor in one picture, and a psychotic, violent killer in the next. They can even "become" someone of the opposite sex, like Hoffman in *Tootsie*, and be totally believable in all instances.

George Raft, on the other hand, always played one character, the tough guy, and in most instances, a gangster—a tough gangster. After meeting him, I came to the conclusion that he didn't require too many acting classes to develop his style. He simply had to play himself. By nature, he projected a stern, austere personality.

I had often seen him in the restaurant but would refrain from approaching a celebrity in that situation. Then one evening, as the other pianist performed, I had the opportunity to meet him without imposing.

On my rest break, I went outside to get a breath of fresh air, returning to the foyer, as he exited. When I realized who stood directly in front of me, I said to him courteously, and with a pleasant smile, "Hello, Mr. Raft, I'm Roger Rossi, one of the pianists in the lounge. I'd like to tell you I really enjoyed you in the movie Scarface."

With that, he gave me a slight affirmative nod and a low-toned "Hmm." The sound resembled a grunt. That was it. For a second, I thought he was clearing his throat. In reappraising the death-cold stare he gave me, and the non-committed reply, I realized that the man was "reserved!"

When I observed his back disappearing into the night, I started to conjure up his probable thoughts about our "meeting." I imagined that he surely contemplated, in that quick passing, whether or not to pull out his .38 and pistol whip me, or perhaps fill me with holes for daring to speak to him. I guess he changed his mind. Several other patrons had come into view, and he might have had witnesses. Now, if it had been Humphrey Bogart, I'm quite certain HE wouldn't have worried about such trivial problems as innocent bystanders. He would simply have shot me in cold blood, and then shot the witnesses, too!

I don't think Humphrey Bogart was necessarily as tough as George Raft. But he certainly made a better gangster—at least in the movies. Then again . . . Bogart was acting!

Joe Louis

Manhattan's Les Champs restaurant was aptly named, as many boxing champions frequented the place.

My meeting the great Joe Louis was an absolute pleasure. He was so warm and cordial he appeared just as interested in meeting me as I was in meeting him. He offered his hand to shake before I did. With a warm smile, the boxing legend said, "I've heard you play that piano, Roger, and you're one mighty fine musician."

I thought to myself, "Gee, what a nice thing for him to say to me." From where he usually sat in the restaurant, he probably couldn't even hear the piano. I believe he had said that simply to be nice and make me feel good.

I will never forget that encounter. It taught me a good lesson in life. You can be nice to other people, no matter how big, successful or great you become. He was a big man, but he was first and foremost a gentleman. Even his shaking my hand seemed dignified. His handshake was firm, but not at all punishing. He probably could have broken every bone in my little palm.

I asked him before we parted, "Can I ask you a question, Mr. Louis? It's something I've always wondered."

"Sure."

"Well, out of all the great fights in your career, which ones gave you the most trouble?"

I expected that he was going to be specific in his answer to me. Something like, "Billy Conn, Jersey Joe Walcott, or even James Braddock." Instead, he replied, "All the ones I lost." He very quickly brightened into a huge smile, as if to suggest, "Did you get it?"

After we both stopped laughing, he said, "Actually, one fight that gave me a lot of trouble was the one I had with my mother when she found out I was quitting my violin lessons . . . to box!"

"I didn't even know you played the violin, but I'm glad you won that fight!" He'd caught me off guard with his answer. If I had known he was going to be humorous, I could have responded with, "In my opinion, the fight that

193

gave you the most trouble was not with your mother, but probably with your Uncle . . . Sam!" (Joe Louis had been hit with a huge back-taxes bill from the Internal Revenue Service.)

Joe Louis never had to talk or act tough. The Brown Bomber accomplished it all in boxing. It was evident that he didn't have to try to impress anyone. His gloves did all that for him! I wasn't old enough to have been there for any of his fights, but I have seen a lot of them on film. He was probably one of the few men in boxing history that could knock out his opponent with only eight or ten inches between his glove and their jaw. In 2003, Ring Magazine ranked Joe Louis "the #1 All-Time Greatest Puncher" in their list of 100. What power he had. Additionally, in 2006 the International Boxing Research Organization ranked him "the #1 heavyweight boxer of all-time."

Joe Louis was tough, but in meeting him I found a true gentleman. Using some of the words he used in describing my piano playing, I'd say he was . . . "one mighty fine" gentleman!

RECORDS AND ACCOMPLISHMENTS

Joseph Louis Barrow (May 13, 1914 – April 12, 1981), known as Joe Louis and nicknamed the "Brown Bomber," held his Heavyweight Championship title for 140 consecutive months, from 1937 to 1949, the longest span of any heavyweight titleholder. During that time, he fought in twenty-six championship fights and won twenty-five. He had a total of seventy professional fights with only three losses, fifty-seven of his wins were by knockout.

Rocky Graziano

One night, on a break at Les Champs, I had the good fortune of meeting the great former Middleweight Champion of the World, Rocky Graziano. Rocky was not only tough, but he also talked tough. He spoke "Brooklynese." A lot of his words were not only mispronounced because of improper diction but often ran into each other, to form one word instead of two or three.

Having spent my first nine years in the Bay Ridge section of Brooklyn, I recognized the lingo immediately. It was typical to utter words like "dees" and "doze" and "dem" for "these" and "those" and "them." People from that part of the country never greet you with "How are you doing?" It's "Howharya?" . . . Janowadiemeen?

Approaching me and the cute hat-check girl with whom I talked, Rocky said to me, "Yeah, gladdameedja!" He extended his right hand in a slightly tilted fashion with the palm up. I wasn't sure if he wanted me to shake hands or tip him until he moved it toward me another three inches. He said, "Yadda piano player, huh? Nice job."

I had played for him on many occasions, but this was the first chance I had to actually meet him.

Rocky appeared either tired, slightly inebriated or both. His normal mutilation of the English language became extreme. Rocky Graziano never seemed to care much for the King's English. That evening, it became apparent to me that he wasn't impressed with the Marquis of Queensbury, either.

After exchanging pleasantries with me, he turned to the hatcheck girl and asked her, "Yagotmy blagh ckhat?" With this, the cute young lady got a little too cute. In a bad attempt at humor, she replied, "Sorry, Mr. Graziano, but we just don't have any cats back here; not even black ones."

This slightly irritated Rocky. He didn't appreciate her having fun with his dictionless speech. He bellowed back at her, "I dint say I wanna blagh ckhat, I saidi wuan my blagh ckhat!"

By this time, several other slightly inebriated patrons had meandered into the area. After hearing Graziano's attempt to clarify his Brooklyn English to this smart-ass girl, they went into hysterics. This intensified his aggravation. It probably sounded hilarious to them, but it was no laughing matter for the Champ. He was pissed!

One of the onlookers was a very big (six foot four or five) local bookie who hung out in the place. He outweighed Graziano by at least 80 pounds, not to mention the enormous difference in arm lengths.

I guess he thought he knew the boxing legend enough to join in the kibitzing. He said nonchalantly, "Come on

Rocky! Don't give the girl such a hard time." Well, this not only compounded Rocky's embarrassment... it just about infuriated him.

Graziano grabbed this mammoth, probably twenty years his junior, and slammed him against the wall like a mere five-pound bag of potatoes. He had the guy by his jacket collar, and he looked up to him saying very forcefully, "Doanja (expletive) wid me or I'll ripya (expletive) headdoff."

This happened no further than five feet from where I stood. I thought to myself, "Wow, this is going to be great! I'm going to see the War of the Worlds, and I've got a ringside seat!"

Rocky was tough, and the bigger man knew it. I didn't think he would take the manhandling, or the lip from Graziano, but he did. Not only did he back off, but he basically begged off.

"No, please, Rocky. I was just kidding with you. I didn't mean anything by it. I'm sorry. I apologize."

When Graziano dropped his hands from the guy's throat and turned toward the hat-check closet, his black hat was humbly held shaking outside the window. Another soft-spoken apology followed the hat.

I never saw Rocky Graziano after that, but the incident left me quite a vivid memory of the boxing great. I never saw him fight in any of his great matches, but I can imagine how great he must have been. He came into boxing in an era filled with such greats as Jake La Motta, Tony Zale, Sugar Ray Robinson, Gene Fulmer, and Willie

Pep, and Rocky Graziano was a World Champion during that time period! He had to be great, just to survive!

He sure as hell was tough!

Tami Mauriello

In December 1967, I took a six-month gig performing at a truly delightful spot in Centerport, Long Island. The restaurant was Glynn's Inn, owned by Tom and Sis Milano. There I met and became acquainted with one of Joe Louis' boxing opponents, Tami Mauriello.

Louis was the world heavyweight-boxing champion from 1937 until he relinquished his throne in 1949. By then, he had dominated the opponents in his weight division.

At one point, he just could not find a viable challenger. Any contender who did fight him had to have the talent, and/or record, to draw an audience for the gate of the bout. After all, each match was for the world championship, so they had to be worthy opponents. Yet, time after time, Louis would dispose of them in good fashion.

These professional boxers had a legitimate chance at acquiring his crown. Nonetheless, they were unkindly referred to as "Bums of the Month." None were bums! At a different time, perhaps against another champion, some probably would have won. A few even put up a good effort against Joe Louis, but he was so great and talented, that he was in a class of his own.

Along came Tami Mauriello, who came very close to beating Joe Louis. I can assure you Tami was no bum.

One evening, finishing my performance at Glynn's, I went over to a club on the south shore of the island, in a small town called Sayville. An old friend of mine, Joe Tuminaro, a car salesman, was picking up some extra cash part-timing as a bartender.

"Hey, Roger, how you doing?" Joe asked.

"Real fine, Joe, and you, and Joan?"

"We're both great, thanks. What can I get you, my friend?"

"Johnny Walker Red, club soda and a twist," I answered.

While mixing my drink, he yelled out to me, "Roger, by the way, a friend of yours has been asking for you. Tami Mauriello."

"Yeah, I heard that he's working here. Is it true?"

"Uh huh, he's our bouncer. He's here tonight."

"Where is he?" I asked, but looking around the club, I spotted him myself. It was very easy to pick Tami out in a crowd. All I had to do was look for numerous bodies being tossed around like mannequins.

I went over to that corner of the room to find Tami taking on not one, but five men, at the same time. As I got closer to the altercation, he yelled out to me, while dumping another body onto the pile that had accumulated in front of him, "Hi, Roger. I'll be done with this in a minute. These guys wanted to have a little fun." He remained in control throughout the episode.

Once, I built up the courage to ask Tami what had really happened in his 1946 bout with Joe Louis. Mauriello was Frank Sinatra's favorite fighter and it was believed that he actually used his influence to help Tami get the title shot against Louis.

Tami told me that, at the time, he was the smaller of the two, as Louis outweighed him.

To Tami, that was insignificant. He

Tami Mauriello
He rocked Joe Louis

had been very confident of his power, although he realized how capable the Champ was.

Tami told me of his own personal shortcoming. He had bad feet—his arches. He recalled for me that in the first round he was lucky enough to tag Louis on the jaw, a solid right that rocked him badly. Unfortunately, for Tami, he just couldn't finish the Champ off. Worse than that, he slightly embarrassed Louis and actually woke him up. Joe came back at him with a barrage of punches which Tami could not defend. His bad arches wouldn't let him back up from the attack.

The fight had attracted a good-sized crowd of almost 40,000 people, who all jumped to their feet. They probably realized that in the center of the ring were two of the world's toughest fighters, with one intention; to give their "all."

My friend continued telling me the details. Louis caught him with a devastating left hook that simply knocked him off his tired feet. When he got up, he still couldn't back up. His arches put him into forward gear only, the opposite direction his brain was telling him to go. Joe Louis finally ended Tami's punishment and his dream of being champion. Louis knocked him out, double-punching him with a crushing left hook, then a right.

Hearing the account of this famous fight right from the horse's mouth was a real thrill. Especially after I'd had the great pleasure of personally meeting Joe Louis only six months earlier. I felt that not only did I meet up with two really fine gentlemen, but two tremendously tough guys. It's a bit sad that only one of them lived their dream of becoming world champion.

After the fight, Mauriello told a reporter on live radio "I guess I'm just an unlucky son of a bitch". However, years later, Louis often said that 'his fight against Tami Mauriello was his last great fight.'

Understandably, Tami Mauriello was nicknamed "The Bronx Barkeep." He was born in The Bronx on September

18, 1923, and died in The Bronx December 3, 1999, at the age of 76. I left New York for Florida in 1972, and never had the chance to say, "Goodbye" to my old pal.

<u>RECORDS AND ACCOMPLISHMENTS</u>

•Mauriello won his pro boxing debut with a first-round knockout against Gilberto Ramirez Vazquez in Queens, NY. He went undefeated in his next twenty-three fights, with fifteen knockout wins.

•In his career, Tami had ninety-six pro matches, with eighty-two wins - sixty by knockout, thirteen losses and one draw.

•Tami also acted professionally. He played the part of "*Tillio,*"a thug in the 1954 film "On the Waterfront" starring Marlon Brando *(Best Actor)* and Eva Marie Saint *Best Actress.*

Jimmy Hoffa

Sal and I took a seasonal, four-month gig at the Boca Teeca Country Club, in Boca Raton. The engagement started in December 1973. We performed as a trio   with bassist Michael Winburn.

The bandstand was in an area that made it the focal point. It was behind the dance floor, not too far from the bar, and adjacent to the dining room. Our location was perfect. All club patrons could listen and dance to our music without our having to turn up the volume.

Our stint at Boca Teeca was without incident except on one occasion. However, I would consider that one episode very unusual for several reasons.

Sal is hardly ever clumsy. She'll accidently break a glass here, or drop a dish there, but basically, she is quite steady and unshakable. However, on one evening in February 1974, she was an absolute klutz! The victim of her clumsiness was a man of extreme notoriety.

It was about nine o'clock when we took our first break. We left the bandstand and I fetched some coffee. Sal went into the dining room to greet some friends. After paying her respects, she started to back away from their table. As she did, she stumbled backward, right onto the lap of a very stern-looking gentleman, dining with some friends at his own table. It doesn't happen too often that a young, good-looking, shapely and exquisitely dressed lady falls onto some stranger's lap. Needless to say, all at his table were shocked. The man said, coolly, "Well, what do we have here?"

Everyone bellowed with laughter, including our friends who had witnessed the whole thing. Sal was actually quite embarrassed. She laughingly apologized for her awkwardness. She said, in sing-song fashion, "Whoa, ex-cuuuuse me!" She got up from the man's lap and said to him and his guests, "I just don't know how that happened. I'm terribly sorry."

"Oh, that's okay. I can see you just slipped." But then, as Sal walked away, he yelled, "Hey! I'll see you next FALL." The house roared.

Sal made her way to me and her cup of java, and said, "Honey, you wouldn't believe what I just did."

"Whatcha do?"

"I was talking to the Turners at their table. As I walked away, like a real clodhopper, I tripped onto this man's lap."

A waitress who had witnessed the whole scene anxiously followed Sal from the dining room. She interjected, "Yeah, and do you know who that guy is?"

Sal and I turned. "No, who is he?"

She exclaimed, "Jimmy Hoffa!" She then covered her mouth as if to emphasize the shock effect. Both Sal and I yelled out in unison, "JIMMY HOFFA?!"

The two ladies laughed uncontrollably, as I stood there amazed. I put in my two cents, saying, "Gee, Sal, when it comes to falling onto somebody's lap, you really know how to pick 'em." The three of us laughed, and I continued. "I mean; the guy has just been released from a federal prison . . . he has all kinds of Teamster union problems. Most people would want to keep out of his way; but here you are, falling all over him!"

He was originally convicted for jury tampering, attempted bribery, and defrauding the Teamster pension fund. He was sentenced to thirteen years in prison. About a year before Sal's encounter with him, the Nixon Administration had pardoned him, eliminating his final six months in prison. After his release, he was known to occasionally get away from it all by visiting some friends at Boca Teeca. That's why he was there on that particular evening.

Later, in the summer of 1975, Hoffa mysteriously disappeared, never to be found. Many people have speculated on his disappearance and probable death. These theories generally point to several facts. One is that he was always involved with underworld figures. The obvious thought is that he was "taken out" by the Mob for some unknown reason. Another theory is that, once out of prison, he was a threat to the new powers in the Teamsters. Hence, they contracted a hit.

Nothing has ever been proven, one way or the other. Additionally, his body has never been found. After he vanished, there was a great deal of media hoopla. Every newspaper, magazine, radio, and television station in the country asked the same question, "What happened to Jimmy Hoffa?"

It was rumored that his remains were buried in Giant's Stadium, but authorities found no trace of any human remains there. The rumors and theories ran rampantly, but none were ever proven.

Several of my personal friends, and a few Boca Teeca employees, aware of Sal's ungraceful episode with Hoffa, thought they knew the answer.

One evening, in the Boca Teeca Lounge, I was confronted with several confusing questions. Jack Miles, the bartender, asked me, "All right Roger, I heard you were jealous but did you have to take such a drastic step?"

I said, "Huh?"

Joan Ryzinski, a waitress, continued with the teasing, "Yeah, Roger, it was just an innocent situation with him and Sal. You didn't have to do what you did!" I responded, "What? . . . What in God's name are you both talking about?"

Finally, club manager Alan Sayer asked, "Come on, Rodge . . . tell me . . . what did you do with Jimmy Hoffa's body?"

The Palumbos

Sometimes in life, you get a real lucky break. Other times, things don't go the way you planned. That's life! In 1964, things were not going especially great for Sal and me. Then I got one of those lucky breaks. I met Tony Palumbo and his wife, Annaleisa. I probably could write a book just about Tony. He was one of those extraordinarily interesting and multi-talented persons. If you meet one in your lifetime, consider yourself very fortunate.

In 1950, Tony, twenty-eight, jumped ship to America. He knew that his father John was somewhere in New York City, but he didn't know exactly where. He had another major problem in locating his father. Tony didn't speak a word of English. Even with those problems, it took less than a day for him to find his father in the Bronx. After that, Tony Palumbo learned how to speak English, and became a master builder.

A few years later, he moved his young family to Patchogue, Long Island, where he did his building. He first bought a strip of land, subdivided it into parcels, and built single-family homes. He sold them for a small profit, and gradually expanded into bigger homes.

When I met Tony in 1964, it was one of my luckiest days. Sal and I were broke and Tony knew it. He actually co-signed a construction loan for me, so that he could build our first home. He also lent me ALL of the down payment! When he did this, he insisted that I did not even have to sign an I.O.U. He flat out trusted me. At that time, not even my own family did! Sal and I regularly made our payments to him, until we paid him back completely. I've always felt I owed Tony Palumbo a lot. I don't know where we would be today if it weren't for him!

We lived directly across the street from the Palumbos. Naturally, we witnessed firsthand the growth of his three children: Gina, Michelina and Johnny. They were a beautiful family to have as neighbors.

Gradually we noticed young Johnny becoming very athletic. His physique grew into the mold of a Greek god. He was something to behold, with muscular biceps, bulky triceps, and tremendous abdominal muscles. His shoulders were huge, and yet, his waistline did not have an ounce of fat. Sylvester Stallone comes to mind when I recall Johnny Palumbo's build. He was a very handsome young man, and through the tutoring of his father, he also was polite and genteel.

Tony, who had boxed competitively while in the Italian Navy, got young Johnny started in the sport. We would often see the two of them in their back yard, working out together. I asked Tony about the young lad. "Tony, is Johnny as strong as he looks?"

He responded as I expected. He said, in his typically broken English, *"Marrone,* he hitsa lika mul-eh!"

Coming from Tony that was a very profound statement, because Tony was a very strong and tough man himself. One of our neighbors, Bruce Loesch, told me how he once witnessed Tony throw a 200-pound man UP a flight of stairs!

One day, Tony decided that he'd had enough of cold weather and he moved his family to Fort Lauderdale. He told everyone, "I want to retire." I later went to Florida to visit him. As he was showing me around, he said, "My friend, you see-eh that duplexa? I builda. You-see-eh that quadaplexa? Me build a too! You see-eh that one a there? Me, too!"

"Gee Tony, it's so nice to see that you're enjoying your retirement!"

"Well, I gotta do-eh sometheeng!" He did something. He talked me into moving to Florida. While Johnny was going to school and training in the gym, Tony became the Chief Building Inspector in Tamarac, Florida. About 1973, one year after Sal and I moved to Boca Raton, Tony quit working for the Building Department. He started building Don Carter Bowling Centers for the Ledbetter Company of Ohio. He built them in Ohio, Louisiana, Pennsylvania, Texas, and Florida — fourteen of them. In Florida, he built the largest, second largest, third largest, etc. bowling alleys that exist today. Some retirement!

In the meantime, Johnny entered in several amateur boxing events. He was great at the sport. He entered himself into the Golden Gloves Tournament in Miami, middleweight (165 pounds) division. Young Johnny went undefeated and became the 1973 champion.

Johnny's amateur record overall was 18-1, with eleven knockouts. His only loss came when he returned to New York, entered, and fought in the New York Golden Gloves. Johnny was twenty-two at the time. In that fight, ahead on points, he received a facial cut from a head butt. Unfortunately, the referee stopped the fight and awarded Johnny's opponent the win. That fighter went on to win the title.

One of Johnny's amateur wins came against a well-known boxer, Jerry Cooney. He won on a decision. Cooney, you might recall, later turned professional and fought for the heavyweight championship of the world in a match he lost to Larry Holmes.

In 1975, at age 24, Johnny moved back to live with and work for his father in Fort Lauderdale. He once again entered into the Golden Gloves Tournament, entering the finals undefeated. The event was at the Flagler Kennel Club. His bout was against Rick Johnson. At that fight, Tony recalls sitting next to some of Rick's fans. They heckled Tony for his verbal support of Johnny. One of them said, "That Italian boy doesn't stand a chance!"

Tony said, "Oh yeah? We see abouta that!" With that said, he yelled out to Johnny, in the middle of the third round, while Johnny was fighting, "JOHN-nee. Come on. Whatta you wait-eh for?" While he was still fighting, Johnny stopped for a split second to yell back to his father, "Aspetti, Papa!" (Wait, Father!) A moment or two later, it was all over. Johnny knocked Johnson out and captured himself another Golden Gloves Championship.

As the reigning state champion, he was invited to compete in the AAU Tournament, in Shreveport, Louisiana. The tournament was looked upon as a stepping-stone to the Olympics.

Johnny, only 5'9", was accustomed to fighting guys 6'2" and 6'3". He decided to shed a few pounds because he knew that the lower weight class would give him guys that were more his size to fight. He moved down to the junior middleweight (156 pounds) division. When he entered, Johnny was considered one of the top four national prospects in that weight class. The other standouts were the fighters from Ohio, New York, and California.

Fighting against those guys was no contest because Johnny had great power and could knock out his opponents with either hand.

Earlier I made reference to luck. When the officials made the pairing selections, Johnny had an unlucky draw. He ended up fighting two of those three other top prospects, in the opening fights of the tournament. He won both of them. In one of those bouts, however, the kid from California broke Johnny's nose in the first round.

Johnny would not let the referee or ringside doctors stop the fight. He told them, "Oh no, I'm fine!" They let him continue and he knocked his opponent out in the next round. Johnny was 3-0 in his AAU bouts, with two knockouts, and made it to the quarterfinals. Unfortunately, he had to withdraw because of his broken nose. Meanwhile, the boxer from Ohio, with lesser opponents throughout the tournament, won the championship. But Johnny had done all the work.

Several of the AAU tournament officials said Johnny was still a top Olympic prospect. They invited him to compete in the Miami Olympic Trials that year. Johnny trained by running eight to ten miles a day, in between sparring two or three rounds. He was in magnificent shape.

Training one day, he was matched up for some sparring against one of the Quarry brothers, Mike. Boxing fans surely remember the bouts his brother Jerry had with Muhammed Ali. The Quarry's were really tough guys. As he and Johnny sparred, Mike made a very aggressive move on Johnny. Young Palumbo then counterpunched him and sent Quarry reeling into the ropes. The trainers thought that it was getting too rough, and stopped it then. However, it didn't go unnoticed.

Angelo Dundee ──the famous boxing clinician, tutor and former manager of Muhammed Ali was sitting ringside. He called Palumbo over to talk with him. He said, "Young man, I like what I see in you. Here's my business card. I want you to come and see me when you're ready to turn professional. I'm going to make you into the champion of the world!"

Johnny responded quite differently than was expected. He said respectfully, "Thank you very much, Mr. Dundee, but I'm not interested in turning professional or becoming the champion of the world. My goal is to win the Gold Medal at the Olympics, PERIOD!"

Angelo was shocked.

In between all his training activities, Johnny worked for his father at the construction site of a Don Carter's Bowling Center. Tragically, one day his boxing career came to an abrupt end when he took a masonry nail in the eye. He suffered permanent damage and could never fight again. All who knew Johnny Palumbo were saddened by his bad luck. We all know he would have won an Olympic medal, more than likely the gold.

Johnny had some altercations out of the boxing ring that deserve comment, especially to illustrate his toughness. He was once confronted by four hoodlums. One held a gun on him, demanding Johnny give them his money. Johnny said, "Okay, I'm going to give you my money, but I don't want any rough stuff."

They took his money, but ignoring his warning, started to shove him, trying to punch him. He said, "Okay, I warned you!" He grabbed one of the guys and threw him into the guy with the gun. The thug accidentally shot his own friend, killing him. He then shot Johnny in the neck. The bullet entered one way and ricocheted out through his shoulder. Johnny grabbed the guy and knocked him out cold. He then battled one of the other hoodlums, and knocked him out, too. The other guy ran off, leaving Johnny to die. Thank God, a concerned citizen, who witnessed it all, called the police and ambulance. It saved Johnny's life.

In another incident, Johnny was awakened by a telephone call. One of his neighbors told him there was an intruder inside Johnny's house. "He's downstairs robbing you, Johnny!" Johnny threw on a pair of skivvies and went down to greet the intruder. As they fought, Johnny and he went crashing through a back window. The brawl continued outside. Johnny hit him with his best stuff, but the guy never gave up. Johnny actually knocked the guy out . . . twice. The thief came to both times and re-attacked Johnny. Johnny then beat him up so badly, the guy never regained consciousness. He went into a coma and died several days later. The post-mortem revealed the guy was on drugs and never registered the pain from Johnny's blows. Thus, he kept coming back for more. It was ruled justifiable provocation. Johnny was never charged.

Unfortunately, Johnny lost his last bout. It was as a passenger in a car crash. The vehicle turned over and

Johnny's head hit a huge boulder on the roadside. He never regained consciousness. It took a car crash to put him down. Johnny Palumbo died at age 37, on February 5, 1989. My heart went out to Tony, Annaleisa and their family.

PART FOUR: The Gangsters

The Patriarca Crime Family
Joseph "Joe Dogs" Iannuzzi
Tommy Agro
Joe Dogs, Maitre D' Joint
Golf Games with A Gangster
Dominick "Little Dom" Cataldo
Brother, Can You Spare . . . A Thousand?
All in The Family

The Patriarca Crime Family

La Cosa Nostra has always financed great successes in the restaurant and nightclub business. I don't know why The Mob likes that business so much, but they do. Perhaps it comes from the love of great food and the pride in food preparation that is so ingrained in the Italian culture. If you'd worked in restaurants and clubs the past fifty-eight years, as I have, you too would have found your path frequently crossing those of the organized crime world.

The tentacles of The Mob have likewise stretched out into the management and booking end of the entertainment field. Many top performers would not have gained their stature in show business if their careers hadn't been handled by organized crime figures.

I am not divulging anything new or earth shattering. I'm merely revealing my personal story, as I viewed it, from the piano bench.

The Patriarca Family was the most powerful organized crime family in New England. The head of that group was the late Raymond Patriarca. In a roundabout way, I was slightly involved with them in 1961 and 1962.

I use the word slightly because I personally never dealt with the Patriarcas. These people managed Gene Stridel for several years, so he took his directions from them. Gene was my employer. They were always around, and I couldn't avoid dealing with them.

We were assigned a road manager   a woman by the name of Madeleine Flanders   who traveled with us. I started to suspect that some of the clubs we worked were Mob-owned and operated. My suspicions started one evening when we were on a rest period at a club in Springfield, Massachusetts. I got up, excused myself from the table where Gene, Madeleine, and I sat and went to the lobby for a pack of cigarettes. Starting back, I realized that I had forgotten the book of matches, and turned to retrieve them. When I pivoted, I had a slight collision with a very big man. I, of course, immediately apologized, but he said absolutely nothing to me in return.

People bump into each other all the time. It goes without saying that it's unintentional. I mean, who in their right mind would purposely bump into somebody else, especially when that person outweighs you by at least a hundred pounds? This guy said nothing. He just stared at me. When my eyes focused on his, I realized that he was not drunk or high on anything. I immediately had a cold feeling wash over me. This was not an ordinary customer or person. I could see in his eyes, a stare of death! I later saw that same coldness in the eyes of the actor George Raft. I also saw it in the eyes of two other people, Tommy Agro and Dominick *"Little Dom"* Cataldo, who WERE gangsters and undoubtedly cold-blooded killers.

I once again apologized to the man. When I finished, he abruptly shoved me aside and continued walking. My Italian temper almost got the best of me. I really wanted to say to him, "Hey Jerk . . . now I think you owe ME an apology, you (expletive!)" Thank God I never said it, because I'm sure he would have made mincemeat out of me. I simply tucked my tail between my legs and returned to the table. Madeleine asked if I had apologized to the man I'd just bumped. I assured her that I did. She said, "That's good. He happens to be a professional hitman just released from prison. I don't think you'd want to mess with him!"

I didn't say anything to her aloud, but I silently thought to myself, "My God . . . what has Gene gotten us into here?"

Admittedly, during the remainder of my time working with Gene, I never witnessed any "criminal behavior." Gene's new handlers never tried any direct intimidation. People in powerful positions rarely have to use crass means to get what they want. In chess, it has been said that the implication of a threat is stronger than the fulfillment of one. With a direct threat, a person knows what consequences to expect. But with the implied threat, one's imagination leads to far more devastation.

I witnessed a classic example of an implied threat while Gene and I sat in the Springfield office of one of his handlers. Because it was over the telephone, I could hear only our side of the exchange. It sounded like this:

"Hello, John? This is Phil from Springfield."

"Fine . . . and, how are you?"

John, as explained to me later, was connected with the production of a Hollywood talent show featured at that time on network television. The format of the show was that celebrities in various areas of show business would come on the program to introduce their protégés, who would then perform to the national viewing audience. It was almost like a forerunner to the *Star Search* T.V. show hosted by Ed McMahon. This show was hosted by the late Jim Backus of *Gilligan's Island* fame. He also did the voice for the *Mister Magoo* cartoons.

The telephone conversation continued with Phil saying, "The reason I'm calling is because I've got this very talented vocalist, Gene Stridel. He's going to be out your way in May. I would like him on your show, introduced by Sarah Vaughan!"

There was a long pause. I surmised that John was discussing the difficulties in such a happening. Perhaps he expressed some indecisiveness and/or reluctance. Gene's handler, Phil, then said, very simply, slowly and softly, "Eh . . . you don't seem to understand! . . . I'm not ASKING you!"

After that, no more was said, except for the typical pleasantries. "Okay, you take care of it. . . . Give my regards to your wife!" He then turned to Gene and said, "That's it. You've got it! You're on for May 18th!" Gene and I were totally shocked.

Soon after, my wife Sal announced to me that she was expecting our first child. After celebrating, then giving it much thought, I decided to resign my position with Gene. I just didn't want to put Sal and our newborn through the stress traveling musicians and their families must endure. Besides, I really wasn't crazy about working for the Mafia, even in a roundabout way. I left Gene when Sal was in her fourth month of pregnancy. We moved back to Long Island, New York to my childhood and family roots.

There I found work performing with various bands. I also started to teach piano. I worked very hard trying to replenish what I had given up in working for Gene Stridel. Sal, of course, pitched in and worked for several temporary secretarial firms. Between the two of us, we were able to make out okay.

In February, our daughter Bonny was born. Mom and baby were healthy and happy, and so was I. After a brief interruption of passing out cigars and breaking open some cheer, I got right back to work. I kept up my end of the ship by teaching some thirty piano students during the day and working five nights per week in various clubs on the island.

Sal and I forgot about Gene Stridel until, one day, one of my musician friends called and said he had seen in *T.V. Guide* that Gene was scheduled to appear on television the following night, May 18th! The following day, I just could not get it off of my mind. In between giving piano lessons to my students, I reflected on the telephone conversation in Springfield, Massachusetts, approximately eight months earlier. I rolled it over and over again, exactly what Phil had said, and what he had meant by it.

"You don't seem to understand. I'm not asking you."

He never completed the sentence with ". . . I'm TELLING you!" Nor did he exercise the ultimatum of a direct threat like ". . . OR ELSE!" None of that had to be said. That comes from the power vested in you when you have tentacles attached to a powerful crime organization.

Pondering the conversation further, I realized he'd probably made another implied threat with the statement, *"You don't seem to understand."* The implication was, "You'd better think twice about this!" The thing that really got me about the whole conversation was the mild manner in which it was all said.

The moment of truth came, and we turned on the television. Jim Backus interviewed jazz legend, Sarah Vaughan. Introducing Gene, she said he was a "protégé and friend for years." I coughed a few times! She continued, "Gene Stridel is one of the most promising young talents I've ever known." Gene came out and sang, sounding as great as always.

Then it hit me. The implied threat really did work! He had not only gotten on the television show but was introduced by this great legend of song. I thought, wow . . . WHAT POWER!

As previously mentioned, Gene drowned years later. I still don't believe it, but the way it supposedly happened was that he got into an argument with his girlfriend and was inebriated when he pushed her out of her apartment. She called the police. They came and demanded he open the door. When he didn't, they broke it down. They found the back window open. Gene had jumped out to avoid confronting the police. He hit his head and rolled into the lake. When they looked out the window, down toward the lake, they evidently didn't see anything. At that moment, he was drowning!

It sounds very *"fishy"* to me, but the investigation did not turn up any evidence of wrongdoing.

Joseph "Joe Dogs" Iannuzzi

My good friend Joe Dogs was not just an ordinary gangster. He was one of considerable notoriety, but with a great sense of humor. When I realized he had been involved in criminal activities, I asked, "Joe, did you ever go to prison?"

"Yeah, but it wasn't my fault. It was a case of mistaken identity."

"Mistaken identity?"

"Yeah. . . . I shot the wrong guy!"

We both must have laughed over that one for five minutes. However, Joe did have a criminal record for burglary, breaking and entering, shylocking and felonious assault.

The assault conviction was more up Joe's alley. He WAS a tough guy, and I could have written about him in "The Tough Guys" section of this book. He was a good boxer in the Army. More important, he's was a great street fighter. I once witnessed him knocking a guy out with one aggressive move. He kicked the guy square in the head with a high kick that was equal to any I have ever seen by any punter in the National Football League, or for that matter, any ballet dancer at Lincoln Center. I don't think that guy will try calling one of Joe's friends a "wop" ever

223

again! Coincidently, that was the precise sound that Joe's foot made, as it met the bigoted idiot's head. However, being tough is not what made Joe famous.

Joe got involved with just about every gangster in South Florida. I met many of these people in social circumstances. A typical scenario: Joe, and I at a restaurant with our wives, and we went to the very best and Joe introduced us to this guy or that guy. It was also common to bump into these people at the racetrack. I didn't know who they were at the time. As long as Joe kept me out of their business dealings, I didn't care who they were.

Joseph "Joe Dogs" Iannuzzi

I met people like Little Dom Cataldo, who I later found out was responsible for the murder of at least ten people. Jiggs Forlano, a retired capo (boss) with the Columbo Family, Tommy Agro, Joe's mentor in the Carlo Gambino Mob; Agro's boss, Joe Piney Armone, a capo with the Gambinos, Louie Esposito, a Gambino associate coincidently from West Babylon, Long Island, my hometown. Freddie Campo, an associate with the Columbos; and one guy who was later murdered, Stanley Gerstenfeld.

Joe's involvement with the Mob was getting so casual that one evening they all had a meeting right at the West Palm Beach club where Sal and I regularly worked. We got off the bandstand and respectfully went to their table to be cordially introduced by Joe. Most of them were polite; but their mere presence in the place got the management, employees and some patrons very nervous, me, too! Later, I quietly said to Joe, "Gee, Joe, you couldn't have made this place more nervous if you had invited *Don* Carlo Gambino himself!"

Joe laughed and said jokingly, "He'll be here later!" For a second, I thought that Joe was serious. I knew that the mafia Godfather actually had a winter residence in West Palm Beach.

In the early days of our friendship, I never even knew that Joe was connected. I always thought he was in the drywalling business. I gradually found out. When I did, I cautioned him about the kind of friendship I would find acceptable. I remember the conversation very well. I told him, "Look, Joe, you have to respect my family, my professional image and my wishes. I NEVER want to know about your business affairs. You have to keep it separated from our social relationship. The moment that you include me in any illegal activities is the moment that our friendship must end. Capisci?" Joe agreed.

As the years passed, I realized that Joe was no longer just some wannabe. He was becoming the most powerful gangster in the Palm Beaches. After (the Godfather) Carlo Gambino died in 1976—his throne was taken over by his cousin Paul *"Big Paulie"* Castellano—business went on as usual. Joe was still backed by the most powerful crime family in America. Throughout that time, Joe never once reneged on our pact, nor had he for the remainder of his life. He never tried to incriminate me, involve me, or manipulate me, in any fashion. Our friendship endured because of that respect he had for my original wishes.

Throughout most of the seventies, Joe and I spent a great deal of time together. We were almost inseparable. We often spent more time with each other than we did with our own wives. I can recall so many occasions that we had an afternoon of laughs on the golf course, followed by an evening at the dog track. It was always fun.

We played golf several times a week. When we played golf, it was for HUGE stakes. I mean a million dollars a side, with automatic presses. At the end of the round, one of us would lose ten dollars or fifteen million. Big deal. It was like winning a pink belt in karate. It meant nothing. We'd settle for who was going to buy lunch!

And the telephone calls that took place were continuous. Joe would call me three, four, five, times a day. He was like a teenager with his little jokes and gags.

"Hey Rodge, whattcha doin?"

"Hi Joe. I have to mow the lawn. Why, what are you up to?"

"Ah, nothin'. Ya wanna play some golf?"

We talked for about twenty minutes and finally hung up. Two minutes later, the phone rang again. With great enthusiasm—the likes of which you might expect from two friends who have not seen or talked to each other for months——he inquired, "HEY . . . RODGE. How the (expletive) are you?"

I answered him with as much fervor, spirit and shock from hearing his supposedly long-lost voice again. "Hey JOE . . . so nice of you to call!"

He laughed and then asked me, "Aren't you done with that (expletive) lawn yet?"

"No. Some a-hole I know keeps calling me and interrupting my work."

We often enjoyed dinner and shows with our wives. I remember how powerful and respected he was everywhere we went. One evening we'd have front seating for the Manhattan Transfer show at Bachelors III (formerly owned by Joe Namath), then three nights later at the Diplomat hotel. A week after that we'd be seated at the most coveted table at the dog track. Everywhere we went, service personnel would bend over backward to accommodate us.

Quite often, Joe would drop in to catch our performances. We always knew when he was in the room because he'd send a waitress up to us with a huge tip, wrapped in a cocktail napkin. It was his usual tip for us . . . a QUARTER!

In between those social occasions, Joe and I would often go to the racetracks. He loved the dogs, and that's how he actually got nicknamed Joe Dogs. But he also enjoyed the "flats," and occasionally we'd even take in Jai Alai.

Joe was like a little kid. He would do almost anything to get a good laugh from you. He loved to shock people, too. I remember one time at Hialeah Racetrack, he said, "Hey, Rodge, watch the number two horse on the tote board. It's a twenty-one horse right now, right? Watch it!"

He disappeared to go and place a bet. A moment later, the odds changed to six to one. When Joe came back, he asked me, "Didja see that?"

"Yeah, Joe. How much did you put on that nag?"

He evaded my question with, "It was funny, hah? Watch. I'll do it again!"

He then brought the odds on the horse down to two to one. I put my five-dollar bet on the horse. It paid $14.60 on a two-dollar-win bet. With a huge smile, he said, "I wonder how I can make such great (expletive) predictions like that?" I found out later that the reason was simple. He fixed the race!

It is said that time passes quickly when you're having fun. The seventies simply raced past us. We were having fun, but more important, we were becoming very successful. Everywhere that Sal and I went, people knew us. It was impossible for us to have a quiet dinner in a public restaurant without being interrupted four or five times by people who knew us from various nightclubs we worked. It must have happened a hundred of times that we were asked, "You're Sal and Roger Rossi, aren't you?"

We would put down our forks and knives and smile saying, "Yes we are."

They would smile back and continue, "Oh we have seen you perform dozens of times. You guys are great!"

Even having dinner interrupted was fun, because we knew that it symbolized the success we were enjoying. If we really didn't want to be bothered, I'd ask the maître d' if he could put us at a secluded table in the back of the restaurant. He would, and then the waiter or waitress who came over to serve us, would ask, "Aren't you Sal and Roger Rossi?" It was getting to the point that we were becoming household names, at least in the Palm Beaches. Besides our performances at popular supper clubs, we were often playing Saturday and Sunday afternoon weddings. The bridal couples were either previous fans, or they'd become new ones.

Joe was having great success too. He was a kingpin in the criminal world of the Palm Beaches. To be truthful, it was getting to the point that I had to be very careful. I was not ashamed of our friendship, but I knew that most people did not understand it. They'd carefully evade the subject, either to avoid embarrassing me or to avoid Joe's retaliation. Many people would have preferred that I cooled down my friendship with him. I knew that I was not doing anything wrong, so the friendship continued.

One day, however, something happened that forced me to distance myself from my friend. Stanley Gerstenfeld died of "lead poisoning." Actually, he took four bullets in the head and one in the chest!

Gerstenfeld was a local bookmaker who used to frequent one of the West Palm Beach nightclubs where my group performed. He was a heavy drinker, into nose candy, and knew a few people from the organized crime world. The combination of all three factors contributed to his obnoxious behavior. He tried to throw his weight around, especially with club employees. One evening, he forced a scene against Joe Dogs. It was the sorriest thing he ever did. Joe kicked the living hell out of him. After that, Gerstenfeld apologized to Joe, and it was considered a closed issue. However, when Gerstenfeld's body was found in a Miami parking lot one morning in February of 1978, most people presumed it was Joe Dogs who did it. I must confess that even I suspected it was Joe. I questioned him, "Joe, who do you think did it?"

He retorted, "He was no friend of mine, but *Minchia,* everybody else thinks I did it. You might as well think it too!"

"Did you?"

"No, I did not! I have an alibi to prove it. I have an idea who did, but don't (expletive) ask!"

I took Joe's word and found out that he did have a legitimate alibi. He never divulged to me who it was that he suspected, and I never asked. But, I realized that I had to be very careful from that day forward.

Often the image of the Mob, the *Mafia, La Cosa Nostra, La Famiglia,* etcetera, can appear glamorous to some people. In many ways, my association with Joe was! But there is never anything glamorous about murder. Just the mere fact that Joe was (wrongly) presumed to be involved in Gerstenfeld's demise was, in itself, dangerous for my image. I had to stretch the distance between myself and Joe because he was getting so involved.

Sal and I took off the whole summer. We took our three children in a travel trailer we bought and went on a ten-week vacation to California.

Shortly after returning, we went into partnership with Jess Santamaria, a local businessman. He and I along with several other investors bought The Royal Inn Resort, located by a lake in a small community called Royal Palm Beach. My ownership lasted seven years. With my business commitment, it was essential for me to live nearby. So, we sold our home in Boca Raton and moved to Wellington, a community located next to Royal Palm Beach.

All of these changes, although never by design, automatically cooled things down with Joe and me. I still saw Joe, but not as often. Occasionally he would come out to my club, and we still had a great time, but we rarely played golf. The geography made it difficult for us to get together.

In 1979, I made another change. I was offered a gig at the 5-star Boca Raton Hotel and Club. I put the operation of the Royal Inn in the capable and trustworthy hands of my partner. Sal and I formed a new band for the three-year stint. That hotel is totally private. I saw Joe only three or four times during those three years. As we lost touch with each other, was when things turned bad for him with his mentor, Tommy Agro.

In Italian, there is an expression, *"Cane non mangia cane,"* which says that a dog doesn't eat another dog. It means that there is honor amongst thieves. However, the expression doesn't account for vicious dogs. Tommy Agro was vicious.

Joe made an appointment to drop off money he owed Agro. When he showed up, he was met by Agro and his crew. They cold-cocked Joe and beat him within an inch of his life with a tire iron and a baseball bat. He was in a coma for two days. Agro wanted to send a warning message to all underlings, by making an example of Joe. When he finally came to in his hospital room, a priest was giving him his last rites. It was probably the only time in Joe's life that a priest was in his presence. One of the nurses incorrectly proclaimed him dead.

The beating knocked out his teeth, broke his nose, ruptured his spleen, busted several ribs and, I'm sure— gave him a long-term headache when he had finally regained consciousness.

Joe was initially hurt that his own mentor would turn on him, and for no apparent reason. Gradually, his hurt grew into revenge-seeking hatred. At first, his get-even scheme was dead set on murdering his attackers, one by one. Then he opted for another route of satisfaction. Joe colluded with the FBI. They talked him into trying to regain Agro's confidence, which Joe miraculously did. Then, they set up a sting operation to trap as many of Joe's colleagues as they could. They did that with great success, too.

The sting operation's code name was called Operation Home Run. It was named after the baseball bat treatment Agro used as he tried to hit Joe's brain out of his head. They opened a private club in Riviera Beach called Suite 100. It was to be an illegal gambling spot, but it was rigged with audio and video equipment. Everyone who entered was recorded on tape.

At that point, I came back into Joe's life. I hadn't known of his beating and close encounter with death. One evening, after his recuperation, I bumped into a rather strange man at the Palm Beach Kennel Club, where I was having a night out with Sal. As I walked by, he said, "Hey, Rodge."

"Yes. Do I know you?"

"What's wrong, don't you know your old friends?"

It took almost a full minute before I recognized who he was. I asked with astonishment, "JOE? . . . My God, what happened to you?"

"Oh, I just ran into a few guys who didn't like the way I looked!"

The broken nose, the complete new set of teeth, and the plastic surgery that was required to make his face into some reasonable facsimile of the original had rendered him unrecognizable. Joe told me briefly, what had happened. He didn't divulge his impending scheme with the Feds. He simply said that he had kissed and made up with his attackers, and he had opened Suite 100. "We're fronting it as a private club. What we're really going to do is run illegal casino-type gambling in the place."

"You're kidding, I hope. How do you expect to get away with that?"

Joe told me, "We're quietly being endorsed . . . by the (expletive) Chief of Police, Boone Darden!"

I knew Boone. Freddie Campo' a local bookmaker' once introduced me to him. Boone was a regular guy who hung out at some of the clubs in his off-duty time. I never figured that Joe and company could get to him through a bribe, but they did. However, Boone didn't know that the Feds were in on the whole thing. Unfortunately, for him, he found out later.

Joe said that he could use some late-night music, and wanted to know if I'd be interested.

I told him, "Look, Joe, suppose I pop in one night and see what your place looks like, and we'll take it from there. Okay?"

He agreed and we stopped in a few nights later, after we'd finished performing at the hotel. Joe introduced us to his new partner, John Marino, who was really FBI Agent John Bonino. They showed us around.

Afterward, while Joe showed Sal another area of the club, Marino showed me the office. He poured me a cocktail while we conversed. He casually questioned me. I didn't know it, but that was the modus operandus they had set up to interrogate everyone who came into the club. While I was questioned, the video and audio equipment were running behind the mirror in front of us. Of course, I did not incriminate myself, because I had never done anything wrong. He asked, "How do you know Joe?"

"Oh, we've just been great friends through the years. We've played a lot of golf, been to the track together, all that kind of stuff. I haven't seen him much lately, though. He's been busy and so have I."

"Have you ever been involved with him on anything?"

"Are you kidding? Music is my business, and that's it. I never got into any of Joe's business. 'Never wanted to!"

Joe never prepared me for the routine, because he knew I had nothing to hide. But that routine eventually incriminated many gangsters who came into the place. Many were big-time lawbreakers, but because of the relaxed mood and high confidence level, they divulged all to either John or Joe; all on video tape.

I told Joe that I couldn't make his gig, but I gave him the name and telephone number of a guitarist who could do the job.

Sal and I left and she immediately told me, "Something is wrong in that place. Joe's new partner is much too square to be involved with criminal activities. I don't know what it is, but he just doesn't fit into the mold."

Sal's ESP, as usual, was correct. The FBI, with the help of Joe's involvement and dedication, put many fast trackers from the Mob on trial, including his old friend and benefactor, Tommy Agro. There were twelve trials in which Joe personally testified against his former colleagues. Those trials occurred during a ten-year span. In the Agro trial, Joe was on the witness stand thirteen days. He smiled through most of his testimony. That aggravated the judge. It infuriated Agro. That testimony helped convict, and ultimately sentence Agro. He got fifteen years to life for loan-sharking, extortion, and attempted murder.

Some of the others sentenced because of Joe's testimony included: Joe N. Gallo, the *consigliere* to Paul Castellano; Little Dom Cataldo (thirty-five years); Carmine *the Snake* Persico, boss of the Columbo Family; Joe Piney Armone; and alas, police chief Boone Darden.

The testimony Joe provided the FBI reached much deeper into the Mob than just the gangsters he had put away. In fact, it went right to the top of the Mafia world. It was the catalyst that began the fall of The Godfather himself, Paul Castellano. Joe's testimony, the trials, and convictions of those associated with the Gambino Family, gave the FBI exactly the proof they needed to use electronic surveillance in the mafia lord's personal inner sanctum, where he conducted his Mob meetings. This intrusion into Castellano's Staten Island home was authorized by a federal judge after the convictions of all those against whom Joe had testified.

The eavesdropping device revealed many of La Cosa Nostra's innermost secrets. That crucial, leaked information caused an avalanche of arrests that weakened Castellano's grip on his empire. Underling John Gotti made a move on him, to stop the decline. He had Castellano and his bodyguard, Tom Bilotti both murdered. Gotti consequently was arrested, tried and convicted. He died in prison while serving time for that crime.

After the sting operation hit the headlines, I did not hear from Joe for several years. I was aware of all the trials taking place, and I had heard through the grapevine that the Mob had put a contract out to terminate his life. He was placed in the Federal Witness Protection program. I was concerned that Joe would take his seclusion and hiding lightly, thereby promoting his own demise. When I didn't hear from him, I presumed he was hit.

Finally, one day the telephone rang. The caller said, "Hey, Rodge."

I immediately recognized the familiar, low-toned, back-of-the-throat utterance of my name. I just said, "Hey…I thought you were DEAD!"

"Yeah . . . I guess a lot of people wish I was!"

"I heard that they have a contract on your life."

"Just one? I'm disappointed. The last I heard, it was THREE! Roger, I got a lot of guys pissed off at me, but I had to do what I did. It was the best way for me to get even with them."

"Joe, after seeing what they did to you, I can't say I blame you. You just better be careful, though, because they're out to get you, now."

"Hey, let them (expletive)'n try. You think some (expletive) punk is gonna make a move on me? Fuhgedaboutit! He's gonna have to watch his own ass, because I'll make a move on HIM! Ya think that's worth it for him? If he IS successful in getting to me, he might not even collect. $#!+! Most of the people that put out those contracts on me, I put away in the pen; and some of them are already (expletive) dead. Who's he gonna collect from?"

I told Joe the story I read in the newspaper, about his testifying. The story revealed that he was questioned, in front of a grand jury, by a defense attorney. The lawyer grilled Joe about the money the FBI funded him for time and salary lost while testifying. Of course, the attorney implied that Joe was testifying against his clients because of the money. The lawyer asked, "Mr. Iannuzzi, what do you intend to do with the one hundred and twenty-five thousand dollars that the Federal Bureau of Investigation is paying you for your testimony?"

Joe flippantly gave the lawyer and the jury some Vintage-Joe-Dogs repartee when he answered, "I don't know. Maybe I'll open up my own hotdog stand . . . I'll call it *Joe Dog's Dogs*!"

Joe said to me, "Yeah that one even got the judge laughing. It was probably the only laugh the defendants had since the (expletive) trials began!"

I have a feeling that if one of those contracts on his life were to catch up with him, he just might embrace the morbid encounter by attempting to tell his assassin some clever joke. He would probably tell the guy, "Hey, I'll give you odds that you forgot to load the (expletive) gun, you (expletive) jerk!"

Joe changed the subject. "Roger, have you read the book, *Boss of Bosses?*"

"No. Why?"

"Pick up the book. It's about the fall of The Godfather, Big Paulie Castellano, who the Mob call *il capo di tutti capi* (The Boss of all Bosses). I'm in there!"

"You mean that you're in the book?"

"Roger, pick up the (expletive) book. It's written by two FBI Agents, Joseph F. O'Brien, and Andris Kurins, and it's published by *Simon & Schuster*. Get it and read it. You'll see!"

After finishing our conversation, I immediately went out and bought the book. It was a terrific book, and when I reached the parts about Joe, I was shocked. The two Feds gave Joe credit for being the turning point in their operation.

They wrote, "Even Castellano's death was connected to Agro's beating of Iannuzzi. Castellano was murdered because he was facing a heavy prison term and had compromised Mob security. Both of these things resulted from the bugging of his house. The bugging of his house, in turn, could not have been accomplished [if it were not for] a subpoena involving Tommy Agro that first allowed law enforcement officers to get beyond the Godfather's threshold."

They reasoned that the Home Run investigation linked Agro to the Mob's *consigliere,* Joe N. Gallo, who had avoided prosecution for four decades. Additionally, it uncovered a Mob mole in the United States District Court, who regularly tipped off the Mafia to sealed indictments. It started the implication of Castellano and underboss, Joe Piney Armone. Reading all of this made my eyes open wide.

About a week later, Joe surprised me with another phone call. "Hey Rodge, ja get the book? Whatcha think?"

"Joe, I was shocked. First of all, I enjoyed the book a lot. Gosh, they credited YOU for being one of the reasons for the downfall of the Godfather."

"Yeah, I know. . . . I'm writing my own book about it!"

"You putting me on?"

"No . . . YOU'RE in it!"

"WHAT? . . . Gee Joe, I'm not sure that I want to be in a book about the Mafia!"

"Roger, you never did anything wrong, and you have nothing to be ashamed of. I only mentioned you a couple of times, where in the story line we came into the places you and Sal were performing because you were our favorite entertainers. That's all. But if you don't want to be in there, (expletive) it. I'll take it out."

"Please do, Joe. I'll rest a lot easier. So, tell me. Have you lined up a publisher for it yet?"

"Yeah, the same people that published Boss of Bosses, Simon & Schuster."

"Wow. They're really big-time. They also publish Rush Limbaugh's books, don't they?" He quipped, "Who the hell is he? . . . I'm only kiddin' you. I know who he is. He's the guy that flew across the ocean with a fly in his plane. Right?"

I continued the bad humor with, "Joe, you don't know nothin' do you? That wasn't Rush Limbaugh that flew over the ocean. That was James Stewart, the actor, who was doing a movie impersonation of the guy YOU'RE thinking of . . . Rush Lindbergh!"

Joe imitated the sound of a drummer punctuating a burlesque comedian's punch line, "Bada bing . . . cheee!"

Simon & Schuster published Joe's first book, *Joe Dogs: The Life & Crimes of a Mobster*. It was terrific, except they didn't include enough of Joe's profanities. At least he didn't think so. My name was excluded, as promised. I'm very surprised, however, that to this day, Hollywood has not made a movie out of that book.

Joe went from bookmaking to book writing. Simon & Schuster published his second book, *The Mafia Cookbook.*

It told about how Joe, who spent a great deal of time cooking in the Army and elsewhere—was a chef for the Mob and the FBI. It includes intimate stories about the Mob and the Feds while serving up the various recipes he concocted for them. He eventually wrote a third book, *Cooking on the Lam.*

Incidentally, Joe Iannuzzi was the one who gave me the initial courage and inspiration to write THIS book you're now reading. He has been highlighted on radio, T.V., and even an HBO special. He was willing to endanger his own life one evening when he accepted a live appearance on the David Letterman Show. However, when he showed up at the studio dressed to the nines, Letterman, and his producer chickened out. They felt it could endanger the welfare of their audience and themselves. I understand that Joe was so angry that he threw the producer into a wall, and he verbally threatened Letterman.

When the T.V. host complained about the incident, the FBI stepped in and said that if Joe was going to misuse his notoriety for financial gain, he could spend his own money in protecting himself. Furthermore, they didn't cotton to his making threats of violence. Joe casually sidestepped the issue by saying, "Nah, I was only kidding about Letterman. Actually, he's my favorite talk-show host!"

My friendship with Joe was a very fulfilling experience. He was one of the most extraordinary people I have ever known. He could have very easily been an aeronautical engineer at NASA or a professor of mathematics at the Massachusetts Institute of Technology. Instead, he chose a life of crime.

But when I suggested that to him, he retorted, "Yeah, but I never would've had as much fun as I do with my job. Besides, how smart do you think those la-de-da professors at M.I.T. really are? . . . Do they know how to rob a (expletive) bank?"

Joe developed an obsession for calling me every Mother's Day. Typically, he'd open the conversation with, "Hey . . . Happy Mother's Day . . . YOU MOTHER!" I spoke with Joe on the telephone this past September. He was at a faraway Hospice facility dying. Aside from his weak mumbling of my name, he was almost incoherent. I felt he had understood my words, but just couldn't reply any more than a low-murmured, "Hmmm." I told him I'd always remember him for the good friend he was to me.

Joe "Dogs" Iannuzzi, my friend for forty-four years, outlived all of his incarcerated enemies, and died peacefully on September 20, 2016.

Tommy Agro

I realized that my friend, Joe Iannuzzi, was connected with The Mob in January of 1973. Until then, we had played golf, and taken our wives to dinner. I thought he made his income from his drywall business. I found out otherwise when he came into Alfredo's, in Boynton

Beach, where Sal and I performed. He entered with his wife, Bunny, and another couple.

I got a little suspicious when the sinister-looking man with him made a bit of a scene, insisting they sit at the table by the windowless wall. The man was particularly insistent that HE had to sit in the chair against that wall! I later found out the significance of this unique fetish. Joe explained that it was essential to the man's security and survival. You see, Mafiosi are constantly aware of the possible hit. If the targeted person has his back to a wall, he only has to watch his front. If that hit does take place, he might see it coming with enough time to counter the foul deed.

People like this are always cognizant of their periphery. While they sit with guests and friends in public places, they continually scan the room. They might be doing normal things like talking, eating, listening, laughing, and drinking, but they don't let their guard down for one second. It could cost them their lives. That's the way things are if you're a gangster. This man's name was Tommy Agro. He WAS a gangster!

After they had dinner, Joe invited us to join them when we'd finished performing the dance set. At their table, Joe did the introductions. "Roger and Sal, this is a business partner of mine, Tommy Agro."

Agro was a short, stocky man whom I guessed to be in his mid-to-late forties. He shook my hand, nodding. He then introduced his lady, "This is Shirley."

"Hi, Shirley."

"Hello." That was the extent of what we heard of Shirley's vocabulary for the remainder of the evening.

Agro said, "Pull up a chair. Would you like some champagne? Joe bought us some Dom Perignon!" I could see Agro was important to Joe. Not only was my friend going all out to accommodate him, but he acted somewhat subservient.

Sal and I stayed about ten minutes. I don't think Agro looked at us more than twice, although he talked and listened intently.

I asked him, "And just what business is it that you're in, Mr. Agro?"

I didn't immediately understand his stab at humor when he replied, "Well . . . you might say it's a family type of business."

They all laughed, so he continued with the one-liners. "Yeah . . . you could call it a Mom and POP type of operation!"

The four of them roared with laughter, yet Sal and I still didn't understand. We simply smiled out of courtesy.

Joe interjected his own attempt at comedy with, "Yeah, and you have to join the _Mothers_ _and_ _Fathers_ _Italian_ _Association_ to work in this Mom and Pop business!"

As they once again laughed themselves silly, the fog suddenly lifted. It dawned on me that Joe was referring to the MAFIA. Agro clarified it further, with all the savvy, confidence and wisdom that one would only accumulate through first-hand experiences, "Yeah . . . and you pray that it involves more Momming than it does Popping . . . but sometimes ya gotta do whatcha gotta do!"

Now it was Joe and Bunny's turn to smile out of politeness. Agro had meant it as a joke, but the truth came burning through the humor. You could see the evil and callousness pouring out of the man in just one short sentence. At that moment, I realized my friend was connected with a ruthless person.

Sal and I smiled through all of this beating around the bushes. After a brief look at my wristwatch, I said with as much composure as I could muster, "Well, thank you for the champagne. We have to get back to the bandstand now. Is there anything that we can perform for you?"

Joe jumped in saying, "Yeah Roger, play that song that you wrote. What's the name of it?"

"You mean, *Ain't Nobody Gonna Change My Mind?*"

"Yeah, that's the one!" Joe turned to Agro as Sal and I headed for the bandstand. I heard him murmur, "Tommy, you're gonna love this song!"

When Sal and I started our music, I had a very hard time trying to keep focused. My mind wandered back to the conversation at the table, while my fingers performed on automatic pilot. As I mulled it over, it became quite obvious that all of the joking around held a definite undercurrent of truth. I saw it all in Argo's eyes when he talked. I saw it in Joe's subservience to Agro. It didn't have to be spelled out anymore. Joe definitely was in The Mob!

Even though I had reached my conclusion, many questions needed to be answered. How deeply was Joe involved? Was it going to involve me, without my consent? What could I possibly do about my friendship with Joe? Did I want to do anything about it?

Sal and I must have performed for more than an hour. I probably should have received only half my pay for it, because my mind was divided between two thoughts. My fingers were on the piano, but my eyes kept glancing over toward Joe's table as if some sort of spell had been cast on me. I didn't miss a note, but by the same token, I didn't miss a trick, either. I watched Joe laughing in his inimitable way. Finally, I came to another conclusion. Joe was already my friend. It was too late to change that now.

On my next break, Joe came over and asked me, "Rodge, you got a minute?"

"Sure, Joe. What is it?"

"Tommy is really impressed with your music. I think he wants to talk about backing you and Sal."

"Well, Joe, I'll listen to what he has to say, but I want to talk to you, too. This is neither time nor the place for it. Maybe we can meet sometime tomorrow."

"Sure. But in the meantime, come back to our table when you can." I assured him that I would, but I needed some time to collect my thoughts.

I knew that a lot of honorable, legitimate, big-time stars had been under the professional and business guidance of La Cosa Nostra. Yet, I really wasn't sure that I wanted to flirt with the idea. In the sixties, I had resigned my position as piano accompanist and music director for Gene Stridel because he was handled and backed by the Raymond Patriarca Crime Family. Why now would I want to get directly involved with Tommy Agro? I quickly talked it over with Sal, and we returned to their table.

Tommy Agro said to us, "You people are really great. I think you both can make it into the big time. I mean, BIG TIME!" He paused. "You've got everything it takes. You're musical, creative, and attractive together and individually." He looked at Sal and said, "You sing like a bird." He then turned toward me and said, "You're very talented on the piano...but you're missing one or two important things that I think I can provide for you. You need backing and promotion. I've got the power and the money to get you where you wanna go."

Joe interrupted him so he could verify just how big Agro and his associates really were. "Roger, I wouldn't lie to you. Tommy is very connected with the right people out of New York. They have unlimited power and funds! They'll make stars out of both of you."

Agro reiterated Joe's assertion. "We'll make another Sonny and Cher out of you. I mean television, recordings, concerts; I can do it all for you!"

Sal and I were taken aback by all of this. Although I had pretty much made up my mind, I thought it only fair to talk with Sal about it further in private. I said to Agro, "Gee, Mr. Agro, I want to thank you for this awesome offer, but . . ."

He interrupted saying, "Please! Call me Tommy. . . . That's what all my friends call me."

I really didn't want to be rude or insulting, but in actuality, he was NOT a friend of mine. Joe was. I didn't want him to get the wrong impression, that I considered him a friend. Yet, I thought it best to simply side step the issue. Purposely omitting his first name and nickname, I simply said, "Well, I do want to thank you. I just feel that when we're talking about our future, it's important that we take some time in making the right decision. Can we get back to you?"

"Absolutely. Take all the time you need. You can let me know through Joe. He's gonna be my partner down here. If you decide you want it, we can start you out by working in my own club, up in Queens. This way we can have you close to all the things we need in New York; you know—the television and recording companies. People who will tutor you and give you any of the polishing touches you might need . . . and then . . . the sky is the limit!" Agro pointed his index finger upward.

Upon leaving Alfredo's, Joe assured me that Agro was "for real." He divulged that Agro was an associate with Joe "Piney" Armone, a very powerful Capo with the Carlo Gambino Crime Family. The strongest crime family in America! "Anything he says he can do, you can almost bank on it," I told Joe that I would talk about it later with Sal, and I'd call him.

Sal and I got into our car for the approximate ten-mile drive home. We really didn't need any more time than that to talk it all out. We came to exactly the same conclusion as a couple as we had individually. I said to Sal, "Honey, I know it might sound corny, or old-fashioned, but I only want happiness for us as a family. We have three beautiful children. We have their future to think about here. I don't like the idea of taking a chance on their lives. If we were to take a shot at the big time, perhaps the stability we're providing them now will continue. Then again, it could very well be thrown into an upheaval. If Agro were to accomplish what he says he can with our careers, what do you think would happen to us as a family?"

Sal pondered my question for a moment. Then she came back with the same conclusion that I had reached. She said, "It would drastically change all of our lives, and I'm not sure that it would necessarily be for the better."

Sal and Roger Rossi
Agro to Rossi, "We'll make another Sonny and Cher out of you!"

"Exactly! The tabloids would get into our private lives with all kinds of negatives like they do with all of the stars today. They'd try to sell their newspapers at our expense.

In the long run, we might end up with fame and fortune, but the price will be all the good things going for us right now. It would be different if we could make only a few recordings. But that's not the way it works. We'd have to promote any product in which they were invested. That would mean a lot of traveling, my setting up promotions here while you're there, and the kids somewhere else. I'm sorry, but that's not for me."

"You're right. I don't want that for our family, either. I'm not so sure that I like or could trust this Tommy Agro anyway. I don't think I want any part of him or his way of life."

I agreed and added somberly, "He is a very determined man. You can just tell that once he gets his claws into your life, there'll be no turning back. He'll own you lock, stock, and barrel."

"I'll tell you right now. He has his claws into your friend!"

"Yeah, I know, Sal. And I don't know how I'm going to handle that!"

Sal nervously questioned me, "You won't ever put yourself into a situation where you become involved with Joe and his new business associates, will you?"

I moved my eyes slowly toward hers, in a very villainous fashion. I slowly smiled while saying, "You never know about us Sicilians. They say it's born in us, you know!" That said, I quickly received an affectionate jab in my right side from the back of her left fist. Nevertheless, I continued with my warped humor. "You mean you wouldn't want me to join the Mothers and Fathers Italian Association? Heck, it's just like the PTA!"

The next day, I told Joe politely, "Joe, please tell Mr. Agro that we're just simple folks, with modest aspirations. Be sure to thank him for his offer. Tell him that we would like to respectfully decline." Joe said that he understood.

Did we make the right decision? I can say unequivocally that we did. Forty-three years after having made that choice, I can look back at the numerous rewards we have enjoyed as a family, in the form of family unity, honor, pride, and security. Our family is the envy of most people who witness the true love and affection that exists between us. Our children are not the typical "showbiz offspring," so often identified by promiscuity, drug usage, mental instability and more. By contrast, our children are God-fearing, productive and successful members of society—the fruits coming from years of parental dedication and love. Our careers have not suffered, either. If you were to compare our successes these past four decades with all the other full-time musicians who perform in their resident locales, I think we'd probably would be in the top ten or twenty percent, nationally.

None of that would exist today if I hadn't steadfastly stood by my convictions to avoid a pact with an obviously unscrupulous and mendacious gangster. Later, we came to find what a truly vicious animal Tommy Agro was. Once, while in his company, he bragged to us how he had "simply warned" a man by biting a huge chunk of flesh out of his cheek. He did this at a popular race track in New York, in full view of many people. But the man and those in the vicinity could do nothing in the presence of Agro's bodyguards and associates. He also boasted about having a man's severed thumb dangling over the cash register at his club in Queens   the same club he wanted us to work at in 1973! Agro said he did this as a subtle message to all employees "that the thumb once belonged to the last person he'd found stealing from him".

Additionally, when Joe Iannuzzi was clandestinely audio taping various members of the Mob for the FBI, Tommy Agro actually confessed to the murders of Anthony Desimone and Thomas Desimone, but Joe was not recording the conversation at that moment, so Agro was never convicted of those murders. Later, in the 1990 Martin Scorsese film *Goodfellas*, the character "Vinnie" played by Scorsese's father, was based upon Tommy Agro. Vinnie was seen cooking sauce in prison when the character "Tommy Devito" was murdered. The Devito character represented Thomas Desimone in real life.

Yes . . . back in 1973, we made the correct decision!

For decades, Joe resided somewhere in the USA under the FBI Witness Protection Program. Unfortunately, I saw him only once in the past thirty-three years. Unexpectedly, one night he called asking, "Hey Rodge, you wanna meet and have some pasta?"

I never thought I'd ever see him again. We met at an Italian restaurant in Lake Worth and had a lot of laughs. BUT, he sat with his back against the windowless wall!

Joe died in a Hospice center September 2016.

Tommy Agro never served his complete sentence. He died in 1987. The world has been a nicer place ever since!

Joe Dogs, Maitre D' Joint

My friend Joe *"Dogs"* Iannuzzi was a very intelligent guy. Joe's upbringing in various tough neighborhoods and his myriad hairy situations produced a rather colorful vocabulary. On the golf course, we all used expletives. Joe used them everywhere he went, and no matter with whom. He vocalized with a constant barrage of profanities and vulgarities. He did try to be on his best behavior in Sal's presence, but even then, I would occasionally have to reprimand him. He would apologize with all sincerity. I would scold him, in Italian, "Disgraziato!"

One night, at Alfredo's in Boynton Beach, my boss, Ozzie Provenzano told Joe (his cousin), "Joe, I need your help. Phil Tulata, my maitre d', is recuperating from a gall bladder operation. He can't make it this weekend."

"Yeah, so what the (expletive) do you want from me?"

"Look, if you don't do it, I've got nobody to take his place."

"Hey, I don't know nothin' about that (expletive) (expletive). Sei pazzo?"

Ozzie said, "No, I'm not crazy, Joe, just desperate. I promise you, all ya gotta do is to seat the customers and cross their name off the reservation list. Please help me, Joe."

Joe was a tough guy, but he also had a heart of gold. He wasn't going to let cousin Ozzie down. "Alright, what

253

the (expletive). I hate to see a (expletive) grown man cry! You owe me one."

"Molte grazie, Cugino (Thanks, Cuz).

"Si . . . e' va fan' culo (Sure . . . and up yours)."

Friday night came. I couldn't wait to get to the club to see just how Joe was going to handle the suppression of his gutter vocabulary. It was going to be a supreme test for him because in all of the time I knew Joe—and I'd spent an awful lot of time with the man—every second (expletive) word out of his (expletive) mouth was a (expletive)! And now, this man was going to play the role of an elegant and suave maitre d'? I had to see it for myself!

When Sal and I entered the club, Joe was on his best behavior. He was a model of etiquette and elegance. He momentarily acted like he didn't know us. He greeted us with, "Good evening Sir, Madam. Are you having dinner this evening?"

I simply smiled and said quietly, "Good luck, Joe."

We went over to the bandstand to prepare for our night's performance. Sal said to me, "So far so good."

"Yeah, RIGHT. Just like a time bomb!"

After setting up, we still had about twenty minutes before our start. We got some coffee from the kitchen and sat down at a table near Joe so that we could observe his debut into the world of fine dining service. We were impressed! He must have thought about all of the swanky places that he frequented and tried his utmost to mimic those people who had served him. He cordially smiled where and when necessary. He even bowed his head slightly, with a subtle hint of dedication and (almost) subservience to all the ladies and gentlemen. If he hadn't been wearing his *Mister B* shirt, with its mafia-type collar, you'd have figured restaurant service was his primary occupation. Sal and I looked at each other with elevated eyebrows.

On break, at the bar sipping a beer, I overheard a lady summon Joe to her table. It was very easy to overhear. She had an extremely high-pitched, nasal quality to her loud voice. The whole restaurant heard her. Evidently, she had a complaint. My ears perked up and my head turned to get a full view of how my friend would handle the situation. Joe never took tough or sassy behavior from anyone, much less from this browbeating, abrasive, "I-want-it-NOW" type woman.

Still sipping my beer, I heard Joe reply, obviously prepared for confrontation.

"Yeah lady . . . whatcha want?" Now THIS was beginning to sound like the Joe we'd all come to know and love.

She didn't flinch at his tough-guy jargon. Instead, equally firm, she said even louder, "Young man . . . do you call this veal? . . . This doesn't taste like veal. It tastes like BEEF!"

That whole area of the club immediately became very quiet. Everyone was eavesdropping.

Finally, as anticipated, Joe asserted himself *au natural*. Slowly shaking his head left to right, sternly looking her right in the eye, he bellowed back to her, "Nooooo shhhhit!

Almost everyone at the surrounding tables went into uncontrollable laughter. Likewise, I went out of control and sprayed a mouthful of beer across the bar top.

The lady and her party, without the same sense of humor as the rest of us, abruptly departed. At exactly that moment, we all saw Joe's career as a maitre d' also depart.

At the end of the evening, Ozzie bought the staff a round of drinks. We all had a big laugh as we reviewed the evening's episodes. Ozzie joked to Joe, "Gee, Cousin, I got a phone call from Phil Tulata tonight. He said he is feeling good enough to come in to be the maitre d' tomorrow night!"

I stuck up for Joe and said, "Hey, Boss . . . you're not firing Joe, are you? I thought that he exhibited a lot of CLASS tonight!"

Joe broke everyone up when he added, "Yeah, I did act with a lot of class but unfortunately . . . it was all LOW!"

Golf Games with a Gangster

There isn't much that you can expect in the way of honesty when playing golf with a confirmed member of La Cosa Nostra. My friend Joe Dogs—an associate of the Carlo Gambino crime family—and I often played golf together. From 1972 until 1979, we played at least once, sometimes as often as five times, a week.

In fact, golf had started our friendship in the first place. It happened shortly after my wife Sal and I began performing at Alfredo's (now defunct) in Boynton Beach, Florida. Joe set up a golf match with my former employer, Ozzie Provenzano, the bartender Rick Phillips, and myself.

Because I was a rank beginner and the worst player in the group, they teamed me up with Rick, who was the best player. That was fine with me. Rick was a good friend and actually instrumental in securing my music contract at Alfredo's.

I did absolutely nothing to help our team . . . until the last hole. I'd hit out of bounds, into the water, into every sand trap there was, and while three and four putting almost every hole. Rick played valiantly and kept us in the game in spite of the heavy load he had in carrying me.

Golfing Buddy, Gangster Joe Iannuzzi

At the eighteenth tee, Rick finally said, "Look, Roger, whichever team wins this final hole, wins it all. You can help us if you listen to me."

257

"What can I do? Tell me!"

"Your problem is that you're trying too hard. Instead of trying to kill the ball, just take the club back slowly and only half way. Then hit the ball easily. With the handicapping, you get two free strokes on this hole. If you keep the ball in bounds, you might help us."

I tried it Rick's way, and I'll be darned, the ball went down the fairway, more than two hundred yards! Rick encouraged me further. "All right! Do it again with this next shot and we'll be in good shape."

I did it again. The ball was now resting only a hundred yards away from the green. It was a par five hole and with the two free strokes I received, I was actually laying a net ZERO! Rick was ecstatic. He said, "You're going to win this hole for us."

I was getting really nervous about my remaining approach shot to the green, but then Joe Dogs—who up to that point had played an honest game and been a model of etiquette—approached my ball with one of his clubs. Rick yelled out to him, "Hey, don't hit THAT ball. That's Roger's ball."

Rick's warning didn't bother Joe in the least. He purposely slammed my ball straight into the middle of the lake nearby. Rick quickly ran up to him and said, "That's it. The rule is that if you hit your opponent's ball, you lose the hole . . . and because you've lost that hole, you've lost the entire match!"

Ozzie, obviously flustered, asked Joe, "Don't you know the rule? You just cost me twenty bucks, you dumb (expletive)! Why did you hit his ball, are you (expletive) crazy?"

Joe just couldn't stop laughing, but he finally did long enough to explain. "Yeah, I know what the rules say. I also knew we'd lose the match, but it was worth it. You see, Roger hit his ball into just about every lake there is on this course. I just didn't want his *perfect record* broken on the last hole!" We all laughed, even Ozzie.

From that point on, Joe and I became the best of friends. We started playing golf regularly. Oh yes, I eventually found out that he was a key figure in the South Florida Gambino mob. I realized that in many of the professional circles I musically performed, Joe was considered *persona non-grata.* But I simply downplayed the issue.

Although my game improved tremendously, I very rarely beat Joe. You see, he happened to be the game's consummate cheater. My friend knew every trick in the book. He would psych you every chance he got. He'd continually move his ball from the rough to much-improved positions on the fairway. When he hit his ball out of bounds, he simply kicked it back in or, with sleight-of-hand deception, secretly introduced another ball to the playing field. That trick also worked for lost balls. If his ball landed in a sand trap, he would always come out with a "miraculous" recovery. Joe threw some great shots from the sand! You might title him *the Willie Sutton of sand traps* because he always found an easy way out!

If none of these deceitful stratagems worked, because you'd either caught him in the act or prevented it in the first place, he'd make up for it in the tabulation of his score. Joe had an amazing knack of reducing a quadruple bogey into a birdie . . . every hole! I never had the opportunity to witness him having a legitimate hole-in-one, but if I had, I know it would have made golfing history. He undoubtedly would have recorded the world's first hole in zero!

Although Joe Dogs was the *World's Greatest Cheater at Golf*, he honestly meant all of his scheming to be just a joke. He would never take your money if he beat you by devious means. Furthermore, if you insisted on paying him, he'd laughingly explain whatever deception it was that he'd employed in beating you. Then he would proclaim, "No, I wouldn't think of taking your money." And with an impish grin and the innocence of an angel, he would state, "That would be dishonest!"

Joe's cheating schemes ran from the sublime to the ridiculous, but he performed them with such candor, you just had to laugh. If he hit his ball into an unplayable lie? Not to worry! He'd calmly pick up his ball from the horrendous spot and ask with superficial naiveté, "Is this my ball?" He'd briefly read the identifying brand name on the ball as he strolled toward the fairway. Then he'd proclaim, with equal innocence and nonchalance, "Ah yes, this IS my ball." He would then place the ball onto a perfect lie, sometimes improving his position by ten or fifteen feet from its original spot. Joe invented the word *chutzpa!*

Many times, he'd beat you on the greens, but it wasn't because of any superior putting abilities. It was because he cheated before he even got to putt. Joe would do this with his ball marker, always an old, dirty penny. If he hit his ball on the green before you hit yours there, he'd prance onto the green and mark his ball, while you observed from your fairway position. As he leaned down to supposedly mark his ball with the coin, he would instead flip the coin with his thumbnail . . . toward the hole! Then, he would pick up his ball and walk off the green to innocently await the other golfers' arrival.

Joe got so good at his "Tiddly Winks" technique that he would inevitably improve his putting distance by as much as fifteen or twenty feet. Nobody would ever see the coin flipped because it was never a shiny coin. One day I finally did catch on. From that day forward, I would simply pick up his coin and move it back to the approximate place his ball legitimately came to rest. Joe would laugh with the giddiness of an eleven-year-old caught kissing his girlfriend.

In order to speed up the game, many golfers will agree on "*gimme*" putts. They're putts that are within such a short distance from the hole that they're considered a waste of time to even bother with. Many golfers implement the gimme putt arrangement, agreeing that it has to be *within the leather*. That means they'll measure the gimme putt with one of their putters. If it is within the leather grip on the putter's handle, a distance of approximately two feet, it is considered an automatic "*gimme.*" That eliminates many arguments as to whether or not a putt is a gimme.

One time, Joe and I were playing two other gentlemen in a very hard fought battle. When we reached the green, we found both of their putts near the pin. Joe's putt was about six feet, mine about five. With a putter, they measured the distance for their putts. They proclaimed that because they were within the leather, both were gimme putts. They picked up their respective balls and stepped out of the way, expecting Joe and me to putt.

Joe shocked the other two gentlemen when he took the seven-foot flag stick and measured his putt with it. Joe proclaimed that both of our putts were also within "the leather," and therefore were gimme putts. He picked up his ball and mine and walked off the green to play the next hole. Somehow, I knew his putt wasn't going to give him any problem! The two golfers stood there, jaws dropped about half-a-leather.

If you happened to get the best of Joe on the scorecard, he then employed every means he could to beat you. Distractions played a big part in his plan. He would loudly cough during your backswing. If that didn't work, he'd make loud choking or gagging sounds. The first time he did that to me, I really thought he was choking. I went to his aid until I realized that he was laughing. I should have finished what he started and choked him myself!

If you were concentrating on a given putt that was essential to your beating Joe on a hole; he would boisterously belch, sneeze, drop clubs, cough, hiccup and hum loudly. He even interrupted your thinking process with some bodily punctuations that were downright crass and unmentionable. One sound he used, for one of our matches, still rings in my mind . . . and my ears.

We played as a threesome, our mutual friend Lou Barone joining us at Cypress Creek Country Club in Boynton Beach, Florida. Joe probably realized that I was becoming immune to his repertoire of psyches and tricks, so he turned to Lou for his target. Lou finally proclaimed with absolute disgust, "Hey . . . wait a second! What the hell is going on here? You're cheating!"

I confirmed his thoughts and probably aggravated him further when I said to him, in between my uncontrollable laughter, "No kidding, Sherlock Holmes!"

Lou didn't realize it was all meant as a joke, and that neither one of us had any intention of beating him out of the six dollars he owed us each. Instead, he was livid. Joe tried to apologize. I tried to calm him down. He wouldn't have any part of it. He said, "I can't play this way. I'm outta here! You both can go (expletive) yourselves!" He said. With that he took his clubs off my golf cart, walked off the course and drove home.

Joe and I continued. I was playing well, even overcoming the deceptive shaving of strokes off Joe's score. In order to beat me that day, he would have had to do something drastic. He did! While I was setting up my ball, preparing to make my drive on this one particular hole, he went to his golf bag. Unbeknownst to me, he pulled out his .38 revolver. In the middle of my backswing, he shot the pistol into the nearby swamp.

In those days, Cypress Creek was not the development it is today. It was relatively barren, but that made Joe's gunshot sound like a cannon. It wasn't just a light cap-pistol sound, but a bellowing BOOM! I'm sure people heard it miles away. Despite blasting one of my longest drives EVER, I think I even soiled my underwear. Turning toward Joe, I nervously said, "Oh . . . so THIS is *golf*!"

Later, we went into the clubhouse to have ourselves a beer. All the employees and several golfers who knew Joe and me looked at us both very suspiciously. We couldn't understand why people, normally friendly to us both, were acting so reserved and remote. I mean, they knew Joe was a mobster. It never seemed to have bothered them until now!

Finally, the bartender nervously asked, "Eh . . . where is your other friend . . . what's his name, Lou?"

Joe said, "We had a misunderstanding, and Lou walked back to his car. He must have gone home. Why?"

The bartender told us, "We heard a gunshot out there, coming from the area that you guys were playing. We couldn't see what was going on by the swamp."

Joe said, "Oh, I shot my gun at this huge water moccasin snake that was climbing up the banks toward our teeing area. *Marrone,* I had to shoot the (expletive) I hope I didn't upset anybody."

The bartender explained further. He said that the golf pro had told him, "Gee, those guys are with Joe Dogs. They went in to play that hole as a threesome. I certainly hope that they come back out as a threesome." The bartender told us, "We never saw Lou come out. When only the two of you guys eventually made the turn and came back toward the clubhouse, we didn't know what to think!"

Joe said, "You thought that we whacked Lou? We'd never kill Lou. He's a friend of ours!"

I added, "No way would we even consider such a thing! Hell, he still owes us six bucks each!"

Joe would deal with hundreds of thousands of dollars in cash every year. He certainly never had to, nor intended to, beat any close friends out of a $6 bet. If you ever forced him to accept the money for a bet, he would spend a fortune on you picking up the bar tab, lunch, greens fees and cart, next time you played. If he couldn't get to pay for any of those items, because you'd paid for them first, he'd insist on going out to fancy and lavish nightclubs, restaurants, or hotel dining rooms with you. Then he could reciprocate for the $6 you paid him on the golf course. He'd end up spending $500 for the night out. Of course, that was $500 by 1970's standards and probably triples that value today.

The next time we went to play a round of golf, we first had lunch together. He offered to pick up the whole tab. I said, "No, Joe, it's my turn. Thanks anyway. If you want to reciprocate, you can start by leaving your gun in your golf bag." He agreed . . . and so the fun (and the cheating) continued.

The biggest golf hoax in which I was ever involved happened during the time Sal and I performed at a wonderful place called *The Margate Resort*. The establishment was owned and operated by the Parisi family. It offered such an enormous array of offered amenities it would be difficult to list them. The highlights included location on the beautiful Lake Winnipesaukee, a good-size nightclub that featured show bands, and a huge dining room in which we performed nightly. We were there for the entire summer of 1975.

One evening, I received a telephone call from Florida. It was Joe. "Hey Rodge, can you do me a favor?"

"Sure Joe, what is it?"

"Look, there's this guy comin' up from Massachusetts to see you. He's gonna give you some money he owes me. I want ya to hold it for me until I see you in September. Capisce?"

"No problem Joe. Did you want to tell me the amount?"

"Yeah, it's no big (expletive) deal. It's two large and a couple of odd!"

"Come on, Joe. You know I don't understand your Mafia language. How much is it? If it's no big (expletive) deal, then you should be able to tell me over the phone."

"*Minchia,* I thought I just did!" Joe laughed, then explained to me that it was twenty-two hundred I could expect from the guy. "He'll call you tomorrow morning to set up a place he can drop it off, okay?"

I agreed.

The next day, the guy called as promised. We set up a time to meet, and he dropped the money off. I counted it out and he left. He didn't want a receipt, although it was all in cash. I put the money away in a safe place and forgot about it.

One evening about a week later, entering the restaurant at the Margate to work, Sal noticed Bunny and Joe seated at a dining table. In a state of shock, I asked, "What are you guys doin' here? We thought you were in Florida."

"When I spoke to you on the phone, we were in Florida, but we left the next day. I had some business to take care of in New York and took Bunny with me. She talked me into renting a car and coming up here to see you both. We took a room in the hotel here and figured we'd spend tomorrow with you if you're free."

"Gee Joe, I wish you had called me. I scheduled a golf game for tomorrow morning with this customer who comes in here and his son. He's a dentist and a very close friend of Mr. Parisi, my boss. But look, I'm positive that it's just the three of us playing, so why don't you join us? I'm sure they won't mind. I'll give them a call."

"Sure, I just have to rent some shoes and a set of clubs at the golf shop."

Joe and Bunny stayed the whole evening. We sat with them on our every break. Sal and Bunny planned out their next morning, while I confirmed things with the dentist. I told Joe, "Okay Buddy, we're all straight for tomorrow. I called Doctor Hanson and he said he's looking forward to meeting you. And then I'll give you that package your friend dropped off to me. Okay?"

The next morning, I picked Joe up at about eight o'clock. At breakfast, I told Joe of a practical joke I had in mind. I said, "Joe, I thought we'd have some fun with this dentist and his son. At the same time, I could give you your money."

He asked, "Whatcha have in mind?"

"Well, they're nice people, but a little square, if you know what I mean. On the way over here, I thought up this little joke we could play on them."

"You gonna joke around with MY (expletive) money?"

"Well . . . YEAH! I thought that we'd make a bet in front of them at the first tee. I'll purposely lose the golf bet, and in paying you your money back, they'll think it's for the bet we made. When they see me paying you twenty-two hundred in crisp one hundred dollar bills, they'll go berserk!"

"I don't give a $#!+, as long as at the end of it all, YOU reach into YOUR (expletive) pocket and come up with all MY (expletive) money!"

We finished breakfast and hastened to the golf course, where Joe got his shoes and clubs. We met the dentist and his fourteen-year-old son near the first tee. I performed the introductions.

I said to the good doctor, "Doc, Joe and I are used to betting on our games. I don't know if you and your son would like to eh . . . participate, or not?"

"Eh . . . well . . . I don't know. How much do you usually play for?"

"I don't know. Joe, what did you want to do? Our usual? A hundred-dollar *Nassau,* with automatic presses?"

Joe played out his part really well. He said to me, almost angrily, "HELL no. I wanna get part of that money back that you took from me last time. . . . How about a hundred a hole! But you have to give me a stroke a hole and two on the par fives."

I asked Dr. Hanson once more if he would like to bet. After hearing "the money" we were tossing around in conversation, he had a hard time talking. He first cleared his throat a couple of times, then said, "Eh …no, eh, eh, eh …no. No, thank you. You gentlemen can bet, and we'll play our own game."

We started out on the first tee with me purposely slicing the ball out of bounds. Unfortunately, so did Joe. I suggested that we hit a (free shot) *Mulligan.* We did, and I again purposely sliced the ball out of bounds. Joe did too!

I was now hitting my third shot from the tee. I purposely hooked the ball to the left side of the fairway, into a forest. He hit the ball out of bounds again. He was now hitting his fifth shot from the tee. He finally drove the ball . . . into the fairway bunker! I poked my ball out from behind this tree and purposely hit another clump of trees. The ball ended up ricocheting down the fairway; in the wrong direction. By then, I was laying four. Deliberately, I hit the ball out of bounds and had to hit my seventh shot from the same position. Joe went to hit out of the bunker, caught the top part of the lip, and rolled back in. He was hitting seven.

THIS went on for the entire hole. I was trying to lose to Joe. No matter what I did to get a bad score, he did worse. I hit three and four strokes to get out of sand traps, just to let him beat me. He, in turn, was trying to win, but playing the ugliest golf in the history of the game! I said to him quietly, "Joe, come on! You're supposed to win. I'm doing everything I can to lose. What must I do, catch yellow fever or diphtheria between now and the next hole?"

He started to laugh and said, "Yeah, that would help! I just don't know what the (expletive) I'm doing wrong."

I said sarcastically, "Well, you can start by playing with BOTH eyes open."

By the end of the hole, I ended up with a thirteen, figuring as we got closer to the green, that Joe would end up with an eleven or twelve. He four-putted and took a fourteen on the hole. We broke even! It was disgusting! The dentist and his son both looked on in astonishment.

The high scores continued as Joe just couldn't find his game. We broke even on the second hole. The third hole got even worse. I won it with an eleven. At that point, I should have theoretically paid back Joe, three of his twenty-two hundred. Instead, he owed me a hundred.

By the end of the first nine, after much hard work on my part, Joe finally had me down, but it was only for two hundred. It should have been nine hundred or better. On the tenth tee, I asked if we could double the bet to two hundred a hole. The Hansons looked at me like I was nuts.

Joe said emphatically, "No way. You're playing TOO GOOD!" I wanted to throw up!

I said, "Come on, Joe. You have me down by two hundred bucks. I just want a chance to get my money back."

He said, with the calm of a professional actor, "All right . . . but you have to give me the extra stroke on the par fives!" I yelled out, "WHAT? You're beating ME!"

Doctor Hanson said, "Gee! If we knew you gentlemen were going to play so badly, we probably would have bet you!"

I retorted nonchalantly, "Well, it's not too late to get into it if you want Doc! We don't have to play for a hundred a hole. We could play for twenty, or five, or even, a dollar a hole if you'd like."

He backed out with, "No, I don't think so." Later, Joe and I had a good laugh about that one. I shot something like a 67 or 68 on the front nine, and he was still too afraid to take me on!

We played the back nine with Joe finally beating me. On the seventeenth, he shot a six, on a par three, because he got hot and only three-putted! We doubled the bet on the eighteenth, and he won. I had to hit the ball three times into three separate sand traps!

I said to Joe, "Well, thank goodness you got me for only twenty-two hundred!" I unceremoniously whipped out the money and peeled it off to him, one hundred at a time.

Joe said, "Thank you!"

Then I said probably the only honest thing I said to Joe all day, "Don't thank me. Thank your mother. She brought a THIEF into this world!"

He winked at me and smiled, saying, "Well . . . THAT'S TRUE!"

The whole club found out about it and was buzzing all night. My boss finally came up to me, and said, "I heard that you lost a lot of money on the golf course today."

"Yeah, it's true, but there wasn't too much that I could do about it. . . . My friend happened to play one of the BEST games I've ever seen him play!"

Dominick "Little Dom" Cataldo

Joe Dogs and I were tired and hungry. Betting on horses at Gulfstream all day can really wear you out. Joe asked me, "Did you wanna spend some of that fortune you made today?"

"What did you have in mind for my fifteen-dollar bonanza?"

"I'm hungry, and I could use a (expletive) drink. We could stop off at the Thunderbird Motel if you'd like. They have a bar there and a Chinese restaurant, too. Okay?"

"Good idea. I'm famished!"

At the bar, Joe recognized a friend. He asked him, "Hey Dom, what the (expletive) you doin' here?" Before the man answered, Joe introduced me.

We ordered our drinks and Joe slipped the cocktail waitress a fifty-dollar tip asking her, "Hey Baby, you think we could eat right in here?" She evidently recognized Joe. She reacted the same way most waitresses did with him. She said, "Joe . . . there isn't a thing in this place that you couldn't have!"

She walked away smiling, as Dom asked him, "Is there a woman in Florida that isn't tryin' to get into the (expletive) sack with you?" Before Joe could answer, I smilingly asked Cataldo, "Oh, you know him, too?"

Cataldo, a short man with a respectable build, asked me, "You're a musician, huh?"

Joe jumped in with, "Yeah he's a great piano player. He works with his wife. They're really great together!" Joe turned to me with a half-smile and asserted, "You know, Dom is a musician, too."

I fell for it asking, "Really? What do you play?"

Joe answered for him, "Well, he's been known to carry around a violin case from time to time!" Joe laughed at his own joke, but Little Dom only smiled.

I asked naively, "You play the violin?"

Joe again interceded with, "I didn't say he PLAYED the violin. He only carried the (expletive) case around with him!" Joe started bellowing his contagious brand of laughter, as I chuckled slightly, out of courtesy. Dom's smile was still low keyed. He didn't say anything, and neither did I. Joe put his hand on my shoulder, leaned in and said with mock seriousness, "He makes a hit . . . every place he goes!"

Joe went into hysterics. I started to laugh, mainly because Joe's laughter was so catching. Yet, Cataldo was still relatively calm. He said to Joe, with a slight smile, "Joe, you're one of kind!"

I asked Cataldo, with a serious tone, "Tell me, Dom, from the horse's mouth . . . were you ever on the stage?" Cataldo started laughing now as he explained, "(Expletive) no . . . but I robbed a lot of them!"

Both of them were laughing with inside knowledge of their jokes. I was laughing because, although I didn't know the inside information, I knew they were both playfully putting me on! I figured that I would do what show business had trained me to do—I played the part of the straight man.

I casually asked, "Well, I mean . . . have you ever been in show business?"

Joe jumped right on that one, answering me with implied sincerity, "Are you (expletive) kidding? He knocked them DEAD in Philadelphia!" Now we were all laughing, and I was getting the gist of their implications. I figured Little Dom Cataldo was a tough guy for the Mob.

There was just no stopping Joe. Once he got started, he could stretch a minute's thought into a postgraduate essay. He resumed by asking me, "Roger, have you ever heard of the Columbia Recording Company?" I nodded "Yes. I have!" He said, "Well, Dom signed a *contract* recently with the COLUMBO Company!"

The highlight of the repartee took place after Cataldo had loosened up from the Scotch he was drinking. Smiling, I asked, "So tell me, Dom, do you sing?"

He thought for a moment and then responded, "No . . . I don't (expletive) rat on anyone! And besides, I've never been to Sing-Sing, so how the (expletive) do you expect me to sing?"

Unbeknownst to me at the time, Cataldo was a hit man with the Columbo Crime Family. I found out later. I had no idea he had murdered at least ten people. He even had his own personal burial grounds for his victims. After a hit, he would transport the body to an area just off the Taconic State Parkway, north of New York City. He called his victim's unmarked cemetery "Boot Hill"!

Years later, thanks to the sting operation that Joe Dogs and the Federal Bureau of Investigation had set up, and Joe's testimony in front of the Grand Jury, Dominick "Little Dom" Cataldo ended up in prison with a sentence of thirty-five years. Joe felt bad about it. Dominick Cataldo was not his original target, Tommy Agro was. Little Dom died in prison.

Brother, Can You Spare . . . A Thousand?

1975 was a formative time for my band's reputation, while we performed at Oliver's in West Palm Beach. It was also a time of growth for the criminal activities and reputation for Joe "Dogs" Iannuzzi.

As Joe's friend, I encountered many people associated with the Mob. One of those was Freddie "Campo" Campagnuolo, an associate of the Joe Columbo crime family. I even became friendly with Freddie and involved weekly in a HUGE criminal business transaction with him. I used to place an enormous $10 football bet through him, twice a week.

Freddie used to take my "action" as a favor out of respect for Joe. I know it must have been a royal pain for him, every time he did. At that time, the minimum bet was $25 and most gamblers would bet in the hundreds and thousands of dollars. I appreciated Freddie doing this for me. It made a normally meaningless football game on television just a bit more exciting for me to watch, although I must confess, I almost always lost!

I gained a reputation for being an incredibly bad football handicapper, to the point that almost everyone, including Joe, insisted on finding out which way I would bet. Then, they would make sure they bet the other way! I would lose a sawbuck and they would win a few hundred. They would buy me drinks, even stick a ten or twenty into the band's tip bowl, just to get my reliable information. It was getting ridiculous. I mean, if the Kansas City Chiefs were my pick and 48 point underdogs to Saint Mary's Girl School, everyone would bet on Saint Mary's that week, simply because I had picked the Chiefs. And wouldn't you know it, a damn miracle would inevitably occur!

Things started to get hot for Freddie. "They" started to occasionally tap his phone lines, so he had to be careful. He had already been arrested several times for bookmaking. It was for that reason he got very aggravated with me when I called him on his betting line and said, "Hey, Freddie, this is Roger Rossi." He had a fit. He very angrily said to me, "Don't you EVER call this number and use your real name!"

"Well, just how would you like me to reveal who I am?" I asked.

"Just say RR. I'll know who you are."

I said, "Okay, no problem."

He then asked, in a much nicer and softer tone, "Alright, whatcha want?"

"What's the spread was on the Baltimore-Miami game?

"Miami is minus three."

"Okay, I'll take Miami . . . for the *usual*." Now I was slightly apprehensive about mentioning the ten-dollar amount. He understood and responded, "Okay, you're in."

I hung up and went to watch the game, which Miami and I ultimately lost. I figured I would try to get even for the day by betting on the four o'clock game. So I called Freddie back. I said, "Hey, Freddie?"

"Yeah, who's this?"

I was so anxious to get my bet in before the game started, I momentarily forgot our earlier conversation. I just answered automatically, "This is Roger Rossi."

Immediately, I realized my mistake and started to laugh, nervous and embarrassed by my stupidity. Freddie must have realized it was an innocent mistake. He didn't blow up, but said, soft and solemnly, "Well, I'll tell you, . . . you can laugh and you might think it's funny right now, but if they come to get you to testify against me, you're not going to think it's so funny! And neither am I!"

"Gee, I'm really sorry. It won't happen again, I promise. And I was just laughing at my own stupidity."

"Okay, whatcha want?"

"What's the spread on the Raiders-Broncos game?"

"Denver is favored by 4."

"Alright, I'm going to take the Raiders and the points, for my usual."

As I sat down to watch the Raiders get creamed by the Broncos, I made a special mental note to be sure to give Freddie the code name of "RR" the next time I called him.

Monday evening came and I figured I would try just one more time, to win at least one game for the week. I called Freddie. This time, I was prepared. I said, "Hello, Freddie?"

"Yeah, who's this?" he asked. I slowly and methodically answered, "This is . . . R . . . R."

"Alright, now you've got it! How can I help you?"

"What's the spread on the game tonight?"

"The Giants are two point favorites."

I thought about it for a moment and then said, "Okay, I'm gonna take the Eagles plus the two points."

"Alright Roger, you've got it. . . . So, how's it going at Oliver's?"

I slowly and carefully answered, "It's . . . going fine."

He continued with small talk. "And how's your lovely wife Sal doing?"

"Eh . . . she's . . . okay."

"You guys are performing there . . . what, from Tuesday to Saturday evenings?"

Now, I was the one who threw a fit. I yelled, "You son of a bitch! You don't want me to give you my name over the phone, and I'm supposed to use a code name, RIGHT? . . . But it's quite all right for you to call me by my real name and to use my wife's name, to mention where it is that we both are working and to establish exactly when the Sheriff can come to get me!"

I slammed the phone down. When Freddie came into the club that week, we had a laugh over the whole thing. He took my thirty dollars in lost bets for the week and then bought my band a round of drinks and hit our bowl with a twenty-dollar tip. I said to myself, "How much did I REALLY lose for the week?"

On another occasion, I called up Freddie to place a ten-dollar bet, but he wasn't the one to answer the telephone. One of the guys who worked for him did. I said, "Hello?"

The guy on the other end said, "Yeah, who's this?"

I answered him very carefully, "This is RR." I wasn't sure if it was someone working for Freddie, or perhaps if Freddie had been arrested and it was the police intercepting his calls. I continued, "Who's this?"

He put my mind a little more at ease when he said, "This is Rob. I'm filling in for Freddie. What do you want?"

I remember Freddie mentioning Rob's name, so I felt that it was all right for me to place my bet. I still tried to be careful in not incriminating myself. I asked, "What is the spread on the Cardinals-Giants game?"

"The Giants are seven and a half point favorites."

I was still slightly nervous about not speaking directly to Freddie, so I tried to disguise my bet's dollar value. I couldn't say, "My usual" because he might not know what that was, so I became creative. I had heard other guys throw around the term, "a dime," so that's what I said. "Alright Rob, I'm gonna take the Giants for a dime!"

"Okay, you're in." I watched the game, and as usual, I lost my bet.

Tuesday evening came and I went to work at Oliver's with Sal. I brought along with me an extra ten dollars to cover my lost bet, just in case Freddie came around. Freddie never charged me "the vig," generally an extra ten percent you have to pay if you lose. Come to think of it, it would have been rather ridiculous for him to take $11 from me on a $10 bet that should have been $25 in the first place. Most of the time Freddie would take my $10 and throw $5 of it back into my tip bowl. He was always very nice to me.

Sal and I were performing with our bassist, Mike Winburn when Joe Dogs walked in. I took a break and joined him. Joe asked, "So Roger, tell me. What is this sudden need you have to become a big-time gambler?"

"What do you mean, big time?"

"Betting a thousand dollars on a football game is what I would refer to as 'big time,' wouldn't you?" Joe asked.

"Well, who bet a thousand dollars?" I asked innocently.

Joe snickered menacingly, "You did, my friend! On the Giant game, Sunday. I heard you lost, too. I didn't realize that you made that kind of (expletive) money!"

"No, no. You've got it wrong, Joe," I explained. "I didn't bet a thousand dollars on that game. I bet ten dollars. I said to Rob, Freddie's partner, that I wanted the Giants for a dime."

"A dime MEANS a thousand, Roger!" Joe proclaimed.

I got up from the table, went over to the bartender and asked, "Hey Bill, you bet on football games, don't you? What does it mean when you bet a dime?"

"A thousand dollars."

I turned pale. I know I felt sick to my stomach. It was just about that time, Freddie Campo came in and sat down at Joe's table. I went over there quickly to try to plead my case. I said, "Hello, Freddie. Freddie . . . I didn't mean a thousand dollars when I bet a 'dime' through Rob. I meant ten dollars."

Freddie sat up in his chair, looked at me sternly and said, "I don't know what you want me to say, Roger! . . . I

281

mean you're a nice guy and all . . . but if you won the bet, I would have come in here with a thousand dollars to put into your hands. Now you're trying to weasel out of this thing with me. I mean, I've got guys that I've got to settle up with and answer to. . . . You know, if they're not satisfied, someone is gonna end up with some broken legs! . . . It's not gonna be me! Capisce?"

I sat there in a total fog. How did I get into this trap? I felt tremendously depressed. Just as I was going to offer to pay Freddie so much per week, I looked up and I noticed both he and Joe wore huge smiles. They started to laugh. Finally, I realized that they were putting me on. Freddie confirmed it by telling me, "When you first placed the bet, Rob asked me 'Who is this guy called RR?' So, I told him, 'Oh that's a guy I know, Roger Rossi. Why?' He then told me that you bet a dime. I told him, 'Oh no. He means ten dollars.' Roger, you never had any more than that on the game. Joe and I figured we'd just have a little fun with you!"

As they both continued laughing, I only had enough energy to say one word, "WHEW!" Then, I laughed with them. However, that evening, I bought THEIR drinks, and put an end to my foolish gambling habit . . . forever!

All in The Family

Our engagement at the Flame restaurant was going very well. Owner Peter Makris had to expand the lounge in which we performed. We played to packed crowds almost every night of the week. Arriving, it usually took us five minutes just to make it past the five and six-deep crowd waiting to get a drink at the bar. Most of the time, when taking a break, we wouldn't even bother going to the kitchen to get some coffee. By the time we'd make it through the crowd, our break would be finished! Makris had to make the room bigger, and he did. He took some of the lobby space from the restaurant and added it to our lounge, and he added seats at the bar so that the lounge could accommodate forty more people. Even so, it was still packed almost every night. That room was one of the most popular places in all of Palm Beach County, and certainly the most exquisite.

Additionally, in October 1977, he signed a new contract with the band that permitted us to add a musician to the group, growing from trio to quartet. I suggested the extra player be a drummer. This way I could take Sal off of the cocktail drums and put her up front as the lead singer she is. Our sound could cut through the crowd without necessarily increasing the volume. Makris agreed, and also gave us a well-deserved raise.

While my music group enjoyed growth and success, my friend Joe "Joe Dogs" Iannuzzi was also moving up the ladder in his business. Through the guidance of his mentor Tommy Agro of the Carlo Gambino Crime Family, he became one of the strongest gangsters in Palm Beach, Broward and Dade counties.

When Joe came into the club to say hello, many times I wouldn't even get a chance to greet him, with anything more than to wave. Sometimes the place was so filled, it was physically impossible to get over to his seat. Thank God that we never had to evacuate from a fire! On other occasions, I did not approach Joe because the place was filled with representatives of the FBI and/or the Palm Beach Sheriff's Department. Many times, the sheriff himself was there as a patron of the club. I knew that they were always investigating Joe. I certainly didn't need to complicate my job by having them investigating me, too. So, I'd wave and keep my distance.

I asked my bassist, Michael Burns if he would recommend someone I could audition for the drummer position. He said, "Yes. I used to work with this drummer before I started with your band. His name is Steve Gambino. I think that he might be available." Steve soon joined my band.

All of the club's customers were delighted with the improved sound. Moving Sal up front added pizazz to the group. Of course, none of this helped to alleviate the tremendous crowd problem, but it did extend good will to the patrons.

One evening, Joe Dogs came into the lounge with his wife, Bunny. It was a typical evening at the Flame. The piano bar was standing room only. The dance floor was packed. As usual, It was five deep at the bar. Naturally, in between the drinking, laughing and dancing, everyone standing had one other very important chore, and that was to grab the very first table or stool that became available.

On my break, I just could not get over to visit with Joe and Bunny. Instead, I talked to Steve, our new drummer. We exchanged musical ideas and suggestions. Then, I jokingly asked him, "Tell me, Steve. Are you any relation to Carlo Gambino, the crime Capo di tutti Capi (Boss of all Bosses) who recently died?"

I was only joking. I NEVER expected to hear what I heard next. He calmly answered, "Yes. HE WAS MY UNCLE!"

"You're . . . not . . . serious . . . are you?" I asked with obvious nervousness. He said emphatically, "Yes, I am!"

I felt queasy. I knew by the way he had responded that he was telling the truth. I quietly asked myself, "How could this happen? Here I am, on the one hand, trying to distance myself from my friend Joe because of his involvement with organized crime and the Carlo Gambino crime family. And now, unknowingly, I have hired the nephew of the BOSS of that family, considered the GODFATHER OF ALL GODFATHERS! Did Mike know who Steve's Uncle was? . . . Nah! . . . Was I becoming paranoid? Was this all happening?"

Steve must have sensed my nervousness. He quickly put my mind at ease. He said, "Roger, you don't have to be nervous about this. Yes, it's a fact that we were related, but I hadn't seen him since I was a kid because my mother hadn't talked to him in many years. We didn't see hide nor hair of him before he died, and we really didn't care to."

My mind and mood relaxed. At that moment, Joe Dogs approached. "Hey Rodge, how you doing? I haven't seen you in a while. Aren't we friends anymore?"

"Hey Joe, how are you doing? Say hello to my new drummer, Steve Gambino."

"Hi, Steve. Good to meet you."

"Joe, I haven't meant to ignore you, and I'm really glad to see you." I added teasingly, "This is as good a time as any for me to tell you that, from now on, I'm taking over all of your business operations! You see Joe, I've got some real heavies working for me now. Steve happens to be the nephew . . . of your late boss, Carlo Gambino!"

I had to laugh at both of their reactions: Joe's, when he registered Steve's last name, and Steve's, when he realized Joe was connected with, and employed by his Uncle Carlo!

Joe recovered quickly and said, "Steve, I liked your Uncle a lot! And Roger, as for you, if you think you can (expletive) operate the Syndicate from your (expletive) piano, you better think again!"

I smiled as the two of them laughed. Once you got Joe started, he wouldn't quit. He continued, "And another thing . . . MINCHIA, how are you ever gonna play the (expletive) piano with broken knuckles?!"

Now, even I joined in the laughter. I asked Joe, "In other words, you think that it would be a good idea for me to stick to just making music, huh?"

"Right. Leave the jokes . . . and the POKES . . . for me to handle!"

Steve eventually had to quit as my drummer. I was getting desperate, trying to find a replacement. I happened to mention it to Joe. He said, "Well, you know my sister is moving to West Palm Beach and her husband, Damon Buckley is a professional drummer. He'll be available for you if you want."

I answered him with excitement, "Damon Buckley?! I knew Damon from Long Island."

Joe teased me with, "You know, Roger, you're getting to be a real (expletive) up. First, you didn't know that Steve was Carlo Gambino's nephew, and now you don't know that Damon is my brother-in-law. What the (expletive) is it with you?"

I did hire Damon, and he stayed with us through the season. Joe asked me, "How is Damon working out with your band?"

"You know Joe, it's much better with Damon in the band," I jested. "Besides the musical part of it, I can sleep better knowing that I've kept it in the family . . . rather than . . . in *The Family* . . . if you know what I mean!"

A frown of bewilderment finally changed to a smile when it all clicked in. He said, "Sure! That's (expletive) easy . . . for YOU to say!"

Roger Rossi

PART FIVE: The Athletes

Maurice "The Rocket" Richard
Whitey Ford
Gardner Dickinson
Tom Fazio
Evel Knievel
The PGA Champion is a Nine Handicap
Lee Trevino
Surprise, Surprise
Fred Couples
"Irish" Mickey McGrath
Jack Nicklaus – Golfer of the Century
Joanne Carner
Bill Parcells
Rick Mears
Jack Nicklaus is The Best Man

Maurice "The Rocket" Richard

After Sal and I were engaged, she began working for a Montreal-based company that supplied temps. She would work for one company as a secretary one week, another a few days as a stenographer, then another firm for two weeks as a receptionist.

One afternoon, I met Sal toward the end of her first day as a receptionist for a sports equipment company. As I waited for her to finish, and then join me for dinner, a gentleman came out of his office and passed us both. He looked at me, smiled courteously and said, *"Bonjour."*

I replied with my own brand of "hello," and Sal introduced us. She hardly knew him herself, but she said, "Mr. Richard (she mistakenly pronounced his name in English), this is my fiancé, Roger Rossi."

He smiled broadly, then spoke in slightly broken English. "Pleased to meet you."

"And likewise, Sir."

When Sal and I left, I said to her, "Well, your boss seems like a nice guy."

"Yes, I think he is. He is a former professional ice hockey player who supposedly played for the Montreal Canadiens. Did you ever hear of him? They call him *The Rocket.*"

My jaw dropped as I asked, "You mean to tell me THAT was Maurice Rocket Richard (pronounced correctly Ree-shard) I just shook hands with?" I proceeded to update Sal on the man for whom she was working. "Sal, he is not just an ice hockey player. He's a living legend. He's one of the greatest ice hockey players in the Canadiens' history."

I went back to his office and apologized. I said, "I'm sorry, Mr. Richard. I didn't recognize you. I'm a fan of yours."

He nodded and said with a smile, "That's okay. I understand. Thank you."

I left his office the second time and rejoined Sal. She asked, "Was he really that good?"

I thought how odd it would be if things were reversed and the same scenario was to take place in the United States, with some young Canadian lad explaining to his fiancée just how good her new employer, Stan Musial, or Wilt Chamberlain, or Johnny Unitas had been. But, you see, Sal had an excellent excuse. She came from England, where ice hockey is one of the last items on the sports menu. She didn't know any hockey teams, much less players. Now if you wanted to talk about rugby or soccer, those subjects would have been more to her liking!

I patiently explained, "Honey, he recently retired, and this is the first time in ten years that the Montreal Canadiens have not played in the Stanley Cup Finals. He was a superstar! The Canadiens have won the last five Stanley Cups because of him! . . . I'm a New York

Rangers fan, and I hate him. Does that tell you something?"

"The Rocket" was a force to be reckoned with, especially in the late 1940's and early fifties. He had great speed, heart, and talent. Real toughness and a fabulous backhand shot added to his arsenal, making him a dangerous scoring threat from anywhere on the ice.

I lived on Saint-Luc Street, right around the corner from the Montreal Forum, the arena where the Canadiens played. Occasionally, I would go to root for the Rangers, when they came to town. I only saw The Rocket play two or three times; and that was toward the end of his career, in 1959 and 1960. Even then, he was still tenacious and tough. Some of Maurice "The Rocket" Richard's records still stand until this day. However, at that point in time, his records were:

- Most goals scored (5) in one Stanley Cup Game (1944)
- Eight goals in all-star games. (Later broken by Gordie Howe)
- Most goals scored (4) in one period of Stanley Cup Game (1945)
- 544 regular season goals in his career.
- 82 playoff goals in his career.
- *Hart Memorial Trophy (1947)* (NHL's MVP).
- 50 goals in 50 games, in the 1944-45 season.
- Member of *Canada's Sports Hall of Fame*.
- Member Stanley Cup Champions 1944, 46, 53, 56, 57, 58, 59, 60.

293

Yeah . . . I'd say, "He was that good!"

Just prior to the publishing of this book's first edition, Sal and I were saddened to hear that "The Rocket" had died of respiratory failure at age 78. A state funeral took place in the Notre dame Basilica in Montreal. Prime Minister Jean Chretien said Richard "defined and transcended the game of hockey."

He was an icon. His death happened during the Stanley Cup series (the ice hockey championship) and four players from one of the competing teams, The Dallas Stars, interrupted the series to attend a memorial service for Richard in Montreal. That says something of the respect they still had for the man. Sal and I will never forget.

Whitey Ford

In 1969, I was called to play at a cocktail party on the north shore of Long Island. I was to perform on a beautiful grand piano in a private home. It turned out to be a very special evening. Not only were the host and hostess super-nice people, but I met and warmly conversed with one of professional baseball's all-time greats . . . all night. Actually, by his own choice, he turned out to be my personal waiter for the evening.

Early in the party, while I played some opening strains on the keyboard, a few guests drifted over. One complimented me by saying, "I haven't heard a piano played like that in a long time. It sounds great!"

I turned toward the gentleman and said, "Thank you. I really appreciate that." I looked him in the eye as I spoke and excitedly continued, "WOW! . . . You're Whitey Ford, aren't you?"

He nodded, and with a smile, answered, "Yes, that's right. What's your name?"

While I continued playing the piano, I answered, "I'm Roger Rossi, and I'm a big fan of yours. I've been to the Bronx to see you pitch on many occasions. I've been a Yankee fan all of my life." I stopped playing the piano right in the middle of the song and emphasized, "Whitey, sometimes that was not easy for me because I grew up in Brooklyn, where it was not exactly 'fashionable' to be a Yankee fan."

We both laughed as I finished the song I had interrupted.

The baseball legend immediately knew what I meant. I had to put up with verbal abuse, year in and year out while living at that time in "Dodger Country." It seemed like a continual pastime for New York City area baseball fans to debate the merits of their respective team. These debates took place in schoolyards, offices, restaurants, bars, on subway trains, and on the streets.

The rivalries were far more intensive than any that exist today. In those days, you could choose between the New York Yankees, who played in Yankee Stadium, or the New York Giants, who played at the Polo Grounds, and of course, the Brooklyn Dodgers, whose home was

Ebbets Field, not too far from my Bay Ridge neighborhood. Naturally, most fans rooted for the team closest to their home. I was one of the few in my neighborhood who committed the mortal sin of rooting for that area's archrivals!

Today, someone who lives in the New York area could contend that a rivalry exists between the Yankee and the New York Met fans. It pales by comparison to the old days. The Yanks still play at The House That Ruth Built—albeit a new exact replica across the street from the original—and the Mets are out on Long Island, two distinctly separate areas. By comparison, the Yankee, Giant and Dodger rivalries of old were truly emotional. Those teams all came from closer proximity. They were always battling it out. The Giants and Dodgers went at it all season long because they were in the same league. They would fight for "the right" to meet their most probable opponent in the World Series, the Yankees. New Yorkers love a "subway series."

The bantering would intensify as the season approached the World Series, but would cease when the Yankees won that Series, which they quite often did. The year would end, with the Giant and Dodger fans saying typically, "Well, just you wait until next year!"

My response to that was, "Hmmm, it seems to me that I've heard that comment before, like . . . eh . . . last year?!"

The Dodgers and the Giants always had great teams, players, and coaches, but the Yankees, in those days, were in a class of their own. In the forty-four-year period between 1921 until 1964, the Yankees were in thirty-four World Series, of which they won twenty. Now if that isn't a monumental and dynastic accomplishment, I don't know what is!

Whitey requested some music choices. When I happily obliged, he returned the favor by fetching us both a beverage. We talked at length about his career, which started out by his winning the *American League Rookie of the Year* Award. That was followed by his astonishing accomplishments in World Series play. Those successes were outstanding at the time of my meeting him back in 1969, but what is more amazing is that now, at the time of this writing in 2016, it's been almost a half century since his retirement and nobody has broken those records!

While pitching for the Yankees in the 1950s and 60s, Edward Charles "Whitey" Ford was fantastic; he was called, "The Chairman of the Board." He played in ten All-Star Games and was a World Champion with the New York Yankees six times.

Ford pitched in the "Fall Classic" in eleven of his sixteen years, and in his first sixteen starts, he had an unbelievable 1.98 ERA in 109 innings. His World Series records include:

- All-time leader in World Series starts (22).
- All-time leader in World Series wins (10).
- The Most Valuable Player Award in the 1961 World Series
- Game one starts (eight).
- Innings pitched (146).
- Wins strikeouts (94).

Additionally, Whitey Ford threw three shutouts in World Series play, and they were in three consecutive starts: Games three and six of the 1960 series; and then Game one of the 1961 series. When I asked him about those great feats, he humbly chalked it up to the fact that he had so many great players on his team. He was right. It certainly did no harm for Ford to have Mickey Mantle, Roger Maris, Phil Rizzuto, Yogi Berra or Elston Howard playing on the team while he pitched. That kind of power and defense would give any pitcher the confidence he needed to win. Of course, a great curveball didn't hurt, either.

The Yankees always came up with fabulous replacements for their retiring superstars. Joe DiMaggio replaced Babe Ruth and Lou Gehrig, and Mickey Mantle replaced DiMaggio.

When Mantle had an "off" year, there was Roger Maris, Berra, and Rizzuto who also won the MVP for the league. When Yogi ended his great catching career, Elston Howard stepped up. They were always the team by which others set their standards. It meant so much to me to nonchalantly chat with one of the Yankees' greatest pitchers.

When I took a break, Whitey went over to talk with some other guests. Shortly after I started again, he returned and said he'd be happy to get me another soft drink, or something "stronger" if I wanted.

"Whitey, you don't have to do that for me."

"Are you kidding? It's no problem at all. What would you like?"

"Thank you. I'll have a scotch and soda, with a lemon twist, please."

When he returned, I played him a couple of selections from the hit Broadway musical, *Damn Yankees*. As I did, we reflected on his winning the Cy Young Award a few years earlier (1961). Today, that award is presented to the best pitcher in his respective league. In Ford's time, it was awarded to the best pitcher in ALL of baseball!

A few years later, my wife and I moved to Florida. In 1974, I felt a touch of euphoria when I read that Whitey and his close pal Mickey Mantle were both inducted into the Baseball Hall of Fame. I reflected back on that evening in 1969, when this great baseball legend used that precious arm to carry a couple of drinks for ME, something that Whitey Ford probably doesn't even remember and I will NEVER forget.

Gardner Dickinson

Professional golfer Gardner Dickinson won quite a few big-time golf tournaments, including a historic playoff against Tom Weiskoph at the Doral Open. His style of play and basic image was often compared to the great Ben Hogan. Gardner was a very talented golf course designer, and one of the finest golf teachers in the world. He worked especially well with the lower-handicap players and taught many of the professional golfers on tour. The list included JoAnne Carner and his second wife Judy Clark Dickenson, who won five professional tournaments but was also the president of the Ladies Professional Golf Association for two years.

I've always been in awe of Dickinson's golf swing, abilities, and accomplishments. So, I was especially hurt, then angry, during my first encounter with him!

In May 1976, my band opened at the Flame, in North Palm Beach, Florida. One evening, our first week there, I noticed he was dining with his then-wife Della. They were in the dining room, adjacent to the lounge where we performed. I said to Gino Ziretti, the bartender, "Gee, I'd really like to meet Gardner Dickinson. I think he's great!"

Gino replied confidently, "Oh, you will. Probably after he has dinner, he'll come into the lounge with his wife."

Later, during one of our breaks, I happened to be seated by the entrance to the lounge. I noticed, through the partially opened wall-divider, Gardner and Della leaving the dining room. I figured they were coming in to hear us, but they walked right past the lounge entrance, toward the exit of the club. Donna Root, the club's hostess, asked them, "Are you going into our lounge, to hear our new music group?"

I was shocked when I overheard his answer. He scowled, and gestured negatively. "I don't want to hear that garbage!"

At first, I felt terribly hurt. Then I became angry. From where he was dining, he could not possibly have heard my band's true sound. It most definitely would have been distorted. I said to myself, "What gives HIM the right to so rudely condemn our music, especially from another room? The guy is a great golfer, but that doesn't qualify him to be a music critic."

I got up and approached the lobby. As I arrived, I noticed that he had already left. I went over to Donna and asked her if I'd heard him correctly. She confirmed it, trying to comfort me with an explanation as to why he would say such a thing. She said, "Roger, don't take it personally. Your band sounds great. However, you happen to be replacing a musician that was here for seven years, and during that time, made most of our patrons his friends. Gardner Dickinson is one of those people. Don't worry, he'll come around."

It was nice of Donna to say that. Nevertheless, I still felt upset. My Sicilian temper boiled. I told Donna, "I appreciate what you're saying, Donna, but that doesn't give him the right to call my music 'garbage.' Look, do me a favor. Next time you see Gardner Dickinson, relay this message to him. Tell Mr. Dickinson that I've seen him on television doing his Buick automobile commercials. I've also seen him playing golf. Please tell him that if he could putt . . . the way Roger Rossi's band makes music . . . he'd be doing Mercedes-Benz, not Buick, commercials!"

I don't know if Donna ever relayed my message, but that very weekend, the Dickinson's came into our lounge after dinner. They sat there, at first just listening to our music. Then, gradually, they started to applaud lightly. Soon, they were applauding every arrangement we performed. Their applause grew louder and louder. They sent us a note, written on a napkin, asking us if we could join them as soon as we finished. I told the waitress that "we would be honored."

When we finished, we went right over to their table and met them. They were absolutely wonderful to us. I couldn't believe it. After that night, we became friends. On many, many occasions, Dickenson, and his party were the last ones in the club, and he was the last one applauding us.

One such evening stands out vividly in my memory. That afternoon, on television, we had watched him and his partner Sam Snead, win *the Legends of Golf* tournament in Austin, Texas. He surprised us when he showed up at the Flame lounge only a few hours later. He must have immediately caught a plane back to Florida and came right into the club. He made all of us in my band feel great when he said, "I could've stayed in Texas, but I wanted to come right in here to celebrate my success with you, folks!"

I said, "Gardner, you make us feel proud to know you!"

Then, innocently, I asked him, "Where's Sam Snead?"

Smiling, he said, "You must be kidding. He won't go for spit. Sammy probably still owns the very first dollar he ever made!"

One day I brought my thirteen-year old son Roger (Jr.) to see Gardner play in golfer Bob Murphy's Pro-Am tournament at Delray Dunes, Delray Beach, Florida. I introduced them both just before Gardner was to be announced at the first tee. Proudly, I said, "Roger, I want you to meet one of the finest golfers you could find anywhere; Mr. Gardner Dickinson."

Roger, the gentleman I taught him to be, extended his hand to Gardner. Gardner smiled, shook his hand, and then proceeded to embarrass all of us with probably the worst drive I've ever seen from any professional! The ball didn't travel any further than 125-150 yards down the fairway.

Roger looked at me with obvious suspicion. I assured him that he shouldn't worry. "Son, believe me! A golfing tournament is not won or lost by the first shot. Gardner Dickinson is a fine golfer, and he'll recover from that bad shot. Just wait and see."

Well, I couldn't have picked a better moment to double-down. With his second shot from the fairway, Gardner advanced the ball onto the green, and he just missed his birdie putt by inches. He not only parred that first hole but also went on to win the tournament. It was a great lesson for my son, and me. Honor was restored because perseverance prevailed!

In 1998, I was saddened to hear that Gardner died at age 70. Shortly afterward it was announced on television during The Masters tournament.

I was happy we patched up our differences in the early going of our relationship, and I was always proud to have been considered a friend. Gardner Dickinson was a great man and golfer. Gardner won eleven professional golfing events, including:

- The Florida Open – 1952.
- The Miami Beach Open – 1956

- The Haig and Haig Scotch Foursome – 1978 (with Ruth Jessen)
- The Legends of Golf – 1978 (with Sam Snead).
- Holds the record for the best winning percentage in Ryder Cup history (minimum of seven matches) with a record 9-1-0.
- In Ryder Cup play, teaming up with Arnold Palmer, he never lost a match. They had a 5-0 record together. In PGA regulation tournaments, he also beat such golfing greats as:
- Sam Snead by three strokes at the *West Palm Beach Open*, 1956;
- Miller Barber by four strokes at the *Cleveland Open Invitational*, 1967;
- Tom Weiskopf by one stroke at the *Doral Open Invitational*, 1968;
- Gary Player by 1 stroke at the *Colonial National Invitational*, 1969;
- In Gardener Dickinson's last tournament (1971), he beat Jack Nicklaus in a sudden-death playoff at the *Atlantic Classic*.
- Dickinson was a published author, penning the book, "Let'er Rip."
- Also, he was one of the founders of the Senior PGA Tour, which is now known as "The Champions Tour."

Tom Fazio

Tom Fazio is a golf course architect – par excellence. I first met Tom under unique but nervous conditions; for me! It was at one of the great golf courses in Florida, the "Hills Course" at Jupiter Hills Country Club, designed by Tom's uncle, professional golfer George Fazio. At that time, it was ranked in the top twenty-five golf courses in the United States.

I had recently signed a six-month music contract to perform with my trio at The Flame supper club in North Palm Beach, owned by Peter Makris, a member of Jupiter Hills. Makris was so impressed with my trio's music and me that he invited me to join him and his golfing friends. I accepted but explained that I was a high-handicap player. He explained, "It won't matter." It did matter!

Prior to playing golf there, I had heard of the greatness of not only the golf-course design and layout Jupiter Hills possessed but of some of its members. Members like entertainers Perry Como and Bob Hope, Ford Motor Company CEO William Clay Ford, and insurance magnate Bill Elliot. That knowledge not only made me feel enthralled but quite nervous.

That Thursday morning, I got up, showered, gulped down two cups of coffee, threw my clubs into the car and sped up to Jupiter to meet my new boss and his pals for breakfast; before teeing it up. They were all exceptional gentlemen, and Peter was nice enough to pick up my breakfast. Additionally, he picked up the green fees, and just before entering the clubhouse at Jupiter Hills, he placed a brand-new box of *Titielist* golf balls in my hand as a gift, saying, "I hope you play well today and wish you good luck. You're going to be my partner!"

Having Peter Makris as my partner helped, as he had a reputation of being an excellent golfer. I found out at a later time that Peter once made a bet with the three other players of his foursome. The bet was that every time he'd shoot a score of seventy-nine or lower, each of them were to pay him one-hundred dollars. But, if he shot a score of eighty or higher, he would have to pay them all two-hundred dollars. I heard he shot fifty-six consecutive rounds of seventy-nine or lower! Nonetheless, that day he had a very heavy load in carrying me, the worst player of the day.

I was amazed and impressed with all of their golf skills and knowledge. Tom Fazio played a very good game, as did Andy Kallas (a junior partner in The Flame), and another player who was a doctor friend to all. They played for much high stakes then what I was used to, but they tolerated my small five-dollar side bet . . . which I lost.

Normally, a foursome is all that's permitted to play in the same group, but it being summertime, less members were playing the course, so we played part of the time as a five some, and later, Tom's uncle George joined us for a few holes, too. He made some awesome shots.

George Fazio played on the professional golfer's tour from the 1930's until 1959. He won the Canadian Open in 1946. Additionally, in 1950, he finished in a tie for first place with Lloyd Mangrum and Ben Hogan, in the United States Open at the Merion Golf Club in Pennsylvania. Ben Hogan won the tournament in an 18-hole playoff. I consider those to be examples of the very highest level of golf.

When I had started out the day, I was excited and hoped to play well, but then, seeing all of these "real" golfers play, I got that much more nervous. I never expected I'd be making a total fool out of myself playing the worst game of my life, on the toughest golf course I've ever played, in front of a fivesome witnessing it all. I was so bad it was hysterically humorous! They laughed, but I did, too.

Knowing I was a lousy golfer in advance, they all were having fun with me but kept coming after my partner, Peter. At one point, because I wasn't wearing a golf cap, my hair became messy from blowing in the wind. I overheard George Fazio whisper to Makris, "Who is this character you brought along with you today?" Between my lousy golf shots and looking like a jerk, I could understand such a comment. But, I smiled when hearing Peter quietly reply, "You're right! He's not a golfer. He is the bandleader at my club, and you should hear what he can do with a piano. He's fabulous!"

Finally, Peter said to me, just before I went to make a crucial shot that HAD to go over a gorgeous lake to its par three flag. It had to go there because of the joking by all of them, including Peter., who said to me, "Okay, I've been carrying you all day. Now, if you don't make a decent shot over this lake to the green, I'm going to talk a lot about you at the club tonight." I said, "Okay, Boss, I'll try my best."

I proceeded to put the ball exactly where they all figured it would go; dead center …in the lake! I said, with disgust, "I guess you'll be talking about me tonight!"

Makris, couldn't control his laughter and had difficulty getting out what he was trying to say. His reply finally came out amidst his chuckling, and snorting, "No, I'm not going to talk anymore. My mouth is too busy throwing up!"

We ALL went into hysterical laughter. They affectionately patted me on the back.

Tom Fazio said with total sincerity, "Roger, I'll make a deal with you. I'll teach you how to play golf if you teach me how to play piano." Peter and Andy nodded in agreement.

I wish I had made that deal with Tom. It was just before he came into national prominence as, arguably, the greatest golf-course designer of our time.

At The Flame one night, I told Tom Fazio that I was planning to build a small chip-and-putt hole in the back of my acre-and-a-half, Wellington, Florida home site. I asked him for a few tips on how I could do it. He picked up a paper cocktail napkin and sketched out the entire design of the hole I wanted, complete with a sand trap. He signed his name and dated it. I should have kept it and framed it.

Soon, Tom Fazio took over where his uncle George left off and became a true star of golf-course designing. His designs are not only great, they are unique. I've played several and was overwhelmed by his creative genius. In Lecanto, Florida, he took a worn out, former-mine quarry, totally useless except perhaps as a garbage dump, and made it blossom into "the Black Diamond," the most beautiful golf course I've ever played.

Tom Fazio has designed over 120 courses and has more golf courses ranked in the top 100 in the United States than anyone else in the business. Three times, Golf Digest Magazine proclaimed him the 'Best Modern Day Golf Course Architect.' In 1995, the Golf Course Superintendent's Association of America presented Tom Fazio with the highest recognition awarded to a golf course architect: "The Old Tom Morris Award. "

FYI, I built that chip-and-putt hole in my back yard, and often humorously bragged that "I am the owner of the World's Smallest Tom Fazio Designed-Golf Course!"

My building it did help my chip shots, but my wife Sal put my bragging into a more accurate light, when she proclaimed, "Our children, with their little pails and shovels actually play the sand trap better than Roger does!

Tom Fazio, a wonderful man, perfect gentleman, good friend, and world-class golf architect. I knew him "when" and I've been proud to know him "always."

Evel Knievel

Bob Allen, one of the patrons of the Flame Restaurant, brought a special guest into the club one night. The legendary daredevil, Evel Knievel sat with Bob's party in the back of the lounge. They listened, danced, and applauded throughout the evening. Taking a break, we were invited to join them. We enthusiastically accepted. Evel seemed not only down to earth, but very charming. He appeared to be more interested in our lives, music, and careers, than in himself.

We did get him to talk about some of his exciting daredevil feats and exciting events that had electrified the country and indeed, the whole world.

We all were having a really nice time at his table when we were rudely interrupted by a man who came over totally uninvited. "Hey, Knievel. . . . I heard you're an Elk."

"Yes. I used to participate."

"Well, you know we have our lodge right next door here. Why don't you come on over and say hello to the guys?"

Evel Knievel, Sal and Roger at The Flame

The daredevil tried to be as nice as he possibly could without hurting the man's feelings. He said, "I'd love to, but I happen to be a guest here. We're between rounds of a business meeting, so I don't think it will be possible. Thanks anyway."

I thought that he was both polite and pleasant. But this arrogant jerk had to push further. "Oh, come on, what's the big deal? Have you gotten so big that you can't spend some time with your brother members?" At this point, I realized how much abuse famous people sometimes must endure.

Knievel still kept his cool. "Well, I'm not a member anymore. I also think that it would be rude for me to leave my hosts and business associates. I'm going to have to decline your invitation. I want to thank you, though."

You'd have thought that would have sufficed, but not for this guy. His rudeness got worse. "Man, I can't believe you. You're really thinking that you're some sort of big deal, aren't you?"

By now, I couldn't control myself and felt compelled to say something before it escalated. "Look, Sir, this man happens to be a guest here. A GUEST! Do you understand? I think you're out of line."

"Hey, come on. What's the big deal? I only want him to come over there for ten minutes."

Evel must have had about as much as he could take of this guy, as had everyone else at the table. Here's what he said: "Okay, I'll tell you what. You want me for ten minutes of my time. I get $25,000 a minute when I'm working. Are you sure you have that kind of money? We're talking about a quarter of a million dollars!"

Well, that did it. It was just funny enough to get everyone laughing. Yet, it was direct enough to put the man in his place. It took the edge off the mounting tension. The rude man simply walked out of the club, and everyone at our table relaxed.

There was a moment, however, following Evel's response, when everyone stopped talking. I guess we were all thinking about what had just taken place. Nobody knew quite what to say. Evel Knievel certainly didn't deserve to be subjected to insults.

My wife, Sal, broke the quiet by asking, "Mister Knievel, could I ask you a question?" He smiled and nodded. She said softly and slowly, "Eh . . . could you give us an estimate on how much you would charge us . . . to have our picture taken with you?"

Everyone at the table went into hysterics. When it got quiet again, Knievel smiled and answered, "For a picture with you guys, I might consider paying YOU!"

We had our picture taken with him in the middle. Sal said that while we had our arms around each other, she couldn't help but feel that he was wearing a body cast all the way up to his shoulder blades. It finally dawned on us why he had looked so stiff while dancing to our music earlier in the evening.

After the pictures, he explained to us that in the course of his various daredevil jumps, and the falls that took place from failed attempts, he had broken almost every major bone in his body, some thirty-four, or thirty-five of them, to be more precise! He once fell off his motorcycle onto concrete, at 100 miles per hour! During his career, he caused enough damage to require fourteen operations.

Evel Knievel died in 2007. Besides being arguably the greatest daredevil of all times, he was an entertainer, a painter, and international icon. In his career, he attempted more than seventy-five ramp-to-ramp motorcycle jumps, and in 1974 he attempted but failed in jumping across Snake River Canyon, Idaho, in a steam-powered rocket. The dirt ramp that was built for that jump is still there and remains a tourist attraction.

Evel was sixty-nine years old when he died of pulmonary disease in Clearwater, Florida. In his obituary, a British Newspaper, *The Times*, described him as one of the greatest American icons of the 1970s. In 1999, he was inducted into the Motorcycle Hall of Fame. The *Guinness Book of World Records* lists Knievel as the survivor of the "most bones broken in a lifetime." He suffered more than 433 bone fractures from his daring feats.

What a price he paid for his fame and fortune. Yet, that evening at The Flame, he continued to smile . . . all night!

The PGA Champion is a Nine Handicap

One evening, Gardner Dickenson came into The Flame restaurant with his close friend, the 1957 PGA Champion, Lionel Hebert. As a 29-year-old, Hebert won that event in his first year on tour. The victory was worth $8,000 and clinched "Rookie of the Year" honors.

Gardner introduced us to each other, then told me that Lionel played the trumpet, "very well." Gardner implied that he would appreciate my letting Lionel "sit in" with the band, normally a frowned-upon practice. Too often, it led to all kinds of problems with other patrons, management and, sometimes, even the stand-in performer.

Lionel Hebert, "Sitting in."

If they were good players, we never minded, but we had to be discriminating and careful. I knew that Lionel was once one of the country's top golfers. I wasn't so sure, however, about Lionel's musical abilities.

At that time, I didn't know that back in Louisiana, at age fourteen, Lionel played trumpet in the Lafayette High School Band, where he also won the high school golf championship.

Later, he went to LSU as a music major. However, while studying music there, he always enjoyed playing golf with the members of the Tigers golf team, which included his older brother Jay, and his friend Gardner Dickinson. Jay and Gardner won the National Collegiate Championship together. Jay, like Lionel, also won the PGA Championship in 1960, and six other tour events.

315

I flat out asked Lionel how well he played the trumpet. He answered me in a fashion that I will always remember. He said, "Roger, I know you and the members of your band are all *scratch*!" That meant in golfing terms that my band members were "experts at music." He added, "I won't embarrass you. I'm about a 'nine' handicap on trumpet. I can play with just about anyone!"

Once again using a golfing term, but applying it to music, Lionel meant that his being a nine handicap meant that although he was not an expert, he was a very good musician. I let Lionel sit in, on that and subsequent occasions. And yes, he played to about a "nine." By contrast, I wish I were a 'nine' at golf!

The PGA was his only major championship, but Lionel Hebert won four other pro tournaments—including the Cajun Classic, played in his hometown, where he shot a total score of twelve-under-par.

His father Gaston Hebert, who served as sheriff of Lafayette Parish for eight years, died in 1955—two years before the first of his son's two PGA championships.

What an interesting and illustrious history that family had!

Lee Trevino

Golfer Bob Murphy had gained tremendous success on both the regular PGA Tour and, later on, the senior tour. For many years, he hosted a pro/am tournament at Delray

Dunes Country Club, in Delray Beach. The event was scheduled annually just before the Doral Open, in Miami. Many of Murphy's golfing pals used his one-day tournament as a "tune-up" for the bigger one. The field was stocked with some fine talent. It was a relaxing and fun-filled day for both golfers and spectators. Through the years, Murphy and friends raised a great deal of money for the local Bethesda Hospital.

I brought my son, Roger when he was thirteen years old. We took some nice photos of the various golfers, including Bob Murphy and the colorful player, Fuzzy Zoeller. I introduced my son to Gardner Dickenson and Lionel Hebert.

While roaming the course in search of the big names in the tournament, we spotted a huge spectator gallery. I said to Roger, "Son, a gallery that big means that it is either Jack Nicklaus or Lee Trevino who they're following." We were both excited as we approached the gallery. Sure enough, there was Lee Trevino in the middle.

He was his usual inimitable self, filled with humorous quips, quick one-liners, great golf shots and from time to time, even some golf tips for the duffers following him. I could see that Roger was impressed, so I said that I'd try to get a picture of the two of them together. The first window of opportunity that I had, I quietly and politely asked the golf legend if he would mind my taking his picture with my son a little later. He said, "Sure . . . I'll tell you, why don't we do it right now?" I was shocked and started getting nervous because it meant holding up

317

his golf game and this big gallery of four or five hundred people.

The next thing you know, I was looking through the lens of my camera at Lee Trevino, holding my son in a playful wrestling headlock. They were both smiling and posing as they waited for me to adjust the lens and shoot the picture. I was so startled by Trevino's graciousness that I remembered almost too late one of the basic rules of photography. The camera was facing into the sun, which was directly behind Roger and Trevino. I didn't mean to impose but I knew the shot would be over-exposed. I said to Lee, "Gee, Mr. Trevino, I'm sorry but the sun is facing right into the camera's eye, and the photo will be ruined. Maybe we can do this later, so I don't hold you up?"

I couldn't believe how patient he was because he courteously said, "No, it's all right. Do it now. We'll wait!"

I made my way into the crowd, behind where they both posed, while the crowd cleared the way for me to try again. Trevino then illustrated his ability to be clever and humorous at the drop of a hat. He said to me, "Well, that should make a better photograph. The other way, you might not be able to tell the difference between the picture of me and the one you take of Lee Elder." The gallery roared with laughter.

Later on, we caught up with Trevino's friend, golfer Lee Elder, who is black. I could see that Roger was confused. He stayed confused until we got the photographs back from the developing lab, and I showed him the photograph's negative.

I must define for younger readers who, in today's world, immediately view their photos without negatives. Negatives are film sheets on transparent plastic, which show the lightest and darkest areas in reverse. In those days, negatives were always enclosed along with the photo prints from the lab.

Finally, understanding Trevino's joke, Roger said, "Ohhhh, now I get it. All of the white people look black and all of the black people look white!"

Surprise, Surprise

Most of the time, Andy Kallas of the Flame Restaurant would personally deliver the band's paycheck to me. When he was out of town, I would pick it up at The Flame Enterprises offices.

For years, I dealt with the same really nice lady in the accounts payable department. She was always helpful. I always asked her how her son was doing with his golf lessons. I knew he was her pride and joy. I didn't really know how good he was, but I used to keep track of his progress. I honestly thought that he was "just another kid who had taken up the game of golf."

One day, she responded to my inquiry with an answer that opened my eyes. She said proudly, "Mark is doing great, thank you. I think he might turn professional one of these days!" I said with glee, "Oh, that's just wonderful Mrs. CALCAVECCHIA!"

As a teenager, Mark Calcavecchia won the Florida High School Golf Championship. In 1982, "Calc" joined the PGA Tour and in 1989 won The British Open by beating Wayne Grady and Greg Norman in a four-hole playoff. When awarded The Open's Claret Jug trophy, he joked, "How's my name going to fit on that thing?"

Mark Calcavecchia now plays on the Champions (Senior) Tour, but continues to live in Palm Beach Gardens, where The Flame Restaurant once existed.

RECORDS AND ACCOMPLISHMENTS

- Calcavecchia won thirteen times on the PGA TOUR, and in 1988 missed winning the Master's Tournament by a single stroke, finishing 2ND behind Sandy Lyle.
- He ranked in "World Golf Rankings Top 10," for 109 consecutive weeks, 1988 to 1991.
- In 2001, he won the Phoenix Open for the 3rd time, but at that time set the tour's scoring record by making 32 birdies in 72 holes. He finished the tournament at 28 under par.
- On July 25, 2009, in his 2nd round at the RBC Canadian Open, he shot nine consecutive birdies, setting another PGA Tour record.

Fred Couples

After a golf tournament in Texas, Fred Couples was making his way from the airport to his home in Wellington. It was getting late. I'm certain that he was tired from the tournament, where he had made a good showing, and of course, from the plane trip. Couples was traveling west on Southern Boulevard. As he approached State Road 7, he turned his pickup truck into the Chevron station on that corner.

My wife Sal and I, also tired, were on our way to our Wellington home too. We pulled into the gasoline bay next to the great golfer.

Unlike so many sports enthusiasts' wives, Sal has sat beside me and enjoyed various boxing, football, and athletic events. She has become rather adept, in not only the various sports rules but in the identification of sports figures. It was only natural that she immediately recognized him. You see, it was only two weeks earlier that we'd both practically worn ourselves out rooting for him when he won the world's most prestigious golfing event, *The Masters*.

Sal spotted him first, as he got out of his vehicle. She said to me, with excitement, "Honey, that's *Boom-Boom* Freddie Couples."

"It sure is!"

When I got out of my car to pump the gas, he was standing not five feet away from me, pumping his gas. I said to him, "Hello Fred."

"Hi."

"I thought that you played well this week."

"Yes, I did, thank you."

I went on to congratulate him on his winning The Masters, and said that we were very proud to have him as a resident of Wellington. He was very cordial, but we were all tired. We finally finished pumping our gas and went inside to the cashier. He paid first and, leaving, wished me a good evening.

As I was reaching for cash, I asked the lady behind the counter, "Do you know who that was?"

"No, I don't."

"That's Freddie Couples. He just won the Masters Golf Tournament two weeks ago."

"Aha? . . . TWELVE DOLLARS!"

While driving home, I told my wife, "Gee, that Freddie Couples is really something. Here's a guy that will make an absolute fortune, in advertising promotions, endorsements and purse money   and he's driving a pickup truck, instead of a Mercedes Benz. On top of that, he's pumping his own gas!"

When Fred's paternal grandparents immigrated from Italy, they changed the family name from "Coppola" to Couples.

His nickname is *Boom-Boom.* because of his long drives

RECORDS AND ACCOMPLISHMENTS

- To date, Fred Couples has enjoyed fifty-seven professional wins, with fifteen on the PGA Tour and eleven on the Champions.
- A former No.1 in World rankings for sixteen weeks.
- Named to the Ryder Cup 1989,1991,1993,1995, 1997.
- Player of the year 1991, 1992
- Winner of the Vardon Trophy 1991, 1992
- He won the Masters Tournament in 1992
- Leading Money winner 1992.
- Winner of the Players Championship twice 1984, 1996
- Winner of the Senior Players Championship 2011
- Winner of the Senior British Open 2012
- Won the Skins Game 1995, 1996, 1999, 2003 and 2004
- To date has won over three-million dollars and seventy-seven "skins" in eleven appearances.
- Nine top ten finishes in The Open
- Inducted in the National Italian-American Sports Hall of Fame, 2007
- Inducted into the World Golf Hall of Fame 2013

Roger Rossi

"Irish" Mickey McGrath

My now deceased, close friend Mickey McGrath, though not a celebrity, is a story worth telling. It has a touch of everything; boxing, humor, and life.

Mickey was an athlete who, if he had set his mind to it, could have probably mastered any sport he chose. He had many chances to be successful in both professional baseball and boxing. He later admitted he never enjoyed total success because he lacked discipline. Mickey never wanted to "work out." Whatever successes he enjoyed came strictly from his natural abilities. He played both shortstop and second base for the Washington Senators' minor league teams. In spite of his fine talent, he never made it into the major leagues. He preferred to have that extra beer, stay and tell that extra story, instead of working to perfect his game.

The same attitude he displayed in his baseball career, he echoed in his boxing career. He fought under the name "Irish" Mickey McGrath and had limited success. His official boxing record was not indicative of his ability. Unfortunately, he lost too many close ones. He had eighteen pro bouts, winning eight and losing six, with four draws. Mickey willingly admitted that he could have easily won nine of those losses and draws if he had only trained for them. None of his wins were by knockout.

Mickey's handlers were very qualified. In fact, one of them worked for the great Jake La Motta. They outlined specific training programs, which Mickey continually ignored! They would inevitably throw up their hands in disgust.

Mickey definitely had talent, though. Even without a work ethic, he was good enough to get on the same card, at Madison Square Garden, that featured Sugar Ray Robinson fighting Gene Fullmer in a championship bout.

One of the sports writers for the New York Daily News quipped, "Irish Mickey McGrath is fighting on the same card at Madison Square Garden that has the Robinson - Fullmer championship match. Now, he shouldn't be confused with any other Mickey McGraths like "Italian" Mickey McGrath, "Jewish" Mickey McGrath, or "Polish" Mickey McGrath!"

Sugar Ray Robinson lost a decision to Gene Fullmer on that January evening in 1957. Because Mickey did not train for his bout, he also lost by decision.

Mickey took all of his successes and failures with total nonchalance. In a relaxed stride, he even joked about his boxing career in much the same manner as Bob Uecker, who played for and later served as a Hall of Fame Broadcaster with the Milwaukee Braves baseball team. The highlight of Uecker's baseball career was when he hit a home run off Hall of Fame pitcher Sandy Koufax. Uecker joked that he felt that home run should have kept Koufax out of the Hall of Fame.

When people found out that Mickey used to be a pro-boxer, they'd inevitably ask about his record. He joked that he had 'one hundred and eighteen fights'. He went further, telling them, 'But unfortunately, only eighteen of those fights were with men. I lost ALL of the fights I had with women. Thank goodness, they were never in the boxing ring. They would 've counted against my record."

Mickey could be very believable when he was in fact, only joking. However, he could give you a charming little grin at the end of his tale, the kind that let you know 'you've been had.' He once said to me, "In one of my fights, they wanted me to take a dive in the third round."

I fell for it. "Oh no, Mick . . . really?"

He replied with absolute assurance, "Yeah . . . but I just couldn't do it." And then, with that telltale grin, he added, "The dirty bastard knocked me out in the second!"

One story that Mickey told quite often, he insisted was true. It seems that there was this guy by the name of Dodo Murphy, who lived in Mickey's hometown of Greenwich, Connecticut. Dodo evidently knew of Mickey's complacency in training for boxing matches. He offered a proposition to Mickey. He said that he could arrange for a local restaurant called The Legion to take out some advertising on a part of the young boxer's apparel. He told Mickey that the Legion would like to advertise "Eat at the Legion," but they would want the advertisement printed on the soles of Mickey's boxing shoes. Mickey told Dodo he thought the whole idea ridiculous. He said, "The only way that the Legion would get their money's worth out of an advertisement placed on my shoes would be if I were knocked out a lot."

Nodding affirmatively, with his eyes closed and eyebrows raised, Dodo replied, "Yeah, that's right! . . . I've been observing your training schedule!"

Mickey laughed nervously and ordered another beer. He did train for, and won, his next three fights, though!

Jack Nicklaus – Golfer of the Century

The Golden Bear was often in my audience. Although just about every person in the universe knows of his unbelievable golfing skills and records, most people would not know that he is the consummate gentleman.

In the late 70's, Jack and Barbara Nicklaus often came into the Flame. The restaurant was basically a driver and a six iron away from where they live. At least those are the golf clubs Jack Nicklaus might have used for that distance.

The restaurant always seated the Nicklaus party in the middle settee of the dining room. Most people who came and went in and out of that room would not even notice that he was there. Those who did notice him usually nodded and smiled, without bothering him. When someone imposed on him, perhaps for an autograph or small talk, he was understanding, considerate, courteous a model of etiquette.

In 1987, I was called by the Jupiter Beach Hilton to play for a banquet by Golden Bear International. That company, owned and operated by Jack Nicklaus, is headquartered just a few miles south of the Hilton. It is multifaceted, dealing in such areas as golf course design, golf equipment, sports management, financial services, and publishing. It is a good-sized company, and I was enthusiastic about playing for one of their "state of the company" shindigs.

Jack Nicklaus

The banquet was set in an "Island Clam Bake" theme. Upon entering, you immediately encountered the buffet line's self-service, with elaborate selections of seafood goodies. At the end of the buffet table was "the lobster shanty," where you could order lobster cooked to your specifications. The lobsters were already partially precooked in the various styles that guests were expected to order. The hotel would put the finishing touches on that order. You could then take your buffet plates, locate an available seat and return to the shanty for your lobster. Seating was on a first come-first served basis.

Jack and Barbara arrived, and I had just started to play and sing Jimmy Buffett's hit "Margaritaville." I couldn't help but notice how uncannily the lyrics aligned with what took place with the Nicklaus's seafood-buffet journey. They made their way past the buffet table and immediately got in line with the rest of the employees and guests.

"Nibbling on sponge cake. Watching the sun bake,
all those tourists covered with oil.
Strumming my six-string, on my front porch swing.
Smell those shrimp, they're beginning to boil."

The Nicklauses finally arrived at the lobster booth and placed their order. They turned to find a seat up front, near where I performed. Jack held the two larger plates, while Barbara had two smaller ones. They looked to the left, then to the right. There were no seats available. They again scanned the whole area and came to the same conclusion. No seats. While they stood there, in the middle of the room, not one employee or guest noticed. Everybody were too busy with their own lobsters and dinner. I'm afraid I was the only one in the whole room, besides Jack and Barbara, who realized that there was a slight seating problem for the Chairman of the Board and his wife. I couldn't very well stop playing the piano and try to fetch someone in authority, to rectify the problem for these very important people. So, while the two of them kept circling the room with their eyes, I continued singing.

"Wasted away again in Margaritaville.
Searching for my lost shaker of salt . . ."

As I played and sang Buffett's strains, I followed Jack and Barbara Nicklaus with my eyes. I watched them look for a place at the far end of the room, quite a long distance from where the speeches would take place. They turned and turned again to scan that part of the room. Nothing. Not one seat was available for the boss and his wife. As they might say in Margaritaville, "NADA!"

"I don't know the reason I've stayed here all season,
with nothing to show but this brand-new tattoo . . ."

Barbara made a slight gesture toward two seats standing against the wall, away from any table. Jack gestured that they should make another attempt at my side of the room. I continued the song, thinking that perhaps it was written with them in mind.

"I blew out my flip-flop. I stepped on a pop top.
'Cut my heel, had to cruise on back home.
But there's booze in the blender, and
soon it will render that frozen concoction
that helps me hang on."

Returning to my part of the room, they still had the same problem. And still no one else noticed. At one point, Jack looked over to me, perhaps because I was probably the only one looking at him. I rolled my eyes, letting him know that I was aware of his situation. He smiled and shrugged.

Finally, the maitre d' noticed and ordered the busboys and waiters to set up another table in the center of the room. At last, they were seated, in the best seats in the house. My music finished at just the right time, and most appropriately, with Jimmy Buffett's lyric . . .

"It's nobody's fault."

After finishing his dinner, Jack came to the piano. I presumed that he was going to make a speech, so I stopped playing. He quickly said, "No, don't stop. It sounds great."

"Oh, I just figured that you wanted to say a few words into my microphone."

"Yes, I do, but for now I just want to hear you play the piano."

With that said, he simply stood right in front of me, listening to what I do best, make music. As I was playing for him, I started up a conversation. "Mr. Nicklaus, you probably don't remember me. I'm Roger Rossi, and I used to play the piano for you all the time when I performed with my band *'Rossi and Company'* at the Flame."

"Yes, as a matter of fact, I do remember. You had that lovely dark-haired lady who sang with your band."

"Yes, that's my wife Sal. And I have to tell you something. She bought me your instructional video, *Golf My Way,* for Christmas. That tape has really helped me a lot. It's taken four or five strokes off my handicap."

Jack Nicklaus replied, "Roger, the way that you play the piano, you don't need golf." He smiled and added, "If you want to know the truth, you should market your OWN video . . . on piano playing."

I quipped, "Sure . . . I could call it . . . *"Piano My Way!"*

When I finished the song, he stood there and loudly applauded me. Most of the people in that section of the room joined in, following his lead. I thought, "I can't believe this. Here is the world's greatest golfer taking time to recognize my talents."

However, it's always bothered me. Jack Nicklaus was born in 1940, 2½ weeks after I was born; and Lee Trevino was born 1939, 4½ weeks before I was born. I mean, c'mon, the three of us are basically the same age. How come they're golfing legends, and my golf shots mostly stink up every golf course I play? I guess should've spent more time at the driving range, and less at the keyboard!

Until the day of this writing, Jack Nicklaus is still considered the *Greatest Golfer of All Time*. I predict that will prevail for many years to come. Albeit, Tiger Woods, considered the greatest golfer of this era, has been threatening to take Nicklaus's overall title away. Well, at least that's what all of the sports intelligentsia have been predicting and printing in our newspapers, ad-nauseum, ever since he was a child. However, at this writing, Woods has been stalled out at winning "only" fourteen major-tournaments. Meantime, Jack has eighteen major trophies resting on his mantle, and wasn't voted "The Golfer of the Century" for nothing!

Maybe someday I will make that video Jack Nicklaus suggested. But for now, it's more than enough to have included such a fabulous sports icon as Jack Nicklaus in my book!

I could go on forever about the many aspects of this remarkable man, like his great golf course designing, Ryder Cup history, business successes and last but not least his wonderful family and parenting with his lovely wife Barbara. They're the very best!

Herein are just a few of Jack Nicklaus's awesome accomplishments:

RECORDS AND ACCOMPLISHMENTS

- Voted Golfer of the Century in 1988 by the PGA,
- Won more major championships (18) than any other player.
- He also came in second-place nineteen times, and third-place nine times.
- In his career, Jack had 116 professional wins and 73 PGA Tour wins
- He shares the record with Arnold Palmer, for most consecutive years (17) with at least one tour victory.
- At 46, he was the oldest player ever to win the Masters, in 1986.
- At The Masters, Nicklaus holds the record for most wins with six, which is two more than Arnold Palmer, and Tiger Woods.

- Nicklaus won The (British Open Championship) three times, and was runner-up a record seven times. From 1970 to 1980, Nicklaus had a record eleven straight top-five finishes.
- At The U.S. Open Nicklaus shares the record (4) for most wins with Willie Anderson, Bobby Jones and Ben Hogan. He was runner-up a record seven times. 1966 to 1980 he never finished worse than sixth.
- At the PGA Championship, Nicklaus holds the record with Walter
- Hagen for most wins with 5. Nicklaus was runner-up four times.

Joanne Carner

My path crossed JoAnne Carner's on many occasions. My wife and I were once seated next to her and her husband at the Palm Beach Kennel Club. We conversed in between eating dinner and placing various wagers on our dog selections. Another time as I warmed up at the driving range of the Palm Beach National Golf and Country Club in Lake Worth, Florida, I looked up to see her hitting balls only ten feet away. I've also been seated at a table at the Wellington Club right next to her on two separate occasions. One of those turned out to be a story to tell.

I used to play golf with a good friend, Al Weil, who worked in the pro shop of the former JDM Country Club, now called Ballenisles Country Club. Al was a strong 10-handicap player. His short game was fantastic.

Al and I had just finished playing a round of golf at the Wellington West golf course. We decided to have our cocktails at the main club, where I was a member. We took a seat at one of the cocktail tables. The bar area was sparsely populated. There were only nine patrons in the entire room. They were Al and I, three other men seated at the bar, a middle-aged couple seated at a table, and seated directly behind Al, two ladies.

Al and I used to goad each other into debates, always in fun. After we received our cocktails, he started in. "Gee, what happened to you out there today? You played golf like a gorilla." I retorted, "You're right. I was driving my ball abnormally past yours all day! How come you hit the ball like such a sissy?"

"A sissy? . . . I beat you! I absolutely devastated you all day. You just couldn't keep up. There's no other way to put it, you were crushed . . . whipped . . . creamed!"

"Al, come back to life. You're dreaming! You nipped me at the final hole of the match. I would hardly call that being creamed!" We both laughed, but I didn't stop there. I went back on the assault. "You are trying to evade my original question, though."

"What's that?"

"Why do you hit the ball like such a sissy?"

"Get out of here. I hit the ball just like Jack Nicklaus today!"

"Al, you hit the ball just like Jack Nicklaus's great-great grandmother. As a matter of fact, I bet she could have outdriven you today! I have no doubt in my mind that she would have beaten you, too!"

"A woman? You're suggesting that a woman could beat ME at golf?" .

I looked around the club and saw that there were three women in the place. I also noticed that the two ladies seated directly behind Al were none other than touring professional Donna White, whom I knew, and Hall of Famer JoAnne Carner. Donna used to hold an annual pro/am charity golf tournament in her name. She was probably discussing details about that event with JoAnne.

I figured I'd take advantage of the situation. I said to Al, "I bet that you couldn't beat two-thirds of the women golfers in the country!" He once again suggested that my statement was nothing less than hogwash. I went further. "I'll bet you a hundred bucks that you couldn't beat two thirds of the women right in this room!"

Al asked, "How could we possibly find that out?"

I leaned past him and said aloud, "Hi, Donna, how are you doing?"

She replied, "Hello Roger. How are things at the Rotary Club?"

"Great. Thank you. By the way, this is a friend of mine, Al Weil. He runs the pro shop at JDM Country Club."

I turned to Al and said, "Al, you've heard of Donna White on the LPGA Tour, haven't you?"

Before Al could respond, JoAnne Carner turned and faced us both. I said with added glee, *"Big Mama!* How are YOU, JoAnne?" She kind of recognized me and said politely, "Well . . . hello. How are you?"

"Really good, thank you. Nice to see you again!"

Again, I turned to my buddy Al and said, "Al, this is Donna White and Joanne Carner!"

Al said humbly, "I'm honored to meet you both!"

I said to the ladies, "We just finished playing over at Wellington West."

Donna asked, "How did you play?"

"Well, let's put it this way. I beat Al out of a hundred bucks today! Didn't I . . . Al?"

I could hear my pal clearing his throat. Before he could answer, I said loudly, "That's okay, Al, I'll call it even if you buy the four of us a round of drinks!"

My friend sighed briskly and said, "That's easy!"

Later, Al whispered in my ear, "You got me good! I almost died when I saw Donna White and JoAnne Carner sitting there!"

A few years later, my pal did die. It was ironic. He birdied the last two holes at the General Course of the PGA, in Palm Beach Gardens. Yet, he didn't have enough energy to walk back to his golf cart. He had to be carried. Later, we found out that he had a bad heart.

As a lady golfer, JoAnne Gunderson Carner was in a class of her own. She dominated women's amateur golf. JoAnne turned pro at age thirty. She had a great career having forty-nine victories. Her husband, Don Carner was her coach and business manager.

JoAnne Carner was truly a superstar. I was thrilled to have had encounters with her.

JOANNE CARNER'S RECORDS AND ACCOMPLISHMENTS

- Won five U.S. Women's Amateur titles.
- In 1969, while still an amateur, she won an LPGA Tour event, The Burdine's Invitational.
- Was the first person and the only woman to ever to win three different United States Golf Assoc. championship events: The U.S. Girls Junior, U.S. Women's Amateur, and U.S. Women's Open Championship.
- Won the U.S Woman's Open in 1971 and 1976.
- Was the LPGA's leading money winner in 1974, 1982 and 1983.
- Inducted into the World Golf Hall of Fame
- Received the highest honor given by the USGA, the Bob Jones Award, for distinguished sportsmanship.
- Joann was the second LPGA player to win over $1 million in career earnings.
- She was the oldest player to make a cut on the LPGA Tour, age sixty-five.

DONNA HORTON WHITE'S RECORDS AND ACCOMPLISHMENTS

- A four-time collegiate medalist, at the University of Florida.
- 1978, was inducted in The University's Athletic Hall of Fame as a "Gator Great."
- She played on the LPGA Tour for fifteen years (1977 to 1992) winning three Tour events.
- Her best finish at an LPGA major was a tie for second in the 1982 U.S. Women's Open.
- She now runs golf operations for Palm Beach County, Florida.

Bill Parcells

One evening in early 1990, at the end of my wedding reception gig at the Jupiter Beach Resort, the loathsome chore of moving my equipment from the banquet room into my van was made considerably easier. Sal, my vocalist wife, collected microphones and wires, and I ferried some heavier equipment to the front entrance. As I crossed the lobby, sitting there all by himself was none other than the great NFL coach, Bill Parcells—nicknamed "The Big Tuna." It was quite late, and there was no one else in the lobby, except for the man behind the registration counter. I presume that the coach was waiting for a taxi, or somebody, to pick him up. He lives in nearby Jonathan's Landing, a very beautiful and exclusive section of Jupiter.

Having been born and raised in New York, I always was a *Giants* (the football team) fan. So, I figured I'd take advantage of the situation and possibly get some inside information right from the horse's mouth. Besides, I'd have considered myself rude were I to constantly walk by him without talking to him. So, I said to him, "Hey, Coach, howharya?"

I tried to sound as New Yorkish as possible, although my New York accent had diminished a lot in the previous two decades living in Florida.

He nodded and smiled warmly, acknowledging that I had recognized him. "I'm feeling really good, thank you."

I continued my roadie chores, having an intermittent conversation with him in the process. While moving my speakers out to my van, I asked, "Have you been over to Alex Webster's?" (A sports bar and grille in nearby Tequesta, owned by another former head coach and former Giants fullback.

"Oh, yeah," the Coach replied. "I've been there a few times. It's a nice place."

I really wanted to talk some nitty-gritty football stuff, but I just didn't have the time to spare. I asked only, "Tell me, Coach, what kind of a year do you expect the Giants to have?"

Enthusiastically, he raised his eyebrows. "We're going to have . . . a GREAT year." He considered. "We may even WIN IT ALL!"

"Hey, SUPER! Good luck, coach!" In retrospect, I couldn't have replied any better had I thought about it for an hour. Bill Parcells and his New York Giants, who had won Super Bowl rings by whipping the Denver Broncos a few years earlier, went on to win the 1991 Super Bowl. They beat the Buffalo Bills, 20-19! After they won, I thought back to when Coach Parcells had predicted victory to me, long before the football season had even started!

<u>RECORDS AND ACCOMPLISHMENTS</u>

- Bill Parcells was head coach in the NFL for the New
- England Patriots, New York Jets, Dallas Cowboys,
- and the New York Giants
- With the New York Giants, he won two Super Bowls.
- He also led the New England Patriots to the big game, but they lost to the Green Bay Packers.
- Parcells is the only coach in NFL history ever to lead four different teams to the playoffs and three different teams to a conference championship game.
- He was voted into the Professional Football Hall of Fame in 2013.

Rick Mears

In December 1991, I received a telephone call from Rick Mears' wife, Chris. She said, "I'm calling because my brother Mark is getting married. My husband Rick and I have offered to have the reception at our home in Jupiter. Roger, you and your wife, Sal, come very highly recommended by several people I know, including my own mother, Mrs. Bowen. She has seen you perform on several occasions."

I said, "Well, please thank your mother for me. It was nice that she recommended us. But did you say that you're

. . . Rick Mears' wife? . . . Like in Rick Mears . . . the race car driver?"

"Yes, that's right. Why, are you a racing fan?"

"Well . . . eh . . . not exactly, but I do know who Rick Mears is. Gosh, who doesn't? He's considered one of the country's all-time greats."

I didn't want her to think that I was basically lost when it came to the subject of race-car driving, which in fact I was. So, I interjected what little knowledge I did have, or at least, thought I had.

"Gee, he's won the Indianapolis 500 at least three or four times, hasn't he?"

She said, with obvious pride, "Yes, that's right. He's won it four times. You must be a fan to know THAT, Roger."

I silently pumped a clenched fist. I didn't know where I had read or heard that bit of information on Mears, but I was certainly pleased with myself when it surfaced correctly.

"We're having the reception on the evening of February twenty- second. Are you available?"

I had to think quickly. The twenty-second of February also happens to be my oldest daughter's birthday. We'd have to push Bonny's celebration to Sunday that year, instead of Saturday. I said, "Yes, we are available. But it's going to cost you dearly!"

"And how much is that?"

"Well, above and beyond the normal fee for our music performance, I'm tagging on a request for a Rick Mears autograph!"

She chuckled and said, "Consider it done. As a matter of fact, I'll make sure that it's done on one of Rick's racing photographs. How's that?"

"Wow . . . that's great!"

Around four pm on February the twenty-second, Sal and I tried to make our way through the typically terrible traffic that characterizes Palm Beach County. I hate driving in South Florida!

We started on State Road 80, a thoroughly abysmal thruway. The State of Florida and its licensed drivers have not yet decided whether this roadway should be treated as an old-aged retirement facility in the passing lane, an alternative site for the Daytona Speedway, or a stage for CNN Television's *Crossfire* debates that would surely result from the first two options!

I once witnessed a young lady using her rear-view mirror to brush her hair, as she filled in that week's lottery card, while driving at least 70 MPH in a 45-mph zone!

Most people who drive on State Road 80, misconstrue the Right-of-way signs to mean, "right-away!"

Since we had to spend the next thirty-five or forty perilous minutes trying to reach Chris and Rick Mears' home, I figured that I'd use the time to give Sal a "crash course" (pun intended) on some auto racing trivia I had recently learned myself. If we were given the opportunity to converse with the legendary driver, I didn't want us to respond like total dunces.

"Sal, are you at all familiar with auto racing?"

At that exact moment, some thirty-year-old in a high-powered Porsche, steering wheel in one hand, a cellular phone in the other, cut us off. He continued speeding down the road, ready to aim his vehicle at other potential victims.

"No, I really don't know too much about auto racing; only what I see!"

"I mean, have you heard of people like Bobby Rahal, Emerson Fittipaldi and Mario Andretti? They're all race-car drivers, Honey. Are you familiar with them?"

"Sure," she said. Zip . . . zip . . . zip. Three cars went by us doing at least 80 miles per hour. "I think they just drove by us. They must be on their way to Rick's house!"

Not to be outdone by Sal's sarcastic humor, I interjected, "No, Sal, that old hag driving that last car was not Mario Andretti. She just thought she was. Did you see the way she held her middle finger in the air as she sped by us? She was trying to tell us that she's number one!"

We finally got on to Interstate 95. It was not really any improvement from the aggravation, abuse and frustration of State Road 80. Most drivers must have thought that the "95" stood for the speed limit. Almost everyone ignored the 55 MPH limit posted in those days, except those who crawled at 45 MPH in the passing lane. Those drivers mistook I-95 to mean THEIR AGE!

We finally arrived, unscathed, at the Mears' residence. We were greeted by a nice, helpful gentleman. I said, "Hello, we're Sal and Roger Rossi. We're doing the music for the wedding." He responded cordially with, "Well, hello. Do you need a hand with your equipment? Perhaps I can help you with some of it!"

"No, that's okay, thanks. I would appreciate it, though, if you could find out where the Mearses would like us to set up."

"That will be easy enough. You can set up around the back, by the swimming pool. And, by the way, Roger . . . I'm Rick Mears!"

"Oh, wow! I'm really happy to meet you!" I said with enthusiasm.

"Can I get you anything? Extension cords, chairs . . . anything to drink?"

"Yes, please. I could use a couple of aspirins and a glass of water. The traffic was horrendous."

He left, returning with my little white tablets of relief. "Which way did you come?"

"State Road 80 to I-95."

"You don't have to say another word. Now I know why you have a headache. That I-95 is probably the most dangerous road in the world!"

I commented to my wife, "And this is coming from a guy who makes his living driving 200+ miles per hour!"

Mears explained, "That's true, but racing conditions are more controlled. Race drivers are professionals who know exactly what they're doing. Many people on I-95 really don't have control of their cars."

"You can say that again. Half of them should be put into straitjackets and committed to a mental institution . . . because they don't have control of their brains!"

Our saxophonist, Ron Nordwell, arrived, my headache left, and we proceeded to make music. Mark and Kelly's ceremony went very nicely. We started their reception by playing *Wind Beneath My Wings* for their first dance.

Two weeks later, we received a photograph of Chris and Rick Mears with his pit crew. It was obviously taken immediately after winning one of his Indy 500 races. The crew is holding the huge, Indianapolis 500 Borg-Warner Trophy, while Rick is holding, of all things, a glass . . . of milk! I guess nobody could find champagne. Both Chris and Rick autographed the photo with a cordial note of thanks for the music we played at their home. It hangs proudly in my office.

The following May, during a practice session for the 1992 Indy 500, Rick's back-up car flipped upside down. Despite a broken foot, he got back in his racecar the next day.

Rick Mears announced his retirement from racing at the end of that same year.

Mears completed his fabulous career having won The Indianapolis 500 in 1979, 1984, 1988 and 1991. The four wins at Indianapolis represent a record that he shares with Al Unser, Sr. and A.J. Foyt.

Confirming that acorns don't fall too far from the oak tree; Rick's nephew Casey is a successful race car driver with the Nascar Racing Series. Casey is the son of Indy Car and off-road veteran Roger Mears.

Roger Rossi

Jack Nicklaus is The Best Man

In early September 1992, Jack Nicklaus was the best man at the wedding of a close friend of his. The affair took place at the famed golfer's home, with the ceremony at the main house and the reception directly across the street at the guesthouse. I fronted the band at the reception.

I was there early to set up all of the speakers, microphones, amplifiers and my keyboards. I was very concerned about the weather; it had already started to drizzle lightly. Dining would occur right on Jack's tennis courts, covered, and protected from the rain by a huge tent. The band was to set up next to that tent, under the guesthouse overhang.

The band and the guests were protected from the rain. However, between us was an exposed gap where the dancing was to take place. I was wary about the setup. If it were to rain heavily, no guests would be able to hear us, much less dance to our music. Unless, that is, they were to drench themselves. I knew that playing the piano keyboard would be an especially difficult thing for me to do . . . with my fingers crossed!

Jack Nicklaus, the Best Man
Photo by Michel Sabourin – At the Nicklaus residence

By the time I'd finished setting up the equipment, the rest of the band had arrived. It was already raining a bit harder. Thank goodness, we were able to get the bride and groom's "First Dance" completed in time. Then, we were able to get a lively dance set going, with all the guests coming out on the dance floor. At that point, the storm broke out heavily, with intervals of thunder and lightning. We had to shut off all our electronic equipment and pull the plugs from the electric outlets. One good jolt could ruin thousands of dollars' worth of music equipment, not to mention the not the danger to anyone holding an instrument.

We took a break and went into the guesthouse, where we relaxed until the rain finally stopped and we got back to work. Turning on our equipment again, we were back in business. Now we had to be very careful where we stepped. A few puddles of water had formed on the patio surface, where we performed. None of us were particularly keen on getting zapped. It really doesn't ease the pain, if you happen to be electrocuted at Jack Nicklaus's house. Once you're dead, you're dead!

We were cranking out some good rock 'n roll for the reception guests, when Jack interrupted. I had known and previously played for Jack Nicklaus on many occasions, and because we are the same age, it wasn't disrespectful for either of us to address the other using a first name. He didn't mind, and certainly neither did I. He said, "Roger, I'd like to make the wedding toast, if I could."

"Sure, Jack. You can use my microphone. Just hand-hold it, and please be careful that you don't step in any of these puddles!"

I got everyone's attention, then I handed the microphone to the golf legend. Immediately, he started moving into the middle of a huge puddle. I quietly warned him, "Jack! You're standing in water!"

"Oh, that's okay. Don't worry about it."

Before I could say another word, he launched into his champagne toast to the bride and groom. I stood there watching and listening, while my heart pounded away at a mile a minute! I'm sure he thought I was warning him only of getting his feet wet. To a seasoned golfer, that's no big deal! However, because of the microphone being connect to an electrical system, he was risking electrocution and death. My lips puckered to warn him again, but I knew I'd have to interrupt his beautiful wedding toast. So, I pulled my lower lip into my mouth and bit on it, quietly praying.

Evidently, God heard my prayers. The toast concluded without any bodily harm coming to Jack Nicklaus. Perhaps God is also one of Jack's fans, and He has gotten as much of a thrill seeing him hit a golf ball, as the rest of us have!

To this day, I'm sure Jack Nicklaus doesn't even know how close he came to his demise. I'm thankful that the next morning, I did not see his name linked with mine on the front-page headlines of the *Palm Beach Post*.

JACK NICKLAUS ELECTROCUTED MAKING TOAST!
PIANIST ROGER ROSSI HELD ACCOUNTABLE.

Roger Rossi

PART SIX: The Musicians

Woody Herman
Errol Garner
Cy Coleman
Liberace
Itzhak Perlman
Chuck Mangione
Vladimir Bakk

Woody Herman

Working with Gene Stridel, I often came in contact with the big-band leader, clarinetist and alto saxophonist, Woody Herman. Gene's manager at the time was Herman Dressel, formerly connected with Mercury Records. Hermie, a musician who performed with such entertainers as Paul Anka, Frankie Avalon, and Little Richard, later managed such artists as Dionne Warwick, Johnny Tilitson, B.J. Thomas and Woody Herman. Additionally, Woody had a theatrical and musicians' booking agency called Woodrow Music, Inc. Hermie would often book us on engagements that came through that office. We found ourselves at the same hotel and nightclub circuits that Woody worked. Often, having finished at our engagement, we would go "down the block" to listen to his fabulous band. Likewise, Herman returned the compliment many times, visiting our performances. When he did, he always brought a couple of his young band members with him. They were always great musicians.

Woody kept changing the name of his band. He called his first band *The First Herd,* then *The Second Herd.* Later on, he had *The Third Herd,* and also *The Thundering Herd.* I listened to him and his band so often, it got to the point that I didn't know which Herd I heard. I finally started referring to his band as simply, *The Herd,* or *The Woody Herman Band.*

Woody was a fine musician. The great Russian composer, Igor Stravinsky, once wrote a composition dedicated to Woody Herman and his The Herd. It is called the "Ebony Concerto," and Herman debuted the work at Carnegie Hall, March 25, 1946 under the guidance of the composer.

As a bandleader, Herman excelled. He had a great talent for putting together a fine blend of sectional sounds. Adding to that blend was the tremendous virtuosity that the musicians individually exhibited. The icing on the cake was that his arrangements were the best of the best with Neal Hefti writing many of them. Together, all of those things made Herman's bands rate as high as any.

If (by enormous stretch of imagination) God were to tell me—and mind you, this is all hypothetical—"Roger, you've made it to heaven. You may bring any five of your favorite big bands with you, to enjoy for the rest of eternity."

I would tell God that I wanted Glenn Miller, Stan Kenton, Artie Shaw, Tommy Dorsey . . . and Woody Herman. I could listen to those bands forever, and never tire of the experience. Their taste and creativity were *heavenly* indeed.

One summer evening in 1962, Woody Herman visited Gene and my trio. It was the last time that I would personally see him. We were booked at Mike Roth's, a fine jazz showcase in Schenectady, New York. Gene and I had performed there on many previous occasions. We always seemed to follow outstanding big names that had been booked there the previous week.

One time, we followed the great saxophonist, Coleman Hawkins who left to tour Russia with Benny Goodman. On other occasions, we followed jazz performers like Teddy Wilson, Carmen McRae and Bobby Hackett. The club was accustomed to having polite jazz fans in the audience. They were always very enthusiastic about our performances, too. When Gene sang, there was always the aura of being in the presence of a future recording star. Gene was on his way up, and everyone seated out there knew it.

The evening started out normally. The first two shows ended with terrific ovations. Columbia recording artist, Dakota Staton dropped by to say hello, and to give a listen. I thought she was wonderful, not only as a jazz singing stylist, but as a person.

Next to Ella Fitzgerald, Dakota was my wife's favorite female singer. Sal had not come to the club with me that evening, so I thought about calling and telling her to come meet Miss Staton. I dismissed the idea because of the hour. I knew she was already asleep.

Sure enough, Woody Herman came in too, with four of his band members. I grabbed a phone and called Sal. "Honey, I'm sorry if I woke you up, but I think that you should get yourself freshened up and take a cab down here. The place is filling up with some VIPs."

"Okay, if you say so. I'll be there in about an hour."

"I love you, Baby. I'll see you then."

Sal arrived toward the end of our third and final show.

I introduced her to Dakota immediately. Sal was impressed. We didn't want to disturb Miss Staton for too long, as she was with several people. We lucked into an available cocktail table right next to Woody Herman and his musicians. As a matter of fact, when we sat down, Sal's right shoulder almost touched Woody's right shoulder. It placed the three of us in a triangular position, although he was seated at his own table.

As I ordered cocktails, it dawned on me that Sal had never met Woody Herman. It went even further than that. Sal, here just a few years from England . . . had never even heard of him. She was a jazz fan, and if you were to ask her about Ted Heath or Johnny Dankworth and Cleo Laine, she knew all there was to know about them. She had even sat in and sung with Johnny Dankworth one evening back in London. But she'd never heard of Woody Herman! That made us even, because I'd never heard of Ted Heath until Sal told me how fine his band was.

I should have thought about this when I said to Sal, loudly enough for Woody to hear, "Honey . . . guess who's sitting right next to you?" I pointed and gestured.

She quietly asked, "Who?"

I said with admiration and pride, "Woody Herman!" I know for sure that he heard me.

Sal inquired, "Who is he? I never heard of him?"

I guess that Herman didn't care to be a party to the education of this young lady, who presumably came from another planet. He simply smiled and turned away, leaving me with the teaching task.

Later, when the club's activities were winding down, we had about a dozen people remaining in the room, including the bartender and waitress, Woody Herman and his band members, Gene Stridel, my trio, Sal and me. We were all standing, gradually saying goodbyes. Gene was talking to Woody and I was in my glory, talking to his quintessential musicians. We all stood close to each other, Sal right next to me.

She nudged me and politely asked, "Honey, it's really getting late. Do you think we could go?"

"Sure, Sal, in a minute."

I continued talking and a few moments later, Sal said to me, "Honey, we really have to go. I don't feel too well."

I knew that Sal wasn't even slightly inebriated, because she'd had only one cocktail. I took her request very lightly, and delayed further. "Sure Honey, in a second." I continued our musicians' conversation.

A moment later, she said to me, "Honey . . . I . . ." With that short utterance, her eyes rolled back and she passed out fortunately into my arms. I carried her to the other side of the club and got her some water. She came to and was extremely embarrassed. "I just don't know what happened."

I said, nervously, "You fainted, Honey. Are you okay? Do you know where you are?"

"Yes. We're at Mike Roth's. We were talking to Woody Herman and his musicians. I hope they don't think I'm drunk! Please, let me go back and explain to Mr. Herman that I am NOT AT ALL drunk."

"Don't worry about what Woody Herman thinks. I'm sure that Gene will tell him that you aren't a heavy drinker. I think that it's more important that I get you home immediately, so you can get a good night's sleep. Furthermore, Sal, first thing tomorrow, I'm going to make a doctor's appointment for you."

It probably did cross Woody Herman's mind that I was not only married to a dingbat (who had never even heard of him), but also to a drunk! In any event, I did get Sal home and to sleep. The next day we scheduled an appointment with a local M.D.

After two appointments, Sal told me, "Well, he found out why I fainted."

This time I listened to her with both ears and eyes wide open. Sal announced with a smile, "He said that people often become faint . . . when they're pregnant!"

"WHAT? . . . Are you pregnant?"

"Yes, I am!"

"Is he positive?"

"Yes, Honey. That's the reason he wanted me to come back for the second visit. They had to run tests to be sure. I'll be delivering our baby somewhere around the third week of February."

"Oh Sal . . . that's WONDERFUL!" We both cried tears of joy as we hugged and kissed each other.

Unfortunately, I never saw Woody Herman again. He died in 1987; but I suspect that if God likes big band music, Woody is playing a Command Performance, at this precise moment . . . with my other four favorites. I'd bet that Gene who died in 1973, is there too!

Erroll Garner

In 1967, while performing at the famous New York nightspot, The Living Room, I unknowingly met and talked with the great jazz pianist, Erroll Garner.

I was between floorshows, which I played with a very talented comedian by the name of Marge Leslie. As I sat at the bar, having a Coke, it started to get busy again, in anticipation of the second show.

A distinguished-looking black gentleman came in and stood behind me, as no seats were available. The bartender came over and asked the man if he wanted a drink, and left to mix it. I felt that, as somewhat of an employee, it was only right that I give up my seat to this paying customer. I stood up and offered my stool.

"Here, Sir, why don't you sit down? I'm sure that cocktail will taste a lot better."

He politely declined. "Oh no, that's all right. You stay there."

"No, that's okay Sir, I'M a pianist. I sit all of the time. YOU sit!"

The man thanked me warmly. He took my vacated stool, while I went to the other end of the bar. The bartender brought him his beverage, then hurried to where I stood. He asked me, "Do you know who that is you just gave your seat to?"

"I don't think so. Let me take another look at him." The bartender stepped out of the way, as I looked at the guy one more time. Then it clicked. "Oh wow! That's Erroll Garner, isn't it?"

"Yup! He's one of the world's greatest jazz pianists."

In the 50's and 60's, there wasn't a jazz pianist enjoying more popularity than Erroll Garner.

He was one of the most popular artists in the Columbia Records stable, and his albums sold like hotcakes.

Erroll Garner

He performed on all kinds of television shows, and his concerts were always sold out. His live recording of *Concert by the Sea* is one of my all-time favorite record albums, as is his hit album recording, *The Most Happy Piano.* They are both simply superb.

Back then Errol Garner was one of the most recognized and imitated jazz pianists anywhere. In those days, you probably could have gone into some lost alleyway bar in Timbuktu, and if there was somebody playing a piano in the place, he or she would more than likely know how to play Erroll Garner's style. French jazz critics referred to him as "the Picasso of the piano," and "the man with forty fingers." Later, in 1971, the Republic of Mali issued a postage stamp in honor of this great musician.

Garner played a unique, solid style of piano. It was full of strong and expanded chordal tones, in the left hand, that laid down a percussive and continual pulse. Simultaneously, the right hand played either a collage of block chords in a staccato fashion, or a movement of singular notes. The overall presentation could be either a slow and feeling tempo, or on other occasions, exhibit his lightning fast and furious, yet impeccably clean technique.

Erroll Garner's improvisational genius went far beyond his style. He was tremendously creative. He never seemed to play any meaningless notes — they were all important! He was, in a word, GREAT! He was also a fine composer, best known for the ever popular, *Misty,* which was a great hit recording for *Johnny Mathis.* What made all of this so very amazing was that he was totally untutored in the piano.

What I said to Erroll Garner finally dawned on me, "I'M a pianist. I sit all of the time. YOU sit." I became red with embarrassment. I hope he realized that I simply did not recognize him. I prayed that he never thought I implied that "Erroll Garner is not a pianist!"

I returned to the bar to apologize for not recognizing him. I was too late. He had already gone. Who knows? Maybe he did mull over in his mind exactly what I said to him and HAD to leave because he was starting to go into uncontrollable hysterics!

Cy Coleman

In 1967, I took a summer gig at a club in Southampton, Long Island, called The Hansom House. Jonathan Jakes, who owned the club, wanted me to feature a mixture of jazz and rock music. I worked with drummer Jim Murphy and bassist Ron Gruberg.

Most of the time, we played to a mixture of (probably) one-third white customers, one-third black customers and one-third Shinnecock Indians. For the most part, we "got down" every night.

Four things about that summer were important enough to remember. For one thing, the waiters and waitresses at the Hansom House were the absolute worst group of amateurs with whom I have ever worked. The place always bustled with business, but didn't make any money, because nobody ever got served! Of course, the band got blamed!

Another thing that I remember about the summer of 1967 was that I casually introduced Jim Murphy to Pat, a girl I had just happened meet a few moments earlier. He ended up divorcing his wife and marrying Pat!

Cy Coleman and Friends – Southampton 1967

I also remember being invited to Yankee Stadium for Carl Yastrzemski Day. I went with about seventy or eighty people from Southampton. Yastrzemski, a Boston Red Sox player who had won the American League Triple Crown Award that year, came from Southampton. I was the only one in the group who rooted for the Yankees. I was very saddened to see Mickey Mantle hurt himself trying to stretch a single into a double. He needed assistance to walk off the field. "The Mick" was plagued with injuries for the remainder of his career.

Memory number four is of playing a cocktail party at a Southampton residence to honor the composer Cy Coleman. When the hostess called me, she said, "I've

365

heard you play the piano at the Hansom House. I wonder if you'd be available to play a cocktail party we're throwing for Cy Coleman, the composer. You've heard of Cy Coleman, haven't you?" I lied! "Oh, of course."

"Well, we have a nice baby grand piano just waiting for you, but I'd appreciate if you would be prepared to play some of his music!" I assured her that I would.

I looked in all the music guides I could find, trying to locate some of his songs. I was pleasantly surprised. Realistically speaking, Cy Coleman was not as well-known as other American composers like George Gershwin, Jerome Kern, Cole Porter, Irving Berlin, or Richard Rodgers. Those composers were, and still are, household names. But Coleman has written some great songs with which we, the listening public, ARE familiar. He'd already had great success with "I'm Gonna Laugh You Right Out of My Life," which was recorded by Nat King Cole. Coleman also had a smash hit when Frank Sinatra recorded "The Best is Yet to Come," and "Witchcraft."

He composed the music for the 1960 Broadway musical *Wildcat,* which starred Lucille Ball. Two other songs from that show are still popular hits, "Hey, Look Me Over," and "What Takes My Fancy." In 1962, he co-wrote with Carolyn Leigh, the music to the Neil Simon musical, *Little Me,* which starred Sid Caesar. The big hit from that show was "I've Got Your Number" and "If My Friends Could See Me Now."

The year before I met him, in 1966, he'd had a big hit with the Broadway show, *Sweet Charity,* which was written by Neil Simon and starred Gwen Verdon. Cy Coleman wrote the music with Dorothy Fields. Bob Fosse choreographed *Sweet Charity*. It was the first new musical for that Broadway season, and the hit songs from the show were very popular, including, "Baby, Dream Your Dream," and "Big Spender," a huge hit recording for Peggy Lee.

I went to the cocktail party well-armed with an arsenal of Cy Coleman compositions. Just prior to playing the party, I asked my musicians, Jim and Ron, if they had ever heard of Cy Coleman. They told me that he was not only a fine composer, but a great jazz pianist and recording artist!

I said, "Thanks a bunch. That makes my day that much easier. . . . Let me see if I've got this all straight. I'm going to be playing the piano for this guy who happens to be a fine composer. Right? Now, in order to make my job *easier*, I have to play HIS hit songs, while HE evaluates my playing! But to make my job that much *easier* again, you're telling me that he also happens to be a great jazz pianist . . . who will be looking over my shoulder and scrutinizing my every note! I don't think I'm going to be able to sleep too well tonight!"

When I arrived at the party, everybody was simply wonderful to me, especially Cy Coleman. I asked him if he would like to honor us by "sitting in" and playing a few tunes. He declined, saying, "Oh no. You're doing great!"

At one point, a bunch of guests gathered around the piano and rendered a couple of his hits in sing-a-long fashion. It was actually a lot of fun, and I enjoyed it

367

thoroughly. When I finished playing, Coleman asked me for my business card. I felt honored.

Three weeks later, I received a telegram. I opened it, wondering who had died. Why else would I receive a telegram? I opened it, and read it with surprise.

ROGER ROSSI • TRIED CALLING YOU TEN TIMES • NEED YOU FOR THREE COCKTAIL PARTIES • CALL ME ASAP • CY COLEMAN

Answering machines were not household items at that time. By the time I called him, it was too late. "Gee, I'm sorry Roger," he lamented. "I really wanted to use you for three separate cocktail parties. I think that you play the piano just great. But I couldn't wait any longer for you to contact me. I've already booked a pianist for two of the parties. Would you be available for the third one? It's for tomorrow evening."

I was already booked elsewhere, and had to decline. He thanked me again for the job I did at the original cocktail party. I felt especially esteemed to have been sought by a composer and musician of his great stature.

Since then, Cy Coleman wrote several more Broadway shows including: Seesaw (1973), starring Tommy Tune and Michele Lee; I Love My Wife (1977); On the Twentieth Century (1978); Barnum (1980); City of Angels (1989); and Will Rogers Follies (1991). He died in 2004, at 75.

Liberace

"Ahhh, damn it, Sal. We have a big traffic jam ahead."

"Oh, I didn't tell you, Honey? I thought you knew. Liberace is at the West Palm Beach Auditorium tonight, and he's performing to a sold-out crowd. They had it all over television and radio today."

"Thanks a lot! I'll be sure to tell the boss that our being late for work is all Liberace's fault. I'm sure it will make a huge difference in the way he tells me that we're fired!" It was Tuesday evening, February 15, 1977. We were on our way to the Flame Restaurant in North Palm Beach—at a very frustrating five miles per hour.

"I've never seen traffic THIS bad for other concerts here. Liberace must really pack 'em in, huh?"

Sal replied, "Well, I'm sure they don't call him the World's Greatest Entertainer' for nothing. . . . Eh, I think you can get into the left lane, just as soon as the next car passes."

Arriving late at the restaurant, we entered the lobby to see the owner standing right there. He said with unexpected cheerfulness, "Hello Sal . . . Roger. How are you both tonight?" I said, somewhat defensively, "We're fine, Peter, but I'm sorry we're late. We got held up in a tremendous traffic jam while passing the West Palm Auditorium. They evidently have Liberace performing tonight, and I-95 was backed up for miles."

"That's all right, Roger. I knew that Liberace is scheduled there tonight." Peter paused briefly and continued with an impish smile. "He's coming here for dinner tonight, right after his show!"

"You're kidding!"

"No, I'm not. He's made reservations for himself and an entourage of about twenty-five people; so, we've set them up in the Key Club."

The Key Club was a private room that shared the same lobby as the rest of the club, but was slightly remote from the lounge where we performed. Actually, it was treated like a separate club. It served exclusive lunches and dinners to the members and their guests. Although most of them would still use the rest of the club's offerings, the private club was perfect for their special parties.

The room itself was decorated in posh red fabric walls, lavish appointments and table place settings, opulent lighting fixtures and rich woodwork. It was a perfect setting for the famed entertainer and his guests to enjoy their dinner and cocktails. That evening, several Key Club members were also using the room. I guess Peter Makris had come to the conclusion that none would object to the slight stretching of rules, to accommodate the superstar. Liberace did request a private dining area. Anywhere else in the club would have subjected him to the constant barrage of autograph seekers.

The famous gentleman arrived at about eleven pm. While someone from his party handled seating with the hostess, Liberace's attention drifted toward our lounge. It soon became apparent that my band's music interested him. While the rest of his party made their way into the Key Club, he just stood there in the lounge entranceway.

Liberace with Sal and Roger at the Flame Restaurant - 1977

Although he was a long distance from where we performed, we couldn't help but notice his huge, inimitable, and contagious smile. His concentration must have been interrupted four or five times, as several in his group tried to steer him into the private club. He would nod appreciatively to them, then turn again to focus his attention on my trio and our music. He stood there quite some time, until several lounge patrons recognized him. Finally, he applauded and waved to us, before turning toward the Key Club.

371

Soon, I was approached at the piano bar by Karen Hudson, one of the hostesses. She said to me, "Roger, when you finish playing your set, come with your band to my desk. I'm going to bring you into the Key Club. Liberace wants to meet you."

"Thanks, Karen. That'll be great, but we do have about another thirty minutes to play for this dance set." I turned to Sal and my bassist, and said to them, "Hey, gang, we're gonna meet Liberace right after this set!" That put big smiles on their faces.

Karen eventually brought us back to meet him. He immediately stood up from his place at the head of the table and came across the room to greet us. He shook my hand first. Karen said, "Liberace, this is Roger Rossi, our bandleader."

"Yes, you're that wonderful pianist I was listening to before, aren't you?"

"Well, thank you. It is such a great pleasure to meet you. And Mr. Liberace, this is my wife, Sal. She is our lead singer and cocktail drummer and this is my bassist, Michael Burns, who also sings and doubles on trombone."

"Your music is wonderful. And Sal, young lady . . . you sing beautifully!" "Gosh, I don't know what to say," Sal said. "We were just talking about you earlier this evening, on our way here. We never would have believed in a million years that we'd be meeting you and talking with you now. You're such a great entertainer. I'm so thrilled!" Mike added, "We all are!" The three of us had basic difficulties realizing we were nonchalantly conversing with Liberace, the highest-paid entertainer in the world.

Liberace introduced us to a fairly tall and good looking young man who was hanging around us. The guy's clothing was overly done with show business flair. To make his flaming appearance that much more pronounced, he was wearing shocking pink silk pants. If the pants were any tighter, he would have been on the other side of them. Although we stood slightly away from the rest of Liberace's entourage, this guy was always in our midst. I thought he was a dancer, or someone in the show. With afterthought, I realized that he was probably . . . a "close" friend of the famed pianist!

After the initial introductions, we engaged in some typical show- biz talk with Liberace. Then he asked me, "Where are you from originally, Roger?"

I told him the story of how I got hooked into show business—by attempting to imitate HIM in a variety show at West Babylon Junior High School, Long Island, back in 1954. It was so successful that the school asked me to do repeat performances from time to time. For quite some time, all my classmates, and even some of the teachers, referred to me with the nickname, *"Liberace!"*

"Well, I'm truly honored to hear that," Liberace said to me.

I happened to mention to him that I was a former member of the Greater New York Musicians' Union, Local 802. Liberace proclaimed, "Oh Gosh, I've been in that office on 52nd Street hundreds of times,"

"Well, perhaps you've come across my father. My real name is Rossitto, not Rossi."

"You mean to tell me that you're Vince Rossitto's son?"

"Yes, that's right. You know him?"

"I should say so! Your father has helped me on numerous occasions. Between your father and Al Knopf, they run that whole union! He's a good man," Liberace said.

That put a big, proud smile on my face. Karen interrupted at this point, saying to me, "Roger, why don't you hold that smile and let me get a photograph of the two of you."

Karen was an excellent

Mr. Showmanship, Liberace

photographer, and always had her camera handy for such occasions. Liberace accepted, and we posed with me shaking his hand and Sal looking on. Karen was ready to shoot the shot, when I halted everything. I asked if we could change positions by putting me on the other side of Liberace. We switched positions and again assumed our hand shaking pose as Karen finally took the photograph. Soon, I felt we had taken Liberace away from his patient friends long enough. We politely excused ourselves and returned to the piano bar.

Later that evening, Sal asked me, "By the way Honey, why did you switch positions with Liberace, in the photograph?"

"Because in the original position, anyone viewing the photograph would have just seen the back of my right hand, instead of seeing HIS right hand with his fabulous rings! You know that they're almost as famous as he is!" One ring was actually a facsimile of his famous candelabra, with diamonds for flames!

"Always thinking, aren't you, Roger!"

Unfortunately, we never saw Liberace again. However, a few years later, in 1982, we did find out who that young, good looking man Liberace introduced us to, really was. He was Liberace's personal chauffeur and live-in lover for five years, Scott Thorson. Thorson, twenty-two years old at the time, became famous for his relationship with — and his palimony lawsuit against — the famous entertainer. Thorson, sued Liberace for $113 million. Publicly, Liberace always denied he was homosexual and refused to admit that Thorson was ever his lover. However, Thorson confirmed he chose to have plastic surgery to look more like Liberace at the pianist's suggestion. One can only imagine that Liberace wanted his young lover to look more like his son, thereby hiding their ongoing sexual trysts. The case was settled out of court in 1986, with Thorson receiving a $75,000 settlement, three cars, and three pet dogs; worth an additional $20,000.

In 2013, much of their bizarre relationship and parting was shown on a Home Box Office movie, *Behind the*

Candelabra. The film features Matt Damon as Thorson and Michael Douglas as Liberace.

Liberace once stated, "I don't give concerts, I put on a show." I believe he was correct in that analogy. To me, he wasn't a great concert pianist, but he was one of the world's greatest showmen. They called him, *Mr. Showmanship* for a good reason!

However, music critics often panned his piano playing. Lewis B. Funke, former writer and critic for the *New York Times*, wrote a horrible review of Liberace's Carnegie Hall concert, panning, "His sloppy technique included "slackness of rhythms, wrong tempos, distorted phrasing, an excess of prettification and sentimentality, and a failure to stick to what the composer has written."

However, Liberace always had the last laugh. He'd often rebut his critics, with wry humor. One such letter stated,

"Thank you for your very amusing review. After reading it, in fact, my brother George and I laughed all the way to the bank."

He started using the 'laughing all the way to the bank' response with such frequency, that it became his standard catchphrase. Once, on *The Tonight Show*, he humorously divulged to Johnny Carson, "I don't cry all the way to the bank any more – I *bought* the bank!"

Unfortunately, Liberace died in 1987 from complications caused by HIV. It was a tremendous loss for his fans and the entertainment world. At the time of his death he was worth (in 1980's value), $110 million. He was truly unique and definitely deserved the label, *"Superstar!"*

We'll never forget how at The Flame, in North Palm Beach, on a February evening in 1977, he went out of his way to be cordial and warmhearted to a few small-time musicians like us.

Itzhak Perlman

My band started performing at the Boca Raton Hotel & Club in May 1980. We were scheduled by a Fort Lauderdale entertainment-booking agency called Florida Attractions International. The name sounded very impressive, projecting an image of enormous size and clout, but in fact, it was mainly a "mom and pop" operation, under the careful direction of Milo Stelt and his wife, Elsie.

Milo was robust in appearance, with a rather austere and businesslike front that camouflaged his warm and friendly nature. Realistically, the displayed seriousness was a prerequisite to his position. Although his agency was really small potatoes, it was the primary booking representative for the hotel—considered one of the top ten facilities in the United States.

Violinist, Itzhak Perlman

Milo became a close friend to many higher-ups at the hotel, including chairman of the board Bert Stephens; general manager George Roy; and executive secretary Dolores Sachs (later, Mrs. George Roy). All of them trusted and relied on Milo's judgment. They expected a continuance of the high-quality music the hotel had staged since its inception in 1926. Milo had nothing to do with the booking of George Liberace (the renowned pianist's brother), Carmen Lombardo (Guy's brother), and the Freddie Martin Band, with Lead Vocalist Merv Griffin, previously booked into the Patio Royale Dining Room. He did, however, book most of the music for that splendid hotel, for many years.

For years, Mobil Travel Guide continually rated "The Boca" a Five-Star Hotel, and the Automobile Association of America rated it Three Diamonds; both ultimate approvals!

The Patio Royale considered one of the "signature" presentations of the hotel had the grandeur and service to match any fine dining room in all of North America. Milo booked us into that room for three years. They were very enjoyable and unforgettable years.

The hotel had a history for attracting guests from all over the world. People of the highest level in every field, endeavor, and position in life, would come and stay there: presidents, senators, kings, queens and royalty; celebrities from the sports world, recording and movie industry; and magnates from the business world. We even had a sheik take over an entire floor of the hotel, using all the rooms for his entourage and their needs. Famous authors, artists, entrepreneurs, scholars and musicians all came. Anybody, who was somebody, stayed there.

One such famous guest was Itzhak Perlman, the great concert violinist. In 1982, he stayed at the hotel with his wife Toby, and their very young children.

I was standing in a corridor outside the El Lago Lounge, talking with Milo Stelt. Milo was trying to impress me with how much he knew about the music business, and how I should listen to his advice more often. His mindset was based upon tradition and only tradition. It differed from my game plan, which suggests that to survive, you must "roll with the punches."

"Roger," he said, "the great music of the past is ALL that is important here at the Boca Hotel. The music of George Gershwin, Jerome Kern and Glenn Miller is the ONLY music you should be playing. Listen to me. I know what I'm talking about. I have a pulse on what's happening in music today. That's my job!"

I was in a hurry and had to cut the conversation short, so I was backing away while talking to him. I said, "Milo, I have a great respect for you. And yes, I too love George Gershwin, Jerome Kern and Glenn Miller. I play their music most of the time. I also play Rodgers and Hart, Cole Porter, Irving Berlin, Benny Goodman and Duke Ellington . . . and, once in a while I break tradition by playing some fifties and sixties Rock 'n Roll. What's the big deal? THIS IS THE EIGHTIES! . . . Look, Milo, I'm late already and I must run. We'll talk about it further some other time."

At that exact moment, I abruptly collided with a man behind me. I yelled out, " . . . EXCUSE ME!"

Simultaneously, the man gasped out a boisterous "AAAAAAAH," from the collision. To make matters worse, prior to my recklessly jolting his body, he was carefully trying to maneuver from his walking canes . . . into his wheelchair. I inadvertently took care of this for him by knocking the man . . . RIGHT ON HIS ASS!

Immediately, I turned to see who I had carelessly crashed into. My worst fears came true when I realized he was disabled. I leaned over to him with outstretched arms and hands to try to aid him.

By now, he was safely seated in his wheelchair. Nonetheless, he was still shocked.

I said with sincerity, "Oh, I'm SO sorry. Are you all right, Sir?" He looked up at me and said with equaled sincerity, "Yes. . . . I'm fine."

As I continued looking at him, I finally realized who he was. But, seeing him out of the normal context—in a concert stage setting— I sputtered my words with uncertainty. "Are you   ITZHAK?"

He smiled and calmly nodded and responded as if asking a question instead of answering one. "Yes?"

"Itzhak . . . PERLMAN?"

Grinning warmly, he said, "Yes, I am."

I could not contain myself. I brought my outstretched hands back to my own body to cover my pounding heart, now beating double time. I whispered, "Oh . . . my God!"

Itzhak Perlman, stricken with polio in Tel Aviv as a very young boy, is paralyzed in his legs. He was discovered by the late Ed Sullivan, and was featured on his show in 1959. His appearance was a tremendous success and gained him instant popularity. Soon, he moved to the United States and attended the Juilliard School of Music. Later, he was befriended by another great violinist, Isaac Stern. Perlman has won many Grammy Awards for his recordings. He has even recorded an album with the great jazz pianist, Oscar Peterson. Perlman is one of the most popular and sought after concert performers in the world.

I knew that this giant of the classical world was in the area. I had seen many television and newspaper advertisements promoting the *"Music at Eight"* concert series at the West Palm Beach Auditorium. Actually, he had just performed that concert the previous night with his piano accompanist, Samuel Sanders. However, in my wildest dreams, I never would have expected to meet him, especially in the manner I did!

Turning to Milo Stelt— who had witnessed the whole incident—I said, "Milo . . . this is Itzhak Perlman, the great concert violinist."

Milo nonchalantly added insult to injury, when he asked Perlman,

"Oh? . . . You play THE FIDDLE?"

I suddenly realized how much of a "pulse" my booking agent REALLY had on what was happening in the music business! I repeated the introduction, "Milo . . . this is the WORLD'S . . . PREMIER . . . concert violinist!"

Milo, then added salt to the wound. He stuttered, "Oh, yes . . . eh . . . I think I've heard of you!" Needless to say, I did NOT introduce Milo to Itzhak Perlman . . . as "*my booking agent.*"

Later, I had *a good laugh* as I recalled my supposedly "knowledgeable" agent's remarks to Perlman. I honestly wondered why he didn't illustrate his obvious stupidity further, by asking the great musician two additionally insulting questions: "So tell me Itzhak . . . are you working New Year's Eve, and do you play any other instruments besides the fiddle, like, eh . . . banjo, ukulele, kazoo? I'd like to book you."

However, I believe Itzhak Perlman may have had *the last laugh*. That evening, he and his family came into the dining room where we performed, and sat fairly close to our bandstand. At my first opportunity, I went to their table, and once again apologized for our collision earlier in the hallway. Itzhak nodded, smiled warmly, and introduced his wife and their young children to me. I asked if they had any music requests, and he answered, "Yes, please, *Gigi.*"

Upon our return to the stage, we started playing their request. But then, immediately, their children came up on our stage, and started running all around while bumping into us and of our equipment. Sal politely tried to show them their way off the stage, but they simply ignored her. I continued playing the song while repeatedly peering over to the Perlman's table and back to their unruly children, but my suggested hints were also ignored. He just kept *laughing*, and having a good time watching his children have fun. So, the song literally ended on a happy note!

Chuck Mangione

Most Valentine's Day celebrations are memorable, but 1997's was outstanding. It was at The Waterford, in Juno Beach, Florida.

We've often performed there, and always with favorable results, so we were very enthusiastic when activities director Luann Hamon called us for the date. "We'll prepare our best love songs for the occasion, Luann. I can't wait!"

Sal and I arrived, set up our equipment, and began. The lyrics and notes flowed easily, and the audience was appreciative. We couldn't have asked for a better setting for our musical arrangements. We finished a medley of three or four love songs to the obvious approval of the crowd. Then Sal asked me, "Doesn't that look like Chuck Mangione coming in, through the back of the room?" I answered with astonishment, "It IS Chuck Mangione . . . and he has his fluegelhorn with him!"

383

Roger Rossi

Sal & Roger with Jazz Legend Chuck Mangione

Mangione was born and raised in Rochester, New York. His list of accomplishments is myriad. After attending Eastman School of Music, he joined Art Blakey's famous ensemble, the Jazz Messengers. Previous greats that held that horn chair were Clifford Brown, Kenny Durham, Freddie Hubbard, Lee Morgan, and Bill Hardman.

Mangione won two Grammy Awards, both in the category of Best Instrumental Composition. His composition "Chase the Clouds Away" was used at the Summer Olympics in Montreal, and later, another composition, "Give It All You Got" was the theme for the Winter Olympics in Lake Placid, New York. In 1981 Mangione composed and performed the theme for the movie "Cannonball Run" starring Burt Reynolds. *Current*

Biography called his hit song "Feels So Good" the most recognized tune since "Michele" by The Beatles.

At The Waterford, the famous jazz musician made his way through the audience to a table near us. I said to him, over the microphone, "I'm sure glad you brought in your horn, man. We'd be honored!"

He simply smiled, nodded, and found his seat at the partially occupied table. As it turned out, one of the occupants was Waterford resident Sue D'Amico, his aunt, with whom he was visiting. Evidently, he was in South Florida to take care of some business for his upcoming concert tour with the famed vocal group, *The Manhattan Transfer*.

Sal and I went into an old chestnut, Duke Ellington's *It Don't Mean a Thing If It Ain't Got That Swing,* and much to our amazement, he simply started to play along with us, from his seat. I said on the mike, "Come on up!" He did. While soloing, he reached across and shook my right hand with his left. Neither one of us missed a note. Sal finished the impromptu arrangement and the audience went wild with applause. I announced what many of them already knew. I said, "Ladies and gentlemen, Sal and I are honored and thrilled to have — the great, internationally acclaimed jazz artist, educator and composer, Chuck Mangione, sitting in with us." They once again showed their appreciation with thunderous applause. I suggested, "Play another one, Chuck."

"How about *I've Got Rhythm*?"

"Great."

Chuck Mangione, "I take my hat off to you"

I gave him a snappy introduction into the Gershwin classic, and he soloed with perfection. Then, I modulated into Sal's key for her to grab a piece of the action. I took a jazz chorus and he finished the song. I don't think many members of the audience blinked during the performance. They didn't want to miss a note of this unique experience. I asked Mangione, "How about a bossa nova?"

Mangione answered, "Sure. Do you know *Manha De Carnival,* from Black Orpheus?"

"Yes, I do. As a matter of fact, if we do it in the key of A minor, I'll even sing a chorus."

"Okay, let's do it!"

386

I was shocked. Most famous performers will do one or two selections and then call it quits. Mangione continued to stay with us throughout our entire allotted hour. We actually went a half an hour overtime because both the audience and we musicians were all having so much fun. We played our special vocal arrangements and he was with us, every note. Years ago, I had written a special introduction for Gershwin's *A Foggy Day*, one of our favorites to perform. Mangione made it even more special with his solo. It sounded as if we had worked together for years.

The only drawback to the entire performance was that we didn't bring Sal's cocktail drums with us for the show. Instead, I had brought a mechanical drum machine. At one point, it was a bit of an embarrassment. Neither the famed jazzman nor I could find the correct rhythm for his own composition, the ever-popular *Feel So Good*. We finally had to go with a poor alternative to what I'm sure Sal could have done wonderfully well with her small, stand-up drum set. However, we did make it through the song and then segued into the great patriotic classic, *America, the Beautiful*! You wouldn't think that the two pieces would work together, but they did, and very well.

Then, Mangione took possession of Sal's microphone and voiced his appreciation for our musicianship and talent. I'll never forget it. He said, "Ladies and gentlemen, I was asked by my aunt to play a few selections with the band today. When I agreed to fulfill her request, I had no knowledge of their musicianship. I didn't know that you have such fine musicians working here, the likes of Sal and Roger Rossi. They're GREAT!"

After the audience showed its appreciation for our efforts, he wowed them with an ad lib version of the Rodgers and Hart standard, *My Funny Valentine.* He started the song alone, and out of tempo. He made his way through the middle of the audience, when I entered musically. We performed it like a classical composition. It brought the house down.

I concluded the performance by asking for one final round of applause for "this great musician. He certainly has given us all a very memorable Valentine's Day."

With my conclusion and the enduring applause, he came directly to the piano, shook my hand, and said privately, "Roger, I didn't know what to expect today. When my aunt asked me to perform with you, I imagined some hokey band accompanying me in a nightmare. . . . You and Sal literally saved me. You made me look good. Both of you are very talented pros."

He then surprised me. Shaking my hand, he pulled my body closer to his, and he kissed me on the cheek, European style, and then he planted a kiss on my other cheek! I thought it was a very special gesture. Italian (and many European) men often kiss each other on the cheeks, but it is usually reserved for relatives, special friends . . . or someone held in high esteem. I was flattered! Sal and Luann both looked on with wide grins. Luann said to me afterwards, "I'll never forget the shocked look on your face!" We ended the occasion with a photo session, and he honored me again, putting his famed hat on MY head! He humbly said, "I take my hat off to you!"

I can personally relate to the fact that New York Yankee fans have enjoyed many fun moments, but on July 4, 1983, it must have been special. Mangione played the national anthem on fluegelhorn for a Yankee game played against the Boston Red Sox. Mangione, a Yankee's fan, joined Phil Rizzuto and Bill White in the broadcast booth, and played a few bars of "Feels So Good". Yankee pitcher Dave Righetti went on to throw a no-hitter, defeating the Red Sox 4–0. Hmmmm that must've felt so good!

Vladimir Bakk

Concert pianist Vladimir Horowitz, considered by many to be the greatest pianist of the twentieth Century, once proclaimed Vladimir Bakk as "one of the greatest pianists of our time!"

How does one explain: the greatness of seventeen-year old Vladimir Bakk playing with The Moscow Symphony; or the incredible quotes by credible pianistic greats hailing him as the genius he was; and why was it that only very few people in America ever heard of him?

Most importantly, how do I, a self-proclaimed *slightly-better-than-average pianist,* write about my encounters and friendship with one of the world's greatest pianists? How does a mere mortal like me, deal with . . . a musical god? I guess I'll have to deal with it by starting from the beginning.

One evening in 2001, I had just finished playing a dance set at a restaurant-night club in Stuart, Florida, when a familiar face approached me from my past. After reminiscing with Ellie Fairchild, she told me about her extremely talented son-in-law, Vladimir Bakk. "Roger, believe me when I tell you that he is one of the world's greatest, classical pianists."

In the past, I have heard similar assertions about other supposed "greats," and time and again I had been disappointed with ordinariness. So, it was probably understandable why I treated her bold claim with calmness. I simply closed my eyes, half-heartedly nodded and grinned, saying, "Aha."

"Roger, I know you don't believe what I'm saying, so I'm going to bring you a few of his recorded CDs. You will not believe his genius! He's a graduate of the Moscow Conservatory of Music, he's often played with the Moscow Symphony, including once when he was a teenager. You'll see!"

A few nights later, Ellie returned with a younger woman holding a handful of CD albums. "Roger, I want you to meet my daughter Brenda, Vladimir's wife."

"I'm pleased to meet you. Ellie told me a lot about Vladimir."

Handing me his albums, she said, "Yes, he is a musical giant. Here are a few of his recordings, and a DVD showing some of his performances. They're gifts for you."

"Thank you so much. Please tell Vladimir I can't wait to listen to them, and also to meet him."

"He couldn't be here tonight, but he's looking forward to meeting you, too."

On the way home, I loaded up my car's CD-player with his discs. Bakk's greatness immediately emerged. Everything they said about him was true, and then some. I've listened to these recordings for hours on end, and loved every single note. Many years later, I still do.

Additionally, I've heard Vladimir play six-ten extremely difficult pieces, in a half a dozen or more concerts, and never once heard a mistake. Not one. He had impeccably clean technique.

Some critics might argue that Bakk often "interpreted" the composer's music, rather than to play it rigidly as the manuscript shows. One could counter that argument that Russian great, pianist Sergei Rachmaninoff also *interpreted*, often. Rachmaninoff, a graduate of Moscow Conservatory and considered one of the foremost composers and pianists of the twentieth century, always searched for expressive pianistic possibilities, thereby giving the appearance of improvisation. Bakk, once pointed out to me that a critic had panned Rachmaninoff for altering a Chopin piece he had played in recital. Sergei's rebuttal suggested that the way he played the piece was actually better than the way Chopin wrote it. Sergei added, "The most important thing for me in my interpretations is *color*. You make the music live. Without color, it is dead."

So, one has to believe that Bakk and Rachmaninoff not only came from the same School of Music, but also the same school of thought. I'd say that Bakk...and Rachmaninoff were both in good company. They were not only great exemplifiers of technical agility and clarity, but also sparkling dynamics and feeling, through color!

Upon visiting Brenda and Vladimir's apartment for the first time, I was impressed by his appearance and demeanor: slightly graying black hair; very austere and robust in size, and piercing eyes that made you feel you were being scrutinized and had to prove yourself worthy of his time.

I opened, "I'm extremely pleased to meet you, Maestro."

He said with a heavy Russian accent, and deep voice, "I'm pleased to meet you, R̊ud-jer."

"I want to thank you for your impressive CD's. I've not been able to stop listening to them."

"You like them?"

I smiled and nodded negatively, "No, Maestro . . . I LOVE THEM! You are the finest classical pianist I have ever heard. Your interpretations are special. Your dynamics are heavenly. Your technique is unbelievable. Your choice in selections are all perfect. Mozart, Scriabin, Chopin, Prokofiev, all of them. . . . I cannot honestly say I've ever heard anyone play them better."

Bakk smiled and nodded. Then, he gestured for me to enter into their "living" room.

Immediately, I realized how poor he and Brenda were. The small room barely had enough room for his baby grand, a small TV, and a very small love seat. That was it; no frills, or room for frills.

Vladimir pointed to the love seat saying, "Sit R̀udjer."

I sat, and he sat next to me, with both of us uncomfortably facing straight ahead. Brenda asked if I would like a cup of tea or coffee. I replied that water would be fine.

"So, Maestro, what are you doing with this superb talent of yours? How come I've never heard of you?"

My questions got to the heart of their problems, and opened up a Pandora's Box! For an hour or more, both Brenda and Vladimir told me of the good and bad things about his life. I quickly noticed that when Vladimir talked of the bad things, he would start stuttering, as he couldn't get it out of him quickly enough. Often, Brenda would interrupt in order for me to understand the essence of his pain.

In 1950, when all those who knew him realized how gifted he was, his father, a graduate of Moscow Conservatory, had young Vladimir study piano from the very best music professors and piano tutors Moscow had to offer. When studying as a child, under Heinrich Neuhaus at a special music school for prodigy children, one of those bad things happened to Vladimir. His mother regularly chained him to their piano; forcing him to practice enough. He finally gave in, and practiced more than enough, but I'm sure the cruelty of her enslavement stayed with him for the rest of his life. I'm sure because he talked about it a lot in his adult life.

He furthered his studies under Raphael Chernov at Moscow College, a pre-conservatory environment, and later, with Yakov Zak of the Moscow Conservatory. At Moscow's conservatory, he learned the invaluable Russian techniques, methods and musical thoughts that they were famous for teaching there. At that time, it was the elite of the world's conservatories.

After his graduation, he quickly became a "rising star," recording six Albums, and concertizing regularly: on Moscow's Radio and Television (fourteen concerts); throughout Europe and South America; and as the Principal Soloist with the Moscow Philharmonic for 18 years.

In the meantime, Russia's state-security committee, the KGB, would not let Bakk forget that he lived in a communist state under the rules of socialism. Everyone except the governmental hierarchy, of course, must relinquish vast amounts of their income to that State. The unfairness that a person who worked as hard as Bakk did, must share their income with others that don't care to work, totally sickened him.

In 1972, Vladimir won 1ST Place in the world-class Montevideo Piano Competition in Uruguay. Newspapers and musicians worldwide were acclaiming him as one of the greats!

Everywhere that Bakk performed, he received the same reviews depicting him as the genius he was.

The more recognition Vladimir received, the harder he worked in augmenting his already superb repertoire. He added extremely difficult pieces by Bach, Schubert, Haydn, Shostakovich, Prokofiev, Schedrin and Galynin.

Vladimir played me a recording made of him performing Rachmaninoff's Rhapsody on a Theme by Paganini, with the Bogota (Columbia) Symphony. It was pure magnificence. After listening to it, he explained what really happened there in Bogota. He was to have only one rehearsal with the orchestra at eleven a.m. and then perform with them in concert that evening. However, Vladimir was out with friends the evening before the rehearsal, and they all got drunk.

The next morning the conductor called him at his hotel room, asking, "Vladimir, its eleven-thirty, and the orchestra's been waiting for you for thirty minutes. Where are you?"

"Oh, no. I over slept. I'll be there soon."

Bakk showed up too late. The orchestra was being paid at an hourly rate, and had to be sent home. He never rehearsed with them. The conductor was there waiting alone. Bakk apologized and the conductor accepted, but said, "Look, Vladimir, I've heard your fabulous recordings, and I know how great you are. So, what I suggest is we just go over the main-transitional tempos together, so I know exactly what you want to do with them."

For about fifteen minutes, Vladimir played those sections, with the conductor conducting them. That was it! Later that evening at the concert, without benefit of any rehearsal with the orchestra, he magnificently played what was recorded, and what I was hearing during my visit at his apartment. Amazing!

However, the Columbian conductor listened as Vladimir continued telling the crux of his story that was not fun. After his performance, the KGB was there to collect his paycheck. Later that night, while celebrating their great performance, he and the orchestra's conductor had a cocktail together. The conductor casually asked Bakk, "Vladimir, was your remuneration okay?"

Bakk replied, "Well, it depends on what you mean by 'okay.'"

The conductor said, "Well, I was paid a total of $2,000 for my conducting the rehearsals and concert. How did you do?"

Vladimir replied, "I received a check for $2,500."

The conductor smiled and replied, "Ah, that's good, my friend. Most of the world-class performers make that amount. Terrific!"

Bakk said, "However, upon my receiving that check, I immediately had to endorse it and turn it over to the KGB. They in turn handed me my pay, which was $300."

That policy prevailed throughout the remainder of his life in Russia. But he also continued using his popularity as a platform for his vocal dissension.

For the time being, the KGB was ignoring him, probably because they were making huge fees for his international performances. Additionally, Russia has always had the propensity to show off their communist systems by boasting of the achievements of their talented musicians, scientists and Olympic-sports star's, versus those of the "decadent" free-world's capitalist systems.

I apologized to Brenda and Vladimir that I had to leave but promised I'd be back. She gave me copies of various newspaper articles written about Vladimir. I left with a lot of thoughts running through my brain. They obviously needed money to pay their rent and bills. Could I help? Is there anything they were not telling me? Slowly, but surely "things" occurred that answered my questions.

A few mornings later I visited them again. I knocked and Vladimir opened their front door. He smiled saying, "Hello, Řud-jer." But it came out sounding, "Hair-woe, Wu-yer."

"Vladimir, I'm fine. But what happened to your teeth?" They were totally gone. He excused himself, to momentarily put his dentures into his mouth. When he returned, he explained.

In 1975, Vladimir Putin entered into the service for the KGB. His service lasted for sixteen years before he retired as Lieutenant Colonel Putin [and entered politics]. Soon after taking reign as a foreign intelligence officer, was when the KGB's toleration of Vladimir Bakk ended. One day, shortly after he spewed out his last outspoken words of dissension about Russian dictators and their communist-socialist dictum, he was attacked by a few Russian goons. They held him down and took turns viciously rocking his head with barrages of punches, breaking his nose and his jaw. loosening all his teeth. They were very careful to avoid hitting his precious hands, arms and brain because they didn't want to lose control of their pianistic, "meal ticket." Finally, when he was able to get out of Russia for good, he traveled to Israel. There, a dentist reported that his x-rays showed his teeth were so weakened by the KGB assault, none were worth saving. It took three days for the dentist to extract all of them, and fit Vladimir with a mouthful of false teeth.

With sadness, I said, "Vladimir, I never knew. I'm so sorry they did that to you. But, if it means anything to you, your false teeth looked so real I always thought they were your originals."

I feel assured that between his mother's earlier enslavement, and the KGB's assault on him, it explained his obvious and deep depression. It must have been there for most of his life. I caught it immediately upon meeting Vladimir during my first visit. He mostly had a low-keyed, lamenting, and 'woe is me' attitude. I don't think he ever wanted to be sad because every once in a while, he would laugh at my stupid jokes, but he'd immediately return to his dismal tone.

I'm a musician, not a psychologist or psychiatrist. But in having dealt with Bakk on many occasions, I developed a simple theory as to why he was always so depressed. He was a one-hundred percent, bonafide-pianistic genius, and all knowledgeable people who encounter him knew it, including I presume, himself. He had to be aware of his enormous and genius-level talents. Therefore, he probably reflected on his life asking himself, "I'm a genuine genius, so why have I been treated so harshly throughout my entire life, and why am I so poor?"

And the more he dwelled on those negatives, the more it became his "crutch" to constantly whine about it to others. Then it became a terrible cycle repeating itself over and over like a mad dog chasing its own tail! The unescapable anguish turned into the deep depression, and then into whining about it to everyone he knew.

Renowned Russian pianist-conductor Vladimir Feltsman, a cohort and friend of Bakk's once stated that after talking with Bakk, I "sometimes need to have a glass of milk!"

On another occasion, he said of Bakk, "His attitude is that life is miserable, and then you die. Many times, I tell him, 'Smile and shut up.' But if there's a chance to put his foot in his mouth, he'll take it."

Music Critic, Stephen Wigler, of The Baltimore Sun, wrote a few quotes about Bakk:

- "His laughter is on the edge of tears. He is someone to whom life, like music, is the stuff of tragedy. He could be a character in a novel by Dostoevsky."
- "Some of Bakk's problems may have been self-inflicted. He never hesitated to share his disdain for the Soviet bureaucracy. And he has an extremely dark view of life."
- "A musician in his position had everything to gain by ingratiating behavior. But Bakk can only be himself. He kept referring, for example, to the miserable piano he had to play as, "Baldwin ka-ka."

However, for the short period of time I knew Vladimir, we had a good friendship. Sometimes we would share thoughts that were interesting and fun.

One time, I happened to notice the enormous length to his fingers. They were easily an inch and a half longer than mine. It made it understandable that his playing the Russian-composed music so much an easier fit than my hands could ever do.

Another time, I remember him asking me to play something for him on his piano. I played a light "bossa-nova jazz" piece. He liked it and said, "I can tell you've had classical training."

"Yes, but nowhere near the training you've had, Maestro! I'm now a dance-band player. I wish I had your technique. Why don't you play something for me?"
He side stepped my request and said, "No, R̈ud-jer, you play ME . . . chromatic scale."

For those who don't know what that is, picture a piano keyboard with its mixture of white and black keys. To play chromatically means you simply ascend (or descend) from one key to the very next key, black or white' with no keys in between.

I asked Vladimir, "From what key, and for how long?"
"Start anywhere, play two octaves."

Bakk meant I had to consecutively play twenty-five notes up or down without repeating or omitting any notes along the way. Using several fingers in my right hand, I fulfilled his request. He said, "Good. Now play fast."

I played it as fast as I could.

"Very good, R̈ud-jer, Now, play using two fingers."

In using several fingers like I did, you have the ability of pivoting your thumb under the next. But using only two fingers, for me, seemed like the two fingers would get in the way of each other making it impossible. I asked, "Well how can you do that?"

He sat at the piano. And because he knew I was watching, in order to make it obvious that he was only going to use two fingers, he tucked away the three fingers he wasn't going to use. Then, using the two remaining fingers, he played the chromatic scale I had played but almost twice as fast as I did. He ascended up two octaves and descended back down two octaves to the original starting note. I still can't figure out how he did it! The only thing I can surmise is that it was a "parlor trick" someone taught him along the way.

Fun times spent with Vladimir were few, and far between. His mental battles were always present. It explained his excessive alcohol problem. He had mentioned his many occasions of drunkenness in his past for it not to be a problem. He obviously self-medicated using alcohol as a comforting agent.

Many people make bad choices in life. I can personally relate. An older brother introduced alcohol to me at a very young age. By the time I attended Crane School of Music, I was hooked and spending most of my time in the bars of Potsdam, NY. After leaving Crane at the disappointment of many professors, I went on the road as piano accompanist-music director for Tommy Desmond, one of Canada's top recording artists. I had to "hide" my problem of consuming huge amounts of beer during the day, and then a fifth of vodka every night. I didn't stop this routine until my future wife Sal came along, saw something in me, and literally saved my life. I made the right choices of marrying her, and "growing up!" Drinking wine can be wonderful, if limiting it to two glasses. I could have rationalized by blaming my brother for all my shortcomings, but that would have only changed wine into . . . "whine."

The first time I noticed Vladimir had a drinking problem was when I went to a late lunch with him and his wife Brenda at a cute Hobe Sound restaurant. We ordered food, and a small bottle of wine. Knowing there are approximately five classes to a bottle, I figured there would surely be enough for the three of us. Upon my pouring, Brenda changed her mind and declined, so I filled Vladimir's and my glass, and we toasted. I sipped a little and put my glass down. He guzzled his glass of wine; took the bottle and poured his second. That was immediately gone, too. He finished the entire remainder of the bottle within five minutes or less. My glass was still full. I didn't say anything, but quickly realized that much of his problems in life echoed mine at an earlier age. The differences were that my problem took place in my late teens, and I quickly got it under control. Vladimir was already into his 60's, and his problem was still prevalent.

Please understand that Russia's way of life, with its hardline dictatorships, has driven many to drink. It obviously is a dismal place to live. According to Wikipedia, "Russia has one of the highest suicide rates in the world." According to The Lancet, a very respected medical journal in the United Kingdom. Russia also has one of the highest rates of alcoholism in the world. It stated that: "25% of Russian men die before they are 55, and most of the deaths are due to alcohol. The comparable UK figure is 7%."

So, Vladimir's problem was typical, and understandable. But, he could have side stepped it all by first "growing up;" and then by softening his tones of dissent. By contrast, his close friend Vladimir Feltsman did side step, and left Russia with his original teeth intact. He came to America and is now one of the most respected pianists anywhere.

I got Vladimir booked at Saint Paul of the Cross Catholic Church, Singer Island. Father Art Venezia, the Pastor, my friend for decades, was also my boss for fifteen years when I was the Resident Pianist there. We set a date for a Sunday of classical music by Bakk. The Pastor and his music director Jeanne Clark went all out in presenting Vladimir. They abundantly advertised his performance through church-network bulletins; they printed posters, and programs. Jeanne Clark told me that their congregation was very generous, and "the artists usually did pretty well with donations received."

I also made preparation for a piano delivery company to pick up, deliver, tune and return Bakk's personal grand. Vladimir had only one concern about his beloved Schubert Grand, and that was "will it be big enough to carry in the church?" I suggested we could test it out together, and if it was inadequate we could mic it; also, testing to his approval. The alternative of renting a concert grand was out of the question, as it would eat up too much donation money. Also, I was very aware that he was very fussy about the pianos he was forced to play on. I felt he would be at home with his own.

I got permission to announce the concert at all of the Sunday Masses, the week before the event. I went from the choir piano to the altar's microphone. There, I briefly told of Vladimir Bakk's great accomplishments. I ended with quotes about him by the legendary Vladimir Horowitz, and Vladimir Feltsman. Then I turned to Pastor Venezia, humorously saying, "You know Father Art, it just dawned on me what MY problem has been all my life. My parents named me Roger . . . instead of Vladimir!"

The concert attracted a full house of classical-music lovers. Vladimir played masterfully and followed my suggestions to a "T." When all was said, and done, he played magnificently for approximately forty-five minutes; the audience loved everything he played which included beautiful, yet difficult piano pieces by Chopin, Bach, Beethoven, Shostakovich and Scriabin, and he amazed them with a Moszkowski piece called *Spanish Caprice*! The results were an audience totally enthralled.

FOUR CLASSICAL GIANTS

Zubin Mehta, Vladimir Bakk, Isaac Stern & Mstislav
Rostropovich.

At intermission, I divulged about Bakk's poverty. It made them dig very deep with thousands of dollars in donations. Vladimir and Brenda were overwhelmed with gratitude, and couldn't thank me enough. They had not received funds like that since being in Florida.

They offered me money and I totally refused it. But, I suggested that Brenda remit a few hundred dollars to the church fund. Shockingly, she snapped back at me. "Oh, (expletive!) em."

Totally shocked, I yelled, "WHAT?"

"You heard me. What the (expletive) did they do, open the doors?"

405

"First of all, I don't like your tone or language. Secondly, they paid for advertising, air conditioning, posters, Jeanne Clark's time and efforts in getting information out to the many other churches were invaluable to attracting the very people who donated as much as they did. At least, give THEM what you would have given to me. Certainly, a booking agent would make far more than what I'm asking you to send them. They already mentioned a return concert for Vladimir. But, if you don't send them at least $300 for their efforts, I'll personally see to it that Vladimir Bakk never plays piano in that church again."

"Alright, here's $300. You pay them!"

I angrily snapped back, "You ungrateful fool. It's not my place to thank them, although I will anyway. But, YOU must be the one to send it to them, and YOU should enclose a nice and polite letter of appreciation, too." Angrily, I turned my back on her and drove home.

I didn't want to mention my conversation with her to anyone. I thought it was so obscene the way she was going to just ignore what would be considered a normal practice. Thankfulness is essential. Benevolence is "a given." Obviously, she didn't learn a thing from her beautiful and elegant mother, Ellie Fairchild.

Monday morning, I called the church and thanked Fr. Venezia and Jeanne Clark for their great efforts. They both stated that Vladimir was indeed the best they ever heard, and truly world-class. They thanked me for bringing him to them, and again, asked me if he would like to play a return engagement. I scheduled it, and got exactly the same successful results, but afterwards Brenda sent them the check and thank-you card without my suggestion.

In the three-year period I associated myself with the Bakk's, I learned much about Vladimir's and Brenda's shortcomings.

One great mistake made was to have located in Lake Worth, Florida, a small town with few opportunities for rebuilding his career. They had no young children to raise, and most definitely should have been in the big cities of New York, Los Angeles, Boston or Chicago.

Another problem was Brenda's attitude. I always felt that she never "pushed" him enough. I offered to put him on tour, lining up available concert dates at the various schools of music and conservatories throughout America. I had envisioned a great opportunity there for him as he had previous successes in staging Master Classes and supervising world-class pianists for competitions, including: The Van Cliburn Competition; the Leeds International Piano Competition, The Tchaikovsky World Competition; The Chopin Competition, and The Palm Beach Invitational Competition. He had a history of feeling comfortable with young students in music schools. I could picture him first giving them a 45-minute recital, and then answer questions, and give instructions to the students for another hour or more. It would have been the perfect venue for him to make very good income, sell his great CD recordings, and for him to "get back in business." I even designed a T-shirt to vend, stating,

"THE FOUR B'S: Bakk playing Bach, Beethoven and Brahms." She nixed all of it!

Additionally, I received a legitimate offer for him to do a return performance with The Bogota Symphony, where years earlier he had received a tremendously long, standing ovation with screams of "Bravo!" That offer was for $25,000 in 2003 currency value. She nixed that, too.

I believe she never wanted to share him with the world, for fright of losing control of him. Then again, in fairness to Brenda, she, in knowing his unstable condition, may very well have been protecting whatever psyche he had left.

However, although she had control of his life, she never had the class to represent him. Her appearance and terribly foul language were too "bohemian." She had a bad attitude with two of the people with whom I dealt with in booking Vladimir. She dropped the "F-Bomb" in both situations, and did so because she didn't want to relinquish a small part of his donations for their costs and time. It was cheap and tasteless behavior. The second time it occurred was the catalyst to ending my involvement with them both.

Roger Rossi and Vladimir Bakk – 2003

From what I surmise, unfortunately, he didn't go much further with his career, and one day I heard of his demise. It saddened me greatly when pondering on 'what could have been.'

Vladimir was one of many great Russian musicians who came to America with hopes of being successful in concertizing, but instead, drastically failed. When he arrived, he got references for agents and managers plus financial assistance from World-renown pianists Vladimir Horowitz and Martha Argerich. It didn't help. As Brenda related to me, one of those management agencies told him, "We are overrun by great Russian musicians. We just don't have room for any more."

As Music Critic Stephen Wigler of the *Baltimore Sun* pointed out: "A young, glamorous winner of a recent

409

international contest stands a good chance of finding a manager and some concerts; an [older] pianist with missing teeth, whose most recent competition victory was twenty-two years ago, has fewer opportunities."

To me, that represented only part of the equation. The other parts were for the Bakks to both have a more focused, energized, upbeat, and "classy" attitude.

QUOTES ABOUT VLADIMIR BAKK

- **Russian-born virtuoso Vladimir Feltsman, Moscow Conservatory graduate and world-renowned pianist-conductor, wrote:** "He's a genuine genius pianist. He plays on a fantastic level that must be heard to be believed. He has absolutely the most incredible piano technique I've ever heard. Certain things he plays better than anyone else alive; he's the last of the dinosaurs from the era that produced Horowitz, [Josef] Lhevinne and [Josef] Hofmann. But he's absolutely unknown."

- *New York Times* **Music Critic, Harold Schoenberg wrote,"** Mr. Vladimir Bakk not only is the greatest technician, he is a huge musical talent. He reminds me of the great Russian pianist Josef Lhevinne."

- *The Jerusalem Post*: "He is a recitalist of the first order, one who bears comparison to [Russian pianistic great, Sviatoslav] Richter."

- *La Prensa*: ". . . a master of expressive range and stylistic eclecticism, and we believe that he is without equal in his generation."
- **Translated from Russian, famous conductor and pianist Maxim Shostakovich [Composer Dmitri's son] said:** "Vladimir Bakk is a remarkable pianist. The interpretive style of Vladimir is characterized with not only technical brightness, but very subtle penetration into the imagination and structure of composition. Sparkling dynamics and infallible understanding of style and form, and his natural sense of ensemble allow him to reach high levels of collaborating with orchestras in concerto repertoire. Bakk is a magnificent musician."
- **Concert pianist, Alexander Toradze, a Moscow Conservatory graduate who studied under Yakov Zak; is a professor of piano at *Indiana University, South Bend*:** "Vladimir Bakk was and remains one of the most stunning piano performers I've ever heard. . . . He is a true keyboard genius!"
- **[Argentina] *La Nacion*:** ". . . a performer whose skills are nothing other than unbelievable given their fullness and quality. We can recall no technique as brilliant as his."
- **World-renowned pianist, Martha Argerich from Argentina stated:** "I think that Mr. Vladimir Bakk is a phenomenon. His playing is simply amazing."
- **[Argentina] *Clarin*:** "Bakk will be the public idol . . . dazzling us with his performance."

411

- **Buenos Aires 1973-Translated from Spanish.** "When, as it happened a few weeks ago, Vladimir Bakk played Tchaikovsky's First Piano Concerto in a concert with the Orquestra Sinfoniaca National, we were as already stated, in the presence of a pianist of extraordinary range."

- "We can recall no technique as brilliant as his. For Bakk there are no difficulties of performance. In his talented hands the most complicated music becomes a simple exercise for beginners."

- **[Israel]** *The Jerusalem Post* **–2 separate review quotes by Dora Snowden:**

- "Once you have heard him play, Vladimir Bakk is a name you will never forget."

- "He is a recitalist of the first order. One who bears comparison with (Sviatislav) Richter."

- **QUOTE BY VLADIMIR BAKK:** "Music is tragedy -- I'm absolutely sure of that. The greatest works -- the last sonatas of Beethoven and Schubert, the Bach Mass, the 'Metamorphoses' of Strauss -- these are not entertainment. They're meditations upon death."

- **BRENDA FAIRCHILD BAKK (Internet Quote)** "He died Dec. 24 (2007) at home; happily. He was tired of the world. He was an honorable person and a great artist; sensitive soul. I am so happy that people are enjoying his art; so is he."

- **ROGER ROSSI** - Bakk's performances were always at the very highest levels of musicianship.

In great parts of South America, Europe, and his native Russia, he was legendary. It's sad that in the United States, few have ever heard of him. Being a believer in God, I feel that right now my old friend is at God's personal piano, taking turns with his pianistic peers: Sergei Rachmaninoff, Vladimir Horowitz, Josef Hofmann, Sviatislav Richter, Van Cliburn, Josef Lhevinne, Arthur Rubinstein, Frederic Chopin, and the grandfather of them all, Franz Liszt. Knowing Vladimir, he's probably complaining about the piano, and demanding that the angels provide him instead with his favorite, a *Beckstein* concert grand. Perhaps, that will make him smile.

PERHAPS!

PLEASE NOTE: To see and hear some of Vladimir's great recordings, go to:

https://www.youtube.com/results?search_query=VladimirBakk

Roger Rossi

PART SEVEN: Looking Back

Roger Rossi

"The Russians Are Coming"

On November 9, 1965, I was in pursuit of a publishing home for two songs I had composed. I arrived at 1619 Broadway in New York City, the Brill Building. That building was the main center of professionally composed rock and roll. It was a "Hub" for professional songwriters, producers and artists, and where many of the 1960's recording successes began. Hits prevailed for such acclaimed artists and composers as Ellie Greenwich, Jeff Barry, George "Shadow" Morton, Hugo and Luigi, The Shangri-Las, Leiber and Stoller, The Drifters, Burt Bacharach, Phil Spector, Neil Diamond, Neil Sedaka, Elvis Presley, Tony Orlando, The Shirelles, Frankie Valli and the Four Seasons, and Carole King, just to name a few.

I knew that to be a successful composer, I had to be there, but didn't quite know the protocol. I realized I made a mistake not making any appointments, but didn't know with whom I should have made them. I didn't have an agent to represent me and my compositions, which was another mistake, but thought I might locate one there. After many hours of sitting and waiting to hopefully meet someone to show my songs to, I realized that I wasn't getting "successful;" I was getting tired!

417

I looked at my watch and realized it was already passed 5:00pm and I was going to be confronted with the problem of driving my car back to Long Island exactly when hundreds of thousands of other people had the same goal.

I immediately boarded the already crowded elevator. We all arrived at floor level; the door opened, and . . . SPLAT! All the electricity went off, seemingly everywhere.

If the electric were to have gone off ten seconds earlier, I and all the elevator occupants may have been stranded for hours before being rescued. Of course, when those doors opened and we all stepped out, none of us really knew the enormity of the problems that would evolve.

Immense turmoil immediately took place. It was the height of rush hour and already dark. Personally, I figured the electric would return with its "steadfast" lighting, I'd find my parked car and drive home. Then, being hungry, I opted to try to find somewhere to eat. I found a restaurant where slight flickers of candle lighting shone. I entered to find a waiter serving only a few patrons. I asked, "Are you open for business?"

"Yes, come in and find yourself a seat."

I perused the menu, and asked if he could prepare a steak without electric. He assured me he could, and I also ordered a glass of red wine. The lights were off for the entire time I enjoyed my meal. I asked for my bill. He replied, "No. There's no charge."

"What?"

"I can't charge you a thing, because I can't get into the cash register. No charge!"

"Well, I could give you what you think the charge would be, couldn't I?"

"No, just be careful going home, and come visit us again."

I couldn't thank him enough. I asked if there was a public-phone booth nearby. He told me there was one a few steps away from the restaurant. As I walked toward the phone booth, I couldn't help but notice the sky. With no distracting city lights, the stars were quite vivid and beautiful. But, the public phone did not work.

I got in my car, and started my trek homeward. The pedestrians were aplenty, and most folks had their thumbs out, hitchhiking. At that moment, I realized that many people leaving the City of New York, normally do so by trains, all powered by electricity. That evening, they were all stranded.

I stopped and asked if anyone needed a ride to Long Island. Within a nanosecond, six other people occupied my vehicle, including one lady sitting on a gentleman's lap. In those days, we didn't have "luxury consoles" between people, so that night we were able to fit in seven riders…all strangers. They were polite, and extremely worried. The lights and electric were off for much too long for it to be the typical "power outage." Something was very wrong, and everyone sensed it.

As we slowly drove by the throngs of hitchhikers, the worrisome group in my car started to analyze our situation. One of them said, "Maybe we're under attack.

I'm not joking. Maybe we're being attacked by the Russians."

Nobody laughed or refuted the comment. With the absence of electrical power for the past few hours, I'm quite sure it had crossed all of our minds. It did mine.

Furthermore, in the 1960's America and the United Soviet Socialist Republic (Russia) had endured many hostile threats from each other. Both countries were caught spying. Tensions escalated. We found Soviet placed medium-range ballistic nuclear missiles in Cuba, 90 miles away from Florida. President Kennedy activated 150,000 reservists, announced a naval quarantine of Cuba, and advised the American people of the possible danger of nuclear attack.

Both countries increased defense spending, and some Americans citizens actually built personal bomb shelters, thinking that that would protect them from a nuclear bomb. Others joked that at that moment, the only thing worth doing besides praying, would be to drop your pants, bend your head passed your knees, and kiss your ass goodbye!

The possibility of engaging in a major war with Russia was very real, and very much on everyone's mind. Additionally, most people did not want to even talk about it. My automobile went silent.

As we traversed toward "The Island," some got off, others got on. They were all very appreciative of my assistance. And, I was happy to help. However, I was not the only driver taking passengers. New Yorkers have a history of being helpful during times of distress. 'Just think of 911.

It took me over five hours to make it home. When I finally arrived my family joyfully screamed, "DAD-DY." We all embraced.

My wife Sal asked, "Do you know what's going on? The phone, radio, and television have not been working for hours. We were worried to death about you."

"Honey, I'm sorry, but I don't know either. I think we should all say a prayer, and let the kids get some sleep. Tomorrow's another day."

Sal put our children to bed, and I poured some wine. I told her about the comments about Russia, made by the passenger in my car. Sal and I shared a very restless night!

The next day it was much the same, no news. But, no news was good news. If we weren't attacked by then, it probably was not going to happen.

Then, the information started to gradually come in. It was a relay switch in one of our power plants that triggered a catastrophe knocking out all the electric in Ontario, New York, Connecticut, Rhode Island, Massachusetts, Vermont and New Hampshire. It was the largest power failure in North American history, affecting over thirty million people.

The amazing thing was that there was no looting by disreputable people. That to me was proof that most people honestly thought it was an attack. Years later, the same basic area endured another major power outage, but then, the looting was immense. What a country!

My Biggest Compliment

I have never been confident of my vocal abilities. Perhaps the feeling exists because I have received adequate training on the piano and have not, vocally. Blame it on whatever you like, but I just don't have the confidence there that I have in other endeavors. Oh sure, I sing on key, but that's about it. When you're making your income by performing music, that's not enough. Additionally, you should have style, timbre and projection. Quite truthfully, I've never felt those qualities coming from my vocal cords.

Piano accompanying such great professionals as Stuart Foster, who followed the vocal tradition set by Frank Sinatra and Dick Haymes with the Tommy Dorsey Orchestra; Jim Nabbie of The Ink Spots; Julius La Rosa; Don Rondo; and Opera Diva Susan Neves—I realize just how inferior my voice is.

I guess I've been spoiled working as a full-time piano accompanist to excellent singers such as three years with Canadian recording artist Tommy Desmond, three years with Columbia recording artist Gene Stridel, twelve years accompanying church soprano Janet Perez who has sparling tones and an enormous vocal range. And of course, my all-time favorite, Sal Rossi, to whom I also happen to be married, and have piano accompanied for fifty years. My working with these fine vocalists has only diminished my confidence that much more. Hearing them, I realize how a voice is supposed to sound. Mine doesn't come close. On many occasions, however, I've received a broad range of comments on my singing. I continue to persevere.

Why is it that some vocalists have "made it" with voices I would not consider great? Perhaps it's because they've had other defining qualities that make them . . . interesting. For example, Jimmy Durante's and Louis Armstrong's voices were not great, but had "warmth." Carol Channing's voice was "grinding," but was cute. Furthermore, Tiny Tim's voice was downright weird and irritating. Yet, he was a star!"

However, all things taken into consideration, the biggest compliment about my voice came from one of America's all-time great singers, Vic Damone. When he visited the Boca Raton Hotel & Club where I was performing with my band, he invited me to the table where he dined with his wife, and his piano accompanist. I'll never forget it. Vic said to me, "Roger, I have to tell you something. . . . That wife of yours really sings GREAT. . . . Eh . . . don't get me wrong . . . your voice is . . . eh . . . okay . . . but she's GREAT!"

For Vic Damone to say that my voice is . . . "okay?" Well, that's simply HUGE! I'll take it!

Roger Rossi

My Biggest Thrill

Probably, the biggest thrill I have experienced as a professional musician occurred on my daughter Bonny's birthday, February 22, 1982, during a performance at The Flame, in Palm Beach, Florida. The episode began when I was asked by the hostess of the posh supper club to make an important announcement. Trying to do that, on that particular evening, in itself, was a unique experience. The place was filled to capacity with an extremely boisterous crowd.

I started by asking for total silence. "Ladies and gentlemen, could I please have your attention." The noise continued so I repeated myself with a touch more emphasis.

"Ladies and gentlemen . . . PLEASE . . . may I have your attention. I have a special announcement."

A few people looked up and stopped talking, but it was still a loud crowd.

One must understand that these were PALM BEACHERS to whom I spoke. (They have been there, done that. They've seen it all. They own it all. They probably invented it all, and yes, they do know it all.) There was very little that I could say, or do, to impress THEM. I was basically ignored.

Finally, out of desperation, I said, "Okay, everyone who can hear me, please say this with me . . . one, two, three . . . shhhhhhhhhhhh!"

Well, I got part of the room to say, "Shhhh," and finally, I became the center of their attention. You could hear a pin drop, which for that place was really an accomplishment. As they gave me their undivided attention, I could see frowns of tolerance on some faces. They were typical Palm Beach frowns, which said, "All right, you've interrupted my very important conversation about my upcoming safari vacation! Now, damn it all, what could you possibly say that is more important?"

I smiled and said unwaveringly, "Ladies and gentlemen, I want to thank you for your attention to this very special announcement. . . . It gives me great pleasure, to announce to you, with patriotic pride, that the United States Olympic Ice Hockey Team has just defeated the Soviet team, in Lake Placid, New York!"

Man, I thought the crowd was boisterous and unruly before. Now it was bedlam. People were screaming out their joy, doing so while smacking palms on knees. Throughout the club, we heard gleeful expressions. "WOW, that's great."

"Yeah . . . ALL RIGHT."

"RIGHT on!"

It was quite obvious that nobody ever expected such an upset. It was the upset of the century! Our team was a collage of, admittedly, the best amateurs in our country. However, they had worked out and trained with each other for such a short time that they hardly knew each other.

By contrast, the Soviet team had trained under a different system entirely. They were classified as "amateurs," but the world knew they were subsidized by

425

their government. Playing ice hockey was their job, their full-time job. It had been their job for years! They were no more amateurs than the Montreal Canadians, or the New York Rangers of the National Hockey League. In fact, they had already competed against, and beat, some of those NHL teams. They'd gotten away with that travesty for years. Up until that evening, the apparently invincible Soviet Union Ice Hockey Team had won the gold medal in six of the seven previous Olympic Games.

Shortly after my announcement, and the ensuing pandemonium, a group in the corner of the restaurant started singing *God Bless America.* I joined in, on the piano, to reinforce their initiative. Immediately, everyone in the place customers, bartenders, waitresses, busboys, and the band all stood up and sang with gusto. That evening, we were all one!

There were no Liberals there; nor were there any Conservatives. No Republicans, nor any Democrats, were present. All the political, racial, religious, economic, and social differences, constant barrier and sources of argument for us all, that night were "put on ice" (pun intended). We were, quite simply, proud Americans, all of us. In my lifetime, I have never witnessed such unity. I had a very difficult time, holding back my tears of pride. I witnessed many patrons who could not restrain themselves. Can you believe it? Palm Beachers with tears in their eyes! It was a proud night for Americans everywhere.

So often we've all seen the constant TV coverage of "the bad things" in our society. I regret that we never had one of those TV cameras there that night, showing the world, and ourselves, what Americans are really made of. Unfortunately, today's ever-popular I-Pads weren't invented yet, so no one saw it but the occupants of that supper club's dining room. Albeit, I'm sure similar celebrations abundantly took place elsewhere. The game that evening was later referred to as the "Miracle on Ice."

It was our year. Our ice hockey team went on to win the gold medal, and the Soviet team came in second with the Silver.

In 1999, Sports Illustrated called the Miracle on Ice the "Top Sports Moment of the 20th Century," and the *International Ice Hockey Federation* labeled it "The Century's Number-One International Ice Hockey Story." For me, it was my biggest thrill!

My Greatest Embarrassment

I'm sure that as people reminisce, they sometimes cringe at the thought of some embarrassing moments in their past. I have many moments of embarrassment in my memory banks. One in particular stands out above the rest.

When Sal and I first moved to Florida, we took an engagement at a small Italian restaurant called Alfredo's, in Boynton Beach. The club had the worst piano on which I have ever performed. It was a spinet, which normally is bad enough. That kind of a piano is usually used for a beginner's practice. Within a few weeks of playing, most professional pianists would destroy a spinet. They weren't built to take the punishment that a console or grand piano can take.

That would account for why this particular spinet at Alfredo's had eleven broken and unplayable notes. They were strategically located across the whole keyboard. I had to constantly avoid them by jumping up or down an octave, in order to continue my melodic ideas. When I did jump to another octave, it wasn't any blessing. The remaining seventy-seven-unbroken notes were out of tune! The situation meant constant aggravation for me, but I persevered. I complained to the owner so often it became a constant source of humor for the patrons. It was our regular, little burlesque routine. I would say to owner Ozzie Provenzano, "Hey Boss, this piano is in bad shape!"

He'd reply, "Ah, don't worry about it. We'll paint it. It'll be fine!"

The customers would roar with laughter; but in the meantime, nothing was done about the piano.

"I needed my own piano on the gig!"

I ultimately bellyached enough that Ozzie said, "All right, already. Go and find me the piano you want for the club and I'll pay for it." I did find a nice Yamaha grand piano and he paid for it. However, the piano didn't arrive for three months, until my last week there. The new pianist reaped the harvest of MY efforts!

I couldn't take it anymore. I needed a real piano for those last three months. So, I had my own Kawai grand piano delivered to the club, at my expense, and for my sanity! I had my grand situated on stage, so that the customers could watch my fingers moving as I played. If I had to sing something, I would simply sit sideways. It was a good setup with only one shortcoming. As the patrons danced by me, they were very close to my keyboard. It was often too tempting for them to avoid tinkling my piano's upper registered notes. When they had their little fun, before I could react, they would already be at the other end of the dance floor.

One evening, it happened five or six times in one song. As dancers swept by, I would hear a rapid series of three or four grossly dissonant notes coming from my keyboard! Dink, dink, dink! I would look down, and the culprit's hand was already gone. Turning to see who performed the rude act, the only clue I got was a distant chuckling couple or two. Oh, I knew they were just having some fun, but the people seated away from the bandstand didn't really know someone else was playing all the wrong notes. I'm sure many patrons thought it was I.

I got so aggravated; I finally decided to take some drastic measures to remedy the problem. I watched my keyboard with askance, from the corner of my eye. As soon as I saw the next hand coming up to tickle the piano's upper register, I was going to smack it!

I waited patiently. Finally came the moment of truth. From the corner of my eye, I could see this guy's hand approaching my piano keys. When it reached the keyboard, I quickly stopped playing with my right hand, reached out to the upper keys and with a sharp downward thrust, I SMACKED the guy's hand very crisply! It gave out a sharp resounding WHACK as my palm hit the top of his hand.

Unfortunately, the gentleman whose hand I had smacked, was NOT the culprit! He was simply putting a twenty-dollar tip on my keyboard! The guy was so nice that in spite of my smacking his hand, he still delivered the twenty on the piano! As he walked away, I couldn't explain to him the reason behind my assault.

I immediately called a break for my band, and went over to where the gentleman was seated with his wife. I said, "Sir, I'm terribly sorry for smacking your hand. I would like to explain to you what exactly happened!"

He courteously said, "Roger, you don't have to explain a thing. I know precisely what happened. We were watching those rude people distort your beautiful music, and we felt very badly about it. I simply wanted to let you know that WE were enjoying your music. So, I decided to give you a tip." He started to laugh, and continued, "But I have to admit . . . that was the first time I've ever been smacked by someone I've tipped!"

Man, was I red!

431

Roger Rossi

Now That's a Little Too Personal

In the mid-seventies, I decided to join the ever-growing ranks of automobile owners with personalized license plates. In Florida, such plates are limited to seven characters   letters or numbers. You cannot use any combination already existing in Florida, and, of course, suggestive or profane language is a definite no-no.

As a musician/bandleader, I naturally wanted plates describing my chosen profession. Yet every combination that I requested was denied. Evidently, someone else was already using it. I had no success in five or six attempts with the Motor Vehicle Department.

It finally dawned on me that Lawrence Welk always set the various tempos for his band by counting them in with, "Ah one . . . ah two . . . ah one, two, three, four." I said to myself, "Ah yes . . . that's for me." Also at that point in time, I was getting into 5 to 18-piece band leading, so it was "ah" definite yes. The end result was my approved personalized plate: "AH 1 AH 2." I affixed them to our car just in time for a trip, with our three young children to North Florida.

In that area of Florida, the local AM radio stations play predominantly two types of music, Country . . . and Western! I actually do enjoy C & W, but not as a continual diet. Yet, in the panhandle, for example, you could change the radio station dial left to right and back again, and receive exactly the same format across the board. It started to put me to sleep, which is exactly what it had already done to Sal and the kids.

After several hours of twangy guitars and bass playing two notes per measure, I opted to listen to my CB (Citizens Band) radio, although it was not without shortcomings, either. My device was partially broken and could only receive radio signals. It was not capable of sending messages. Still, I turned it on, just for the change. I listened in on a conversation between two truckers within my limited reception range.

Driver one said to driver two, "Hey Joe . . . wadya say we stop off ahed and gid some there coffee, eh?"

His friend in the other truck replied, "Good idea Ray. I be widya."

I figured these two truckers to be in convoy with each other, so I looked in my rear-view mirror and spotted them approaching us from behind. Suddenly, as one of them went to pass us, I heard him call out to his friend, "Hey Joe . . . ya not believin' what I jus saw on these people's license. It says ASSHOLE ONE AND ASSHOLE TWO!"

Sal woke up, startled by the loud broadcast. She said to me, "Honey, I think they're talking about us!"

Immediately upon our arrival home in the Palm Beaches, I changed our license plates back to their original state-issued letters and numbers. I also got rid of my CB radio!

Roger Rossi

That Was My Joke

Many people, who enjoyed my first edition of this book, have asked if I've ever encountered the world's all-time greatest crooner, Francis Albert Sinatra. I did not and it is one of my greatest regrets. But, I do have distinctive personal memories of one of his performances that are worth telling. In early January, 1979, we saw him and his featured "warm-up" act, comedian Pat Cooper at The Sunrise Musical Theatre, in Sunrise, Florida; a suburb of Fort Lauderdale.

My story starts back in the 1960's at Carl Hoppl's Valley Stream Park Inn, where I was enjoying a steady gig. The quality of musicianship and floor-show entertainment there was excellent. One of the very best acts in entertainment, comedian Marty Brill, was often booked there.

Marty was also a writer, actor and musician, and in the 60's and 70's appeared regularly on the top TV shows, including The Merv Griffin Show, The Tonight Show, and The Ed Sullivan Show. He was also a regular actor on two popular sitcoms: The New Dick Van Dyke Show and The Mary Tyler Moore Show. He also did some writing for the (New) Soupy Sales Show.

Marty and I hit it off personally, and when he was in town performing at Carl Hoppl's, we often went out for a "nightcap" after his show. One night, I told him that I had thought of a punchline for a joke that could be added to his already written and performed routine, if he wanted to hear it. He said, "Sure. Go ahead and tell me."

Herein, is my abridged version of Marty's routine to his audiences, he said, "I think everyone in the world should walk around undressed. If everyone was nude, we would never have any wars. For one thing, the soldiers would not have any place to hang their hand grenades."

The audience laughed. He continued, "I mean, just think about it. No one would fight because they could never tell the difference between one army and another!"

At the bar with Marty, I suggested, "Marty, why don't you simply add to that line, 'With perhaps . . . the exception of the Israeli Army!'" Marty said, "That's not funny."

"Marty, don't you get it? The Israeli Army is made up primarily with Jewish men, who have all been circumcised, so automatically all of the soldiers would NOTICE the difference."

Marty said adamantly, "Roger, I don't see ANYTHING funny about it."

About two months later, Marty was booked for a return engagement at Hoppl's, and when he ran through his "being naked would end all wars" routine, he used my addendum, stating, 'With perhaps . . . the exception of the Israeli Army!'" The audience went into terrific laughter, and I was happy to have contributed.

Later, Marty and I went out for our typical nightcap and chit-chat. I expressed how happy I was that he added my comedic insert to his routine. He frowned questioningly, and totally denied that it was my joke. "I've had that joke in my routine since I created it, decades ago!"

I thought he was 'putting me on,' but when he avowed that he was telling the truth, I got slightly perturbed. I responded, "Look, Marty, I'm a musician, a fan and mostly a friend. I'm not some comedy writer asking you to pay me for that line, and I'd be insulted if you offered. But a simple, honest "thank you" would have sufficed, but now you're basically calling me a liar."

Carl Hoppl's had a major fire on Christmas Eve that year, and everyone was out of a job. I didn't work with Marty until many years later when he did a show at the Boca Raton Hotel in Florida. He told me he often opened for Ann Margaret in Las Vegas, but he also did a life-changing move, by trying out for and becoming a member of the California Highway Patrol. Occasionally, when he could get off from his CHIPS job, he still did his act. I never saw Marty again.

At The Sunrise Musical Theatre, Sinatra was as great as ever. The City of Sunrise actually brought him a gift, center stage; a beautiful horse. Sinatra pulled on the reins, and the sold-out audience laughed aloud when he told the horse, "Behave yourself, or I'm gonna serve you for dinner!"

Pat Cooper was Frank's opening act, and he was excellent. Cooper has "done it all" in show business. Born, Pasquale Caputo, he did a lot of shows for Italian-American audiences, The Friars Club, radio talks and even acting. He played the role of a mobster—Salvatore

Masiello—in the movie "Analyze This" and later, "Analyze That." Billboard Magazine once said that Pat Cooper has done for the Italian-Americans, what Jackie Mason did for the Jewish-Americans.

Pat opened with many of his Italian routines, but then stated, "I think everyone in the world should walk around undressed. If everyone was nude, we'd never have any wars."

My eyes opened wide and I thought, 'Uh-oh, I seem to recall hearing this before!'

Almost verbatim, he stated the routine Marty Brill had used many years earlier, back at Carl Hoppl's Valley Stream Park Inn. The audience was very responsive, and then, he made the crowd go wild when he stated (totally verbatim) the punch line I had given to Marty Brill:

'With perhaps . . . the exception of the Israeli Army!'"

As the crowd was roaring with uncontrollable laughter, I yelled out to Sal,

"THAT'S . . . MY . . . JOKE!"

I was happy to hear it again, knowing that I had contributed to many audiences enjoying themselves, even if I was never given the credit for it. However, I realized that it's almost a written rule that most comedians steal their jokes from other comedians. But, to be fair, we musicians also learn our trade by imitating other musicians, don't we? So, what's the difference?

Hence, some good old adages apply here. Sayings like: "what goes around comes around," and the old Spanish one, "Live with wolves, and you learn to howl."

The Most Difficult Music

People often ask me, "Roger, you've done it all in music. What music have you found to be the most difficult to play and read?" My answer is simple. After studying Bach, Beethoven, Mozart, and Chopin, making a living for over sixty years playing various floorshows accompanying vocalists, jugglers, magicians, comedians and flamenco dancers. And after playing years of band engagements featuring Dixieland, jazz, pop, rock, disco, society, island, big band and Latin American music; I can unequivocally say, the most difficult music there is to play is the music at burlesque shows. I played it for a full year, so I should know! Do you realize how hard it is to keep your eyes on music while ten feet away, beautiful young ladies are taking off their clothes?

What made it technically difficult was that the band HAD to watch the dancers for the various *bump and grind* cues, and naturally, you kept losing your place with the music. It was difficult!

Buffalo Bob and Clarabelle of the Howdy-Doodie Show

AL-RIGHT . . . I KNOW! It was only the drummer who REALLY had to watch for cues, but the rest of us in the band were watching... 'just to make sure he was doing it right!'

In those days, I became inventive in making extra income. I used to write and copy music arrangements. At the Burlesque, much of the dancers' music arrangements were previously scribbled on by other musicians.

Later, when I went to play them, they were almost unreadable. So, I'd suggest to many of the dancers that for a fee, I could "clean up" their music. Well, one day, I knocked on a dancer's dressing-room door. She inquired, "Who is it?"

"It's Roger Rossi, the piano player. I have your cleaned-up arrangements."

"Oh, C'mon in Roger."

I opened the door, walked in, and there she is stark naked. Immediately turning away, I said, "Sorry, I didn't know you were undressed. I'll be back."

"No, it's all right Roger. Stay here. You're one of the boys!"

I said slowly, "Yeah, I AM one of the boys, and THAT'S one of the problems!"

In 1962, burlesque was having a revival. The legendary Ann Corio, directed and was featured in the off-Broadway show, *This Was Burlesque*. Meanwhile, out in Jamaica, Long Island, I was playing 2-3 burlesque shows per week, filling in for the regular pianist at the Hillside Theater. There, they featured comedians like Tommy Moe Raft, and sensational lady dancers like Cindy Ember, and bust-developing queen Virginia Bell. Her dimensions were 48 - 24 - 36!

When I went back to play at my regular gig at the Valley Stream Park Inn, the musicians in that band, having seen Virginia Bell's ads and proportions, asked me, "What does she do in her show?"

Cindy Ember

The Girl Who Brought
Burlesque Back!!

With a poker face, I quipped, "Well, she crawls out to the center of the stage . . . and her act begins . . . when she tries to stand up!"

441

Look, it was a tough job . . . but SOMEBODY had to do it!

The really tough part about the job carried over into my family's disapproval of the newly acquired music genre in my repertoire; "stripper music."

My mother continually yelled at me, "What happened to the young man I raised with integrity and morality?" She continued, "You're playing piano for naked women is disgraceful! I'm ashamed of you! You must go to confession!" She went on and on and on.

Then, my father started yelling at me, "Son . . . when you gonna TAKE ME WITH YOU?"

The Piano Player is a "Sicko"

This is a story that I would never tell, if it wasn't for the fact that the victim survived.

It was a Saturday evening in 1978. My trio performed to a very large crowd at The Flame, in North Palm Beach, Florida. We were playing the typical requests and selections that had been our bread and butter for success in the place. The dance floor was packed. One gentleman, especially, got into our music, dancing up a storm with his partner. They were requesting and dancing to very lively music, including Jitterbugs, Rock n' Roll, a Peabody, and finally, a Polka.

Suddenly, that area of the club went silent. I looked up from the piano keyboard to notice nobody dancing. Instead, they all stood around the enthusiastic dancer, now lying on the dance floor, unconscious. He had suffered a massive heart attack.

The bartenders, waitresses and hostess all followed the proper procedures for such emergencies. They promptly moved the crowd off the dance floor to give the guy some room. They summoned paramedics and loosened the man's tie and collar to give his windpipe and lungs a fighting chance to do their jobs. It was not working. The man had stopped breathing and was turning blue from lack of oxygen.

I'm sure that practically everyone witnessing this terrible thing also had difficulty breathing, as our hearts went out to him.

Of course, we had stopped playing our music. No band members were schooled in C.P.R. There was really nothing else that we could do.

Slowly putting down our instruments, we started to leave the stage.

The hostess approached and asked me, "Roger, why are you stopping?"

"Donna, we can't play music while that poor man is dying. It would be disrespectful."

"I understand," she said, "and don't think for one moment that I don't have any feelings myself. Everything is being taken care of. We called 911; the paramedics will be here very shortly. In the meantime, people in the back have no idea what's going on, and they might leave. Keep playing, but just don't play anything loud, or with a beat."

Palm Beach - 1978

I understood exactly what Donna meant. She wasn't a heartless person, but a warm hostess whom practically everyone liked. She was simply thinking rationally, while I was not. It was a Saturday evening, and if you lose the crowd then, you will no doubt have a losing week, economically. It is the "night of nights" for the restaurant business.

Every employee and employer just depends on it. She was correct in asking for some background music. Nothing that would stand out.

I told Sal (playing drums that night) and Mike, our bassist, "Let's get back to work. Here's what we're going to do. Sal, play some very light cymbal stuff. Nothing with a definite beat. Don't even play the snare drum. And Mike, you play rubato, with a lot of whole and half notes. Nothing busy. Above all, we must play very quietly, got it?"

They both nodded, always cooperative and helpful. We restarted with Sal and Mike following my directions to a "T." We didn't sing. I noodled, playing idly just some chords, with a slight touch of melody. I was intensely concerned for the helpless gentleman, on the dance floor fighting for his life. My fingers were doing the work while my mind was elsewhere on the dance floor.

The paramedics did their best to revive the man, while they put him onto a rolling stretcher. As they worked, my fingers solemnly continued their unplanned movement.

Sal suddenly turned and whispered sternly to me, "Roger . . . do you know what you're playing?"

I continued playing, but now I did so with total concentration. I said, shrugging my shoulders, "No, I've never played this song. I recognize it, but don't know the name of it. What is it?"

Sal replied sharply, with disgust, "MY HEART STOOD STILL!"

I immediately stopped playing the *Rodgers and Hart* standard, and segued into something else as the paramedics wheeled the gentleman out of the club. It might have been my imagination, but I could swear that as they left, they gave me disapproving looks.

Mike, our bassist had a sense of humor, and realized that I would never do something like that deliberately. He turned to me and teased, "Man, you're a disgrace! . . . The poor guy is dying of a heart attack, and you're ushering him out to the strains of *My Heart Stood Still.* I can't wait to tell everyone at the next Musicians' Union meeting!"

445

I can tell this story and even laugh about it now. About two months after the incident, the heart attack victim came into the club and identified himself. I, in turn, told him what had happened while he was unconscious.

He said to me, "Oh boy . . . I can't wait to tell all of my friends and family. That is truly funny!"

Well, it might have been funny in retrospect. I certainly didn't think so at the time. I can still imagine my audience looking past the prostrate man, to me playing the piano and saying to themselves, "Listen to what that piano player's playing. . . . He must be a real "sicko!"

I'm on "Leader of the Pack," Not Billy Joel!

Many years ago, I found out that while I was the Staff Pianist at Ultrasonic Recording Studios, in Hempstead, NY, recording star Billy Joel also did some recording there. I presume it was for that reason the rumor innocently started that he played the piano part to "Leader of the Pack," where it was recorded.

Billy Joel is a confirmed composing and performing pop-star giant, who has accomplished it all in music, selling more than 150 million recorded songs he composed, sang and played on. To date, Joel has had 33 top-forty hits and twenty-three Grammy nominations.

Additionally, he's received just about every honor and award available including honorary doctorates from major universities and music schools. Billy Joel has received accolades in almost every corner of the Earth, and he rightfully deserves them all.

It's true that imitation is the sincerest form of flattery, because during my performances, I often have sung and played his great hits, especially: "I love You Just the Way You Are"; "New York State of Mind"; and "Piano Man," which I can really relate to. I AM a fan!

However, it is perplexing for me to read and hear comments by astute journalists and commentators who "suggest" that Joel played piano on The Shangri-Las #1 hit, "Leader of the Pack." Billy Joel did not play piano on the hit record, "Leader of the Pack." I did!

It first came to my attention when one of my close friends politely asked,

"Roger, I thought you said you played piano on "Leader of the Pack."

I answered, "Yes, I did . . . why?"

"Because, I read an article in Wikipedia.com stating that in a November 16, 2010 Howard Stern radio interview of Billy Joel, Joel suggested that he thinks he played piano on it, when he was fifteen years old."

I wasn't aware MY playing on "the final recording" was EVER questioned.

I told my friend, "I, in fact, DID play piano on the hit record. I've been the one receiving residuals from the Musicians Union for my piano part on the hit record, not

Billy Joel, but I'll check out the Wikipedia article, and the Howard Stern interview to see what was stated."

I checked, and here is the applicable part of that interview's transcript, as stated verbatim, by Howard Stern and Billy Joel in their radio broadcast.

STERN: "I've always heard this rumor. Did you play piano on "Leader of the Pack?"

JOEL: "I played on a demo of "Leader of the Pack__. In other words, eh, before the actual recording session when the girls sang it, I played on an instrument-basic track__ of "Leader of the Pack."

STERN: "So, did that make it to the record that they sang on?"

JOEL: "I don't know___. I really don't know, but . . ."

STERN: "Couldn't you find out?"

JOEL: "You know the guy that told me that it was__, was Shadow Morton. He was the Producer."

STERN: "But, how does that happen, that you don't know if that's your work?"

JOEL: "I was like fifteen years old."

STERN: "That was an iconic song. It would be so cool if you were to say that you played on it."

JOEL: "Well, I did play on it, but I'm not sure if they used my final piano part on it__. Eh, Ellie

Greenwich; I think she may have done it___. She wrote it."

I believe that rumors sometimes start by someone saying, "I've always heard this rumor. . . ."

From the time I completed the piano part at the Ultrasonic Recording Studio session THAT was the final, recorded piano part released to the public. It was my piano playing on that hit record, not anyone else's!

With Billy Joel's use of the word, "demo," there should never have been a question of who played the final piano part. A demo is a recording that is typically used ONLY for demonstration purposes.

Since then, others have added to "the rumor." There was a piece written in Newsday, a Long Island newspaper, titled "Sounds etched in our memory." Writer Glenn Gamboa wrote: "Billy Joel believes he played piano on the demo as a 15-year old session musician, though he isn't sure whether his playing appears on the final version."

My question is: will future writers or commentators describe "Leader of the Pack" by completely eliminating the word "demo "from Billy Joel's comment? If they were reckless in not applying the demo word initially, why will they bother including it at all, in the future? For example, a future commentary may thoughtlessly state: "Billy Joel played piano on "Leader of the Pack" as a 15-year old musician!" [PERIOD]

"A side issue that also developed was that shortly after "Leader of the Pack" hit number one on the Billboard Hot 100 list, in 1964, a very similar spoof was recorded and released by The Detergents. That song was called, "Leader of the Laundromat" and in January 1965 it also was a hit, reaching #19 on the Billboard Hot 100 list chart.

"The Laundromat" version sounded almost exactly the same as "The Pack" version, including an almost exact duplication of my piano part. I guess that piano part was important enough that at the very end of their recording, one of the Detergents asked, "Who is that banging on the piano?" Who knows, maybe that initiated Howard Stern's and Glenn Gamboa's "rumor?"

I don't blame Billy Joel for any these "problems." I blame scriptwriters and journalists who don't properly research their subject matter. I also blame the producer-composer George "Shadow "Morton, who wouldn't take the time to remember the help I was to him when recording the hit at Ultrasonic Studios, nor the time to remember my name thereafter.

He had forgotten my name when I encountered him coming out of a Broadway restaurant, just a few weeks after the song was released. Additionally, he forgot my name when he came into the Valley Stream Park Inn where I was playing piano; again, when I saw him at a Grand Opening of another recording studio on Long Island; and finally, when conversing with Billy Joel. Methinks that Shadow Morton has a memory problem!

Furthermore, the subject probably never would have been broadcasted by Howard Stern, or written about by

Newsday if they had knowledge that it was a basically unknown, musician (ME), who played that final piano part. They had to give their meaningless storyline credibility by attaching superstar Billy Joel's name to it, and then, by calling it . . . a rumor!

My question is why didn't anyone from the Howard Stern Show, or Newsday, do some research? It would not have taken much time to realize that:

CLUE #1 - because Leader of the Pack was recorded at Ultrasonic Recording Studios, in 1964; and,

CLUE #2 - at the time of that recording, a Babylon boy by the name of Roger Rossi was the Staff Pianist there. OBVIOUSLY, (DUH!) Roger Rossi would be (at least) one of the leading candidates in answering the question: . . . who was banging on that piano?

I Was Mauled by Marilyn Monroe

I received a phone call in May 2001. "Hi Roger, this is Bob Davis, the bassist. I'm calling to see if you and Sal would be available to work with me for a high-end gig, cruising on a large-sized party boat on Tampa Bay. It's for my girlfriend's father, Dave Corriveau. Have you ever heard of him?"

"No, I have not."

"Dave Corriveau, is one of the owners of the national restaurant chain, *Dave and Buster's*. He's holding a 50th

Wedding Anniversary celebration for his mother and father, and the date is July 15th."

I told him that July 15th is also Sal and my anniversary, but we would still be available for the gig.

Dave and Buster's is a good-sized company with eighty-three locations across the United States and one in Canada. You'd never know it the way Mr. Corriveau behaved; down to earth, friendly and a gentleman. I'm not sure if I met his partner, James "Buster" Corley.

Bob Davis explained that he'd play bass; we'd have a drummer; but wanted me to lead the band, and my wife Sal the lead vocalist. He gave me directions to where the party boat was docked.

He continued, "They have a grand piano on board, a sound system, the money is great, and Mr. Corriveau is putting us all up for the night in the 5-star, Ritz Carlton right across the street from the pier. The drummer and I will be sharing one room, and you and Sal will get the suite."

Jokingly, I said, "SWEET . . . but I'm shocked. Don't we get round-trip limousine service from my Wellington home to the pier?" He chuckled.

Early morning, July 15th we traveled to Tampa, found the pier and boarded what was a very large party boat which accommodated several hundred passengers. We found Bob and the drummer at the bandstand. Dave Corriveau approached saying, "You must be Sal and Roger Rossi. We were told a lot about you, and can't wait for you to perform."

We all started setting up and testing the piano and sound system. The provided equipment was all First Class. Bob said we would have enough time to check into the hotel, get changed into formal attire, and return to the boat before the guests arrived. Everything ran smoothly,

In our first set, our musicianship blended very well, and Bob Davis was happy to let me "run the show." Many guests remained on deck watching the ship depart, while inside we had our fair share of people dancing. We answered varied requests, played Standards, Swing Jazz, Latin-American, light Rock 'n roll, and soon, had the dance floor jumping.

David Corriveau approached the bandstand and taking microphone in hand, welcomed his guests, and introduced his parents who danced to "The Anniversary Waltz." When done, he acknowledged, "The Bob Davis Quartet featuring Sal and Roger Rossi."

With the boat speeding out to sea, and guests on the buffet line, we played Jimmy Buffett's "Cheeseburgers in Paradise."

Then, in the middle of our set, the Captain turned on the boat's main microphone for all passengers to hear. He sounded very alarming with his important announcement.

"Attention please. This is your Captain. Please don't be alarmed, but we want you to know that on our radar we've spotted a small craft approaching us at very fast speed. We've not been able to contact them. They're definitely aiming their high-speed boat right at us. We've contacted the United States Coast Guard, and we'll continue to keep you informed, so please enjoy your celebration."

Well, the guests all looked at each other, smiled, shrugged their shoulders and continued having a good time. We musicians did the same, and played more music.

Several minutes later, the Captain interrupted all with another announcement.

"Ladies and Gentlemen, we can actually see the approaching speed boat with our naked eyes, and the Coast Guard has informed us that they have a vessel racing to intercept them."

With that said, the whole dance floor immediately emptied, and all the guests went out on the decks to try to spot the craft for themselves. We musicians followed.

Shortly, the Captain stated,

"We can see the occupants of that boat, and, eh . . . eh . . . OH, MY GOD, it's . . . I CAN'T BELIEVE IT . . . IT'S ELVIS PRESLEY, AND . . . OH, NOOOOO, HE'S WITH . . . MARILYN MONROE!

All of the guests screamed with the relief they were not going to be accosted, and the joy that they were going to be entertained with a floor show, set up "Corriveau Style!"

I asked Bob Davis if he knew about any of this. He smiled nodding negatively. We went inside where Corriveau mentioned he wanted us to accompany the two impersonators. "They're onboard and being ushered up to us very quickly. We'll talk with them in a private area."

We all went to a small room, arriving about the same time Elvis and Marilyn did.

Elvis looked like the real Presley, but Marilyn was the absolute spitting image of Monroe. They both were very nice, extremely talented and professional.

Corriveau said to the two, "I want you to meet the Bob Davis Band, with Roger Rossi, their pianist who will direct the music for your performance."

Elvis said, "Well, there's no need for that. We have our own accompaniment on tapes."

David Corriveau was emphatic. "No, you don't understand. This band is one of the finest you could find anywhere. They're amazing musicians. They WILL accompany both of you."

I interrupted, asking, "Do you have any music for us?"

Marilyn said, "No. Just tapes!"

"Well, do you know the keys you sing in?"

She said, "Not for all of them." Elvis said, "I know a few."

I realized that this situation had to have musical leadership, and there was nobody else on the entire ship that could exhibit that leadership but (Gulp) . . . ME! I put my shoulders back, and took control.

"Look, here's what we must do. You must give me three or four opening songs in the sequence that you'd like to perform. Before there is a big crowd in the main room, let's go in there, and find the keys for those songs. Then, we'll play a few dance songs for the guests while you go, freshen up, collect yourselves, and think about what you're going to do after those openers. In the meantime, after we start, I'll get an idea of what your vocal ranges are, and we'll "wing it" after that. Okay?"

Elvis: "You Ain't Nothin' but a Hound Dog"

Everyone nervously smiled and nodded. None of us really knew what would happen. Would we have chemistry between us? Or, would one spoke of the wheel fail, letting the entire wagon train disastrously topple into the impending ravine . . . or sea? I reassured, saying, "Look, we're all pros. We've all been there. Let's put smiles on our faces, do what we do best, and have some fun!" They all went along and echoed my thoughts. We relocated to the piano where I quickly found their opening song keys; they went to freshen up, and the band played on. David Corriveau came onto the stage in the midst of guests dancing and introduced us all by saying, "Ladies and gentlemen, Mom and Dad, I've brought in two of the finest impersonating performers in the World, directly from Universal Studios, in Orlando. They're going to help us celebrate your anniversary. And although they are performing with the band for the very first time, and the band will accompany them without benefit of music arrangements, I feel totally assured that we're in for a GREAT show. Ladies and Gentlemen, please welcome, ELVIS PRESLEY."

The crowd went wild while Elvis went into, "Blue Suede Shoes." Man, he sounded and looked great. He really made you feel he WAS "The King," reincarnated. He brought thunderous applause, and nodding his head with approval, gestured towards the band. He even sounded like the real thing when thanking the audience with his patterned, "Thang ya very much!" Then, he introduced his next song, "Ladies and gentlemen, here's a song written by Jerry Leiber and Mike Stoller that I recorded back in September 1957. It was released as a 45-rpm single about the same time my motion picture came out with the same name. Maybe you remember it . . . "Jailhouse Rock." I thought, 'Yeah, like RIGHT! Who could forget that huge hit?' He absolutely tore the crowd up. Similarly, he followed it up with, "Are You Lonesome To-Night," and "You Ain't Nothin' But A Hound Dog."

After taking his bows, he introduced, "Our next guest is a great friend of mine, eh . . . but just don't tell Joe DiMaggio about that."

457

The crowd laughed aloud. He continued, "You might have seen her in some of her movies like; *Some Like It Hot, The Seven Year Itch,* or *Gentlemen Prefer Blondes.* Ladies and gentlemen, you know who I'm talking about, everyone's favorite blonde, super star, Marilyn Monroe.

Marilyn came out with a sultry-white dress on, singing, "Diamonds Are a Girl's Best Friend."

My goodness, she sang just like her, she spoke and gestured like her. She looked exactly like the famous actress, and it was hard to believe that in reality she was . . . Heather Chaney, Marilyn Monroe's impersonator. I mean, performing on stage, or up close, you were being held in a trance. She WAS Marilyn Monroe!

My reaction only echoed what I knew the audience felt. They were ecstatic. Every time she went near any of the men in the audience, they put wide smiles and charm on their faces to try to attract her nearer to them. The ladies, noticing their reactions simply sat back laughing and enjoying the fun. Then she sang one of her favorites, "I Wanna be Loved by You," but she slowly walked around the room in her known-for sexy manner, making the men that much more nervous. They fell for it, and she had them eating out of the palms of her gloved hands. She took her well-deserved applause, smiled, nodded, and walked off.

Peter sang some of his up-tempo rock n' roll hits, like "Heartbreak Hotel," "I'm All Shook Up," "Return to Sender" and "Don't Be Cruel". And in between those songs, he changed the tempos and mood by going to his slower hits like "Love Me Tender," "My Way," "It's Now or Never," and "Amazing Grace."

Marilyn Monroe "My Heart Belongs to Daddy"

The audience reacted to every song with roaring applause. He again, presented Heather, who came out singing, "My Heart Belongs to Daddy." But, this time, she made David Corriveau's father her target. She gradually moved to his area of the room, and without taking her eyes off him, she finally wiggled on to his lap. The crowd was elated. She imitated what Marilyn Monroe did at The

White House when she sang, "Happy Birthday, Mr. President" to John F. Kennedy. But, although she sang the music to Happy Birthday, she changed the lyrics to, "Happy Anniversary, Mr. Corriveau."

The entire show was well over an hour, and there was only one-way it could have properly ended, and that was for Elvis to join with Marilyn and the audience in singing, "Happy Anniversary" to the happy couple, Corriveau's parents. Corriveau stepped to the microphone, and asked his guests "Ladies and gentlemen, how about these great artists?" Everyone immediately stood up and gave a well-deserved, standing ovation. While they were applauding, Corriveau singled us all out by gesturing with his pointing hand, and saying, "Our excellent impersonating artists, Peter Alden and Heather Chaney." He continued, "And how about that band? Bob Davis and his musicians, Roger Rossi and his lovely wife, Sal. I heard it's their anniversary, too."

With the audience, still standing, and applauding, we played some "chaser music" for Peter and Marilyn to take final bows and exit the room. When we were finished, I announced that we would take a short break and return for some more dance music. We put on an intermission-music tape, and all parted our own ways. I went down to the lower level of the boat, and after using the men's room I noticed there were only three people on that level: me at the bow, and at the stern, the other two, Peter and Heather.

When Heather noticed me, she yelled, "It's YOU!"

I turned to see if there was somebody behind me. There wasn't, and she started running towards me, yelling out compliments and superlatives at me. "You were fabulous. You saved us!"

She ran closer and closer while continuing her enthusiastic remarks. "We just couldn't have done our show without you!"

By now, she reached me and threw her outstretched arms around me, hugging me and kissing me on both cheeks. She was elated, and I was, too. I told her, "You and Peter were the TRUE stars. YOU made the day! We were only doing what we always do . . . making music!"

Finally, we parted. They got on the speed boat and headed back to Tampa, and I went upstairs to rejoin the band. I didn't realize that Heather's lipstick was smeared all over my face. The band members all smiled with elevated eyebrows. Bob Davis asked, "Roger, is that lipstick?"

Neither Heather nor I did anything but express our enjoyment in working together, but for some reason I felt almost like a kid just caught with his hand in the cookie jar. Smiling while cleaning the lipstick off with a napkin, I replied, "Hey guys . . .what can I say? Eat your hearts out. I was just mauled by Marilyn Monroe!"

Heather Chaney and Peter Alden
www.heatherchaney.com
www.peteraldenentertainment.com

A Few Snafus

During a sixty-year music career, you would almost expect the unexpected. Weirdness and oddities have often occurred in my professional life, but I'll relate only a few in this writing.

ODDITY ONE – I tell my friends and fellow musicians that in the spring of 2002, my wife Sal and I played for golfer Sam Snead's 90th birthday party.

Slamming Sammy Snead was the winner of three Masters' and many other major tournaments and he was truly a golfing legend. His birthday party took place at the former *Meadowood Golf and Tennis Club*, now called Panther Woods, in Ft. Pierce, Florida. He resided there during the wintertime, for fourteen years, and was called, "the Resident Golf Pro Emeritus."

Of course, if any of my friends or fellow musicians were to follow up on my truthful statement, they would immediately challenge me. Although I did play Sam Snead's ninetieth birthday party in Fort Pierce, Florida, he died shortly after ceremoniously teeing off the "First Official Drive" of the 2002 Master's Tournament in Augusta, Georgia . . . at eighty-nine years of age!

ANOTHER ODDITY

My Dixieland band, Red Onions, was asked to play for the groundbreaking ceremonies for the Kravis Center for the Performing Arts, West Palm Beach on January 12, 1989.

The Kravis is a good-sized performing arts center where "no expense was spared" in building it. It routinely presents the very best of musical talents America and the World have to offer. I was honored to be able to present my fourteen-piece Roger Rossi Big Band there in December 1998.

My band played for the groundbreaking, which took place at John Prince Park in Lake Worth, Florida. I have a beautiful commemorative metal memento to prove it.

Then, pray tell, why is that The Kravis Center is actually located on Okeechobee Boulevard, in downtown West Palm Beach, and not John Prince Park, Lake Worth?

Did they run out of money before it was built and couldn't afford to have another coin minted showing its correct location? Or couldn't they afford to have another groundbreaking ceremony at its proper location?

Odd? Yes, but laughingly, I'll keep the erroneously minted coin just in case I ever decide to sell it to the highest bidder on E-Bay!

ONE MORE . . . A QUIZ

Robert Cleveland (now deceased) was a music educator, bandleader, and trumpeter. He was my music teacher at Amityville Memorial High School, Long Island, and afterwards became a good friend.

One day after playing a round of golf with our wives in Fort Lauderdale, we met up with mutual friend, bandleader-saxophonist Pat DeRosa, and his wife. The sextet went out for dinner and cocktails.

We all were having a grand time joking and reminiscing about life, family, and sports but mainly about "the Music Business." At one point, I thought I'd stump them with a trick question.

I asked, "In history, there was one person who played for *The New York Rangers* ice hockey team, *The Brooklyn*

Dodgers baseball team, and *The New York Knicks* basketball team. Who was it?"

When they finally gave up, I divulged that it was a trick question, and the answer was Gladys Gooding . . . the organist!

After the laughter subsided, Bob Cleveland said, "Okay, I've got one for you. Who played for *The New York Jets* football team; *The New York Mets* baseball team; *The New York Nets* basketball team, and *New York Islanders* ice hockey team?"

I said, "Uh-oh, I know the answer to that question . . . It was YOU, Bob Cleveland."

With dropped jaw, he asked, "How in the world did you know that?"

"Because, you gave it away when you said, *The New York Jets*. You probably have forgotten that I played piano and was with you when you auditioned for that gig. I never played for the games because they would never put a piano out there in the cold football weather."

That day, two excellent musicians prevailed in our conversation. Gladys Gooding and my friend Bob Cleveland. Both are now gone.

ONE LAST, WEIRD, BUT FUNNY SITUATION

Sal and I had neighbors living next to us in Patchogue, Long Island, Bruce, and Marie Loesch. They were not just friends, but fans, often coming to see us perform. One day I received a phone call from Bruce, asking, "Roger, we have some dear friends coming to visit us next week.

Would you and Sal be performing anywhere that we could come to see you?"

"Gee, I'm not sure Bruce. I'm kind of in between gigs. I may be at the world-famous Living Room in Manhattan, but I also have an offer to perform at New York's Americana Hotel.

As it turned out, I was able to land the piano gig at Glynn's Inn, in Centerport, Long Island. I always enjoyed performing there previously, but the only thing was I couldn't start until four days after finishing at the Living Room.

Upon finishing at the NYC bistro, and starting to relax with a few days off, I received a phone call from a Long Island entertainment booking agent.

"Roger, this is Arnold. There's an Italian Restaurant about forty-five minutes from where you live, and their piano player was called out of town for a medical emergency in his family. Could you fill in for him tomorrow night?"

The pay was acceptable, and so I said, "Sure, Arnold. I'll do it."

The moment I hung up the phone, my neighbor called.

"Roger, our friends just called. They're on their way here to stay with us for two nights. Are you still working at the Living Room?"

"No, Bruce. I gave my notice and finished there last night."

"Oh, Okay. They'll only have tomorrow night to see you. Have you taken the gig at the Americana Hotel?"

"No, Bruce. I'll be working at an Italian restaurant on Long Island. I turned down the New York City gig because I would rather work closer to home, on Long Island.

"What's the name of the place?"

"Tony's Pizza!

There was a pause. "Geez, Roger! You're the only musician in the world who'd give up performing at world class venues like the Living Room and The Americana Hotel, to work at . . . a pizza joint!"

A Final Word

People spend considerable time with their memories. Let's face it; we cherish them more and more as we grow older. From the piano bench, I have accumulated a true-treasure chest, chock full of poignant memories. Good, bad, happy, sad, exciting . . . all pieces of Roger Rossi.

Did I tell you that this *"slightly-better-than-average piano player"* is richer than a sultan?

No . . . I didn't sign a contract with the "big boys." Nor have I recently won the Florida Powerball jackpot. What I do have is a beautiful wife, wonderful children and grandchildren. I've got dear, life-long friends, a good, honest reputation; and now a book under my belt; with memories made immortal.

From the piano bench, I've seen six and a half decades come and go. It hasn't all been happy, easy, warm, and glowing. There have been some frightfully cold, hard, rough times.

I've made my income performing as a FULL-TIME musician. It's quite unique that I never had a second job outside of music, and did it while avoiding big-city residences. Most musicians either treat their music as a sideline, or they're full-timers and live in the big city. I opted for suburban living, where my family could live in a cleaner and less "complicated" atmosphere. One where family values flourish and prevail.

Amazingly, we were always punctual in paying our bills and taxes; always lived in nice homes; paid for our children's schooling, weddings, family's health care (canine pets included), and still found the funds for one or two family vacations every year. Most importantly, we always tried to make Sunday Mass services, despite arriving home from Saturday's gig early Sunday morning.

Perhaps, we could have done it on my own income, but our lives were so enhanced with the help of my best friend, fellow musician, lead vocalist, part time drummer, chief budgeter, secretary, gardener, house-keeping wife Sal; the love of my life. Sal's always been there beside me, and her efforts have "put us over the top" It's all been so fulfilling. Our life together is full. God has been on our side . . . I AM a rich man!

However, I do worry about the future for our youth. In today's world, mega-corporations are swallowing world-wide markets, while at a rate never before seen, small independent businesses are going belly-up. Life is moving much too fast, while honesty and morality are being drastically diminished!

Additionally, I'm not really enthralled with the direction that music has been going for the past thirty or more years. Like everything else, and perhaps more than most, music is a reflection of the times. Today's "artists" have become much too electronic and digital. Not too long ago, I could never have visualized the decisive manner in which D.J.'s have seized their prominent place in the music entertainment industry. D.J.'s are disc jockeys. They spin records! But, with their lasers, strobes, smoke and Karaoke machines, they are the definitive choice of millions. Where's the outrage? They're not musicians. It's all much too mechanical! Give me a good acoustic pianist, bassist, saxman, and drummer . . . please!

Today, we traditional musicians often "out skill" our audiences who have extremely limited musical tastes and knowledge. It's really sad. The overwhelming majority of America's youth are not really getting proper music education.

Past generations learned about the classy and classic music of the "3- B's," Bach, Beethoven and Brahms, who were symbolic of all the great masters. Most of today's youth don't even know who they were. The result is that standardized, one-dimensional musical minds have filled up the void. It's just another tragic example of out-of-control, collective culture-cide.

Don't get me wrong. Rock and Roll has been with us since the 50's, but the harshness of those sounds has risen to abominable levels, with no end in sight. The raunchy Mick Jagger's presentation replaced the classiness of Sinatra and Tommy Dorsey. Then, the downward cycle continued with the Rolling Stones being replaced by "Rap" superstars, who have totally abolished Harmony 101. Not only don't they have an affection for melody and harmony lines, but they've totally omitted them. Their focal point is strictly on using mechanical drums, and broadcasting profane messages of lawlessness and misogyny. And now, that's what mindlessly-brainwashed America is calling . . . "music??"

When scanning across radio dials in search for anything tasteful like jazz, classical or Latin-American music, I must first jump passed myriad of stations of ear-piercingly loud, screaming, screeching, and angry sounds. How did we ever get to this point of permitting our youth to replace historically classy music and values with . . . garbage?

Nonetheless, please allow me to change the mood by finishing on a positive, pun-intended "note"; the applause. I regularly try to perform to older crowds, who have not let their good tastes wane. I play to them for their genuine and unabashed applause. God, I love the applause. The phenomenon of clapping hands together in utter appreciation is so important, so motivating. The performance of great music is very emotional as it is. But, give me five hearty clappers, and you give me a good case of goosebumps and tremendous joy. If you happen to be someone who has bestowed that wonderful gift to my ears and spirit, I thank you from the bottom of my heart. If we've never met, I regret it now.

Life's too short.

Friends are too few.

This "slightly-better-than-average piano player," bids you, *adieu.*

CPSIA information can be obtained
at www.ICGtesting.com
Printed in the USA
LVHW02s1737040118
561822LV00014B/1431/P